The Rising State

The Rising State

How State Power Is Transforming Our Nation's Schools

Edited by

Bonnie C. Fusarelli
Bruce S. Cooper

SUNY PRESS

Published by
State University of New York Press, Albany

Printed in the United States of America

For information, contact State University of New York Press, Albany, NY
www.sunypress.edu

Production by Kelli W. LeRoux
Marketing by Fran Keneston

Library of Congress Cataloging-in-Publication Data

The rising state : how state power is transforming our nation's schools / edited by Bonnie C. Fusarelli and Bruce S. Cooper.
p. cm.
Includes bibliographical references and index.
ISBN 978-0-7914-7693-2 (hardcover : alk. paper)
ISBN 978-0-7914-7694-9 (pbk. : alk. paper)
1. Education and state—United States—States.
2. School improvement programs—United States—States.
3. Educational accountability—United States—States. 4. Government aid to education—United States—States. I. Fusarelli, Bonnie C., 1968– II. Cooper, Bruce S.
LC89.R57 2009
379.73—dc22

2008018957

10 9 8 7 6 5 4 3 2 1

Contents

Part II
Comparative and National Trends

Part III
Trends and Conclusions

Figures and Tables

Foreword

Michael W. Kirst

Ever since the mid-1960s, state government has increased its intervention and scope of control in local education. *The Rising State* documents and analyzes the most recent phase of state activism in education policy. Before exploring this recent upsurge, it is useful to ask why this has happened. Indeed, the hallmark of American education is local control through a local property tax. At the turn of the twentieth century, many state education departments had less than ten employees.

A crucial reason for a fundamental shift in the state education role is the widespread loss of confidence in local educators and their communities. The federal government led in 1965 with the Elementary and Secondary Education Act that embodied a view that local educators could not be trusted to improve education for low income and minority children. As state governance capacity grew, states passed laws that were votes of no confidence in the local ability to improve education for handicapped children, English learners, and other special categories. Then the key instrument of local control—the property tax—began to diminish through equity and tax limitation assaults.

By 1983, the public and state policymakers believed that local communities could no longer adequately educate the typical student with no special needs. So systemic standards-based reform began by influencing what and how teachers taught. No Child Left Behind was the capstone of accountability pressure on local schools, and is administered through states. State policymakers now have the instruments to connect the capitol to what goes on weekly inside local classrooms. At the same time, forty states passed charter school laws to allow more parental choice, and create competition.

The loss of confidence in local education is palpable and documented through the details of each chapter in this book. It varies in form and intensity by state, but the trend is similar. However, we must be careful not to view the aggregate impact of state policy growth as strictly a zero sum game whereby one level gains and another loses influence on policy and school administration. Rather, the result can be an increased volume of policy and control at all levels.

For example, state academic standards policies can stimulate more curriculum activity at the district and principals' offices. State policies can be the local springboard for local authorities to devise new solutions. State education departments have grown because of federal subsidies to administer national categorical programs. The federal government began its long campaign to enhance state education department capacity with general-purpose grants of $27 million in 1965. So, as you read the chapters in this book, be aware of the complex mutual adaptations and interventions among the three levels of education governance.

States are still searching for the right blend of mandates, sanctions, incentives, and deregulation to galvanize their desired local changes. Cuts in state education department staffs after the 2001 recession are serious, and impede the execution of the policies in this volume. For instance, California had less than 1,200 employees in 2006, compared to over 2,000 in 1978 (80 percent of California employees are paid by the federal government for federal purposes).

This book provides new insights and data for understanding the diversity of state policies and politics. Readers will discover that no such thing as state education policy exists. The operational reality embodies differential state responses to specific external and internal events as they play out through a federal system.

After reading this book, you can ponder if the state role has become too large. Do we have the right balance between state and local education? Who should control what? What if the same trends for the past forty years continue for the next forty years? What should be the limit of state control of local education? Readers will need to decide these questions, so get ready for a stimulating experience.

Chapter 1

Setting the Stage

Where State Power and Education Meet

Bruce S. Cooper and Bonnie C. Fusarelli

States—their governors, legislatures, and state education agencies (SEAs)—play a pivotal role in education policymaking. The state level of government, constitutionally bound to establish education for all children in their jurisdiction, determines the funding, operation, and structure of school districts, and the curriculum, staffing, and programs in schools. The policies of the state determine the nature of the educational experiences for the state's students.

State education policymaking used to be a good deal simpler than it is today. Throughout much of U.S. history, education policy was shaped by a small handful of key education professionals whose expertise was generally unquestioned. Conflict was largely limited to disagreements between school board associations, school administrators, and teachers' unions. State lawmakers, overworked and understaffed, did little except appropriate funding for schools.

America's long-standing, deeply embedded fear of large government, coupled with high levels of local funding, likely forged a preference for local control of schools (Theobald & Bardzell, 2000). Although contemporary scholars do not cast local control strictly as a matter of "those who pay the piper call the tune," financial considerations are often cited as a major force explaining the preference for local control (Fuhrman & Elmore, 1990; Theobald & Bardzell, 2000). Theobald and Bardzell (2000) note that "until the twentieth century, local sources provided all or nearly all of school revenues . . . in such an environment, it is easy to see how a strong tradition of local control of schools would naturally develop" (p. 4).

Still, even as the state portion of school revenues increased substantially over the last century (by the 1990s, the average state contributed slightly more than 50 percent of all education funds), local control remained strong as long as local schools adequately carried out their responsibilities (Fuhrman & Elmore,

1990). In an attempt to ensure that local schools are adequately educating students, various accountability measures have been enacted in recent years.

As a result, state and national policymakers are increasingly important actors in shaping the nature, scope, and direction of education initiatives (Mazzoni, 1995). Educational reforms, such as higher standards, testing, and accountability, seek to improve student achievement through tightened centralized control and more effective command structures. Within the past forty years, local control over education has slowly eroded, as the federal and state governments exert ever-greater control over the educational process (Tyack, 1990; Wirt & Kirst, 1997).

As this book will show, the authority of the state in education is not static. Since the passage of the No Child Left Behind Act (NCLB) in 2001, states have assumed many of the responsibilities and much of the decision-making once reserved for local districts and communities. However, the states were ready to assume this newfound power, as the role of the state in education has increased since the 1960s.

As a prerequisite for increased state activism, state legislative capacity has increased dramatically in the last four decades, as legislatures have established numerous oversight committees, installed sophisticated data processing equipment, and substantially enlarged their staffs. Passage of the Elementary and Secondary Education Act (ESEA) of 1965 energized state education departments and initiated a much larger role for the state in shaping local education policies. Almost overnight, state education departments were transformed from sleepy little offices into large, active bodies with oversight capability and significant control over local education initiatives.

Elementary and Secondary Education Act (ESEA) funds helped to build the capacity of state education agencies across the nation. This "ramping up" stage was followed by a focus on equity. State education policymaking began to change in the 1970s and 1980s as state legislatures were forced by a variety of outside actors and institutions to confront a host of educational challenges, including inequities in school finance, the education of students with special needs, and the push for higher standards, more intensive assessment, and greater accountability.

By the 1970s, reformers began to argue that states were not meeting their constitutional responsibility to educate all children equitably because of the vast disparities in per pupil school expenditures. Constitutional challenges to school funding formulas in the 1970s and 1980s (*Rodriguez v. San Antonio Independent School District*, 1973) resulted in more centralized control over school funding and schools. Many states engaged in school finance reform and increased state aid and regulation of local districts, and, after the publication of *A Nation at Risk* (1983), most states engaged in major school reform initiatives that focused state attention on curriculum, standards, and quality. Spurred in part by school finance litigation, as well as a perceived decline in the quality of schooling, state legislatures and, more recently, governors, have become much more active in crafting education policy.

Since the 1980s, there has been a shift away from local school boards toward state-level decision-making institutions. In virtually every state, legislation has been passed in an effort to enhance knowledge about school performance. The current reform movement follows decades of an expanding state role, which grew along with the enrollment booms of the 1950s, and 1960s (Fuhrman & Elmore, 1990). Fuhrman and Elmore (1990) explain that "though characterized by shifting themes—from local district consolidation to school finance and equity to testing and accountability—state leadership steadily escalated, with each new policy adding to rather than replacing previous laws, regulations, and structures" (p. 84). A unique feature of contemporary reforms is that many state policy objectives are "expressed as mandates or rules, as opposed to efforts to build local capacity, and thus they reinforce the image of an increasingly obtrusive state presence" (Fuhrman & Elmore, 1990, p. 85). Statewide testing programs and tightened teacher certification requirements are prime examples of the increased state presence in education. Nevertheless, most states lack the capacity to assure compliance with reform policies (Fuhrman & Elmore, 1990), and these externally initiated reforms are highly variable in the extent to which they are implemented by local schools.

In the 1980s and 1990s, state involvement increased with federal deregulation, block grants, and various school reform imperatives. Power and policymaking have gradually returned to the states and the result has been an unprecedented growth of state influence over local education.

In the 1990s, National Assessment of Educational Progress (NAEP) tests were administered to students in a voluntary sample of states. The results highlighted differences between states and further fueled the reform movement. Although disagreements remain among educational researchers and policy analysts about the consequences of shifting educational decision-making and curriculum policy away from local schools, by 1998, forty states had statewide curriculum standards, forty-eight states assessed student learning, and thirty-six published annual "report cards" on individual schools (Grissmer & Flanagan, 2001).

In some states, results from school-level report cards have spurred school choice movements. A growing number of states enacted charter school laws and now voucher policies that allow students to transfer out of failing schools with public funds following the student. Since the passage of NCLB in 2001, virtually every state has engaged in systemic reform. These reforms often come at the expense of local control, and they strengthen state authority despite countervailing rhetorics of local control, privatization, choice, and school-based management (James, 1991).

The passage of the NCLB would not have been possible without the prior ESEA buildup. NCLB is not totally new (although it has new elements), but should be seen as a reauthorization of ESEA as well as new policies. Many states were already setting some standards, working on curriculum, whole school reform, testing, and choice; so NCLB is both a continuation of the old and a taste of the new. It builds on but also goes further and beyond what was. The new part is the universality of this law: forcing all states to do what only some were doing—and then some. NCLB is not a "flash in the pan" reform; rather it sits astride almost forty years (1965–2005) of rising state power and potential.

Today, states are the primary policymakers in K–12 education in that they determine the curriculum, teacher licensure or certification requirements, and other important policies such as class size, graduation requirements, assessment of student performance, and school accountability measures. The case study chapters in this book trace the development of increased state control of education in specific state contexts and they explore what the future may hold in state level educational policymaking.

Outline of the Book

In this book, we weave together comparative case studies of six critical states, written by leading national experts, with a series of thematic chapters. The states selected for the case studies were chosen based on their geographic diversity, activist state legislatures, and visibility in the educational reform movement. This book compares major developments such as equity, accountability, and choice across the six states and it offers policymakers, teachers, administrators, and the public some means of understanding the changes occurring around them.

The book has three major parts. The first examines the growth of state power in six key states. The six case study chapters explore in detail the policy developments, reforms, and politics that have resulted in a decrease in local control over education. In the first chapter, Lawrence O. Picus uncovers historical events that shaped the political terrain in California. Tricia Browne-Ferrigno follows with a comprehensive review of educational policymaking in Kentucky—especially since the passage of the Kentucky Educational Reform Act (KERA) in 1990. Next, Bruce S. Cooper and Philip H. Nisonoff explore the politics of educational reform, with a focus on school funding and other reforms in New Jersey. Sandra Vergari's chapter follows in which she writes about the difficulties of implementing reforms in New York. Brendan D. Maxcy, Andrea K. Rorrer, and Enrique Aleman, Jr.'s chapter includes information on the rise of state power in Texas. Continuing the focus on the states, in the last chapter of this part, Bruce D. Baker and Preston C. Green analyze Kansas's educational policymaking history.

The second part of the book includes four thematic chapters focused on equity, comparative differences in state educational policies, agenda setting, and the nationalization of educational policy. They address the major areas of recent state activity in education including educational equity (including finance), accountability, and curriculum policy implementation. These chapters expand on and extend the case studies presented earlier, drawing parallels to the expansion of state power in other states. Karen Seashore, Molly Gordon, Judy Meath, and Emanda Thomas open the part with a chapter focused on the roots of differences in state policies across the states of Oregon, New Mexico, and Missouri. Kevin P. Brady's chapter devoted to equity issues follows. Next, is Kathryn A. McDermott and Elizabeth DeBray-Pelot's chapter, which is broadly cast around issues of accountability and nationalizing educational policy. In the final chapter in this part, Mengli Song reviews recent activities and developments in the reading policy domain in nine states, and highlights the dominant role of the state in developing reading policies. She focuses on the loss of local control to state authority over reading curriculum and instruction. Her chapter rounds out the part by comparing and contrasting policy developments around a particular issue.

The last part of the book, the conclusions and future developments, provides some concerns, warnings, and possible new directions in state support for education, from a national view. To that end, Lance D. Fusarelli examines the success and failure of the growth of state power and centralization of control of education in the United States and forecasts future developments. This part brings the reader full circle from the introduction and early chapters, where we offer a historical analysis of the rise of state power, to an examination of potential future developments.

Audience for the Book

While other books have examined parts of this process, none to date has considered the evolution of the power of the state in education from the 1960s into the twenty-first century, comparing six key states—California, Kentucky, New Jersey, New York, Texas, and Kansas—which gives us a wide geographic spread and case studies of states that have witnessed major changes in the role and power of these jurisdictions to control education. Further, the cross-state and thematic chapters help to draw a national picture of the rising power of the state in educational policymaking.

This book should be of interest to educational leaders, policymakers, and policy analysts both in education and in the general field of public policy. Teachers, school administrators, business officials, and others—and those who train and prepare these educators—should find this book essential for understanding the linkups among federal and state capitals, school boards and schools, and teachers and students all of whom are being changed by the rising power of the state in education.

References

Fuhrman, S. H., & Elmore, R. F. (1990, Spring). Understanding local control in the wake of state education reform. *Educational Evaluation and Policy Analysis, 12*(1), 82–96.

Grissmer, D., & Flanagan, A. (2001). Searching for indirect evidence for the effects of statewide reforms. Brookings Papers on Education Policy.

James, T. (1991). State authority and the politics of educational change. Review in *Research in Education 17,* 169–224.

Mazzoni, T. L. (1995). State policymaking and school reform: Influences and influentials. In J. D. Scribner & D. H. Layton (Eds.), *The study of educational politics* (pp. 55–73). Washington, DC: Falmer Press.

Theobald, N. D., & Bardzell, J. (2000). Introduction and overview: Balancing local control and state responsibility for k–12 education. In N. D. Theobald and B. Malen (Eds.), *Balancing local control and state responsibility for K–12 education: 2000 Yearbook of the American Education Finance Association* (pp. 3–19). Larchmont, NY: Eye on Education.

Tyack, D. (1990). Restructuring in historical perspective: Tinkering toward utopia. *Teachers College Record, 92*(2), 170–191.

Wirt, F., & Kirst, M. (1997). *The political dynamics of American education.* Berkeley, CA: McCutchan.

Part I

State Case Studies

Chapter 2

California

Lawrence O. Picus

Who's in Charge Here? State Educational Governance in California

During the first six months of 2006, California residents witnessed two dramatic events that exemplify the strength of state control over local education policy and the chaos with which that state control is exercised. Beginning with the graduating class of 2006, students who had not passed the California High School Exit Exam (CAHSEE) were to be denied diplomas. In June 2006, approximately 47,000 high school seniors had not passed the test and were at risk of not graduating with their class. However, on May 12, Alameda County Superior Court Judge Robert B. Friedman issued a preliminary injunction against the test. He ruled that the CAHSEE placed an unfair burden on poor and minority students attending low-performing schools. This move gave many of the students who had not passed the test hope that they would still get a diploma, although anecdotal evidence suggested that over two-thirds of those students had not taken all of the courses also required for graduation. The expectations of those high school seniors ended a week later when the California Supreme Court overturned Judge Friedman's decision.

The second event has been the ability of the California Teacher's Association (CTA)—the largest and most powerful collective bargaining unit for teachers in California—to carve away at Governor Arnold Schwarzenegger's once lofty public support and to force the governor to increase state funding for schools as estimates of state revenues improved.

What these two events emphasize is that despite the very high level of state control over local schools in California, there is little coherence or consistency in the policies the state enacts governing those schools. This chapter describes the ascent of state control over public education in California during the past forty years, examines the multiple forces that exert influence over state policy, and makes suggestions for ways state education policy could be made more consistent and coherent—ideally to the benefit of the six million children who attend public K–12 schools across the state.

The story begins with the tale of how education policy has shifted away from local school boards and to the state in recent decades. This policy shift can be understood by following two parallel paths. The first considers education programs and state policies that focus on reform, standards, and accountability, while the second path looks at school finance policy and how it has driven the shift to nearly total state control over public K–12 education.

The second section of this chapter describes the current organization of state education policy, depicting five loci of control—the governor and education secretary, the Superintendent of Public Instruction, the State Board of Education, the California Department of Education, and the state legislature—along with the organizations, such as the CTA, that often drive much of California's education policy.

Finally the third section offers some suggestions as to how California can adjust its governance and finance system to provide more support for school districts as they work to meet state and national goals for improving student performance.

The Story of State Control

Professor Jim Guthrie often talks about his experience as a member of the Berkeley, California, school board. He routinely points out that local school boards in California have no power to raise local revenues and are, in effect, completely dependent on the state for resources to operate their schools. At the same time, California has developed a comprehensive—and often confusing—patchwork of educational standards, policies, rules, and procedures that often tie local administrators' hands as they seek to make programmatic educational decisions. State control of education policy in California has been all-encompassing, removing local influence over what is taught, and taking away local authority to determine how much is spent. This discussion on how state control has evolved begins with the role of school finance and then considers how the growing control over money has led to increasing state intrusion into other aspects of schooling.

State Control of School Finance

Finding the exact point in time at which the state started taking on more responsibility for education policy in California is probably impossible, but if the story is viewed through the lens of school finance reform, it begins in 1968 with the filing of the *Serrano v. Priest*[1] school finance lawsuit. *Serrano* is the first of three major school finance events that have shaped recent school funding issues in California. In addition to *Serrano*, the other two are the passage of Proposition 13 and that of Proposition 98 (see, e.g., Picus 1991, 1992, 1998, 1999, and 2004).[2] Each of these events has led to greater state control over the funding of California schools. In recent years, the trend continued through recessions and large state deficits and through good times when the state budget provided lawmakers with large annual surpluses to distribute throughout the state.

Today, education represents the single largest component of the state's general fund budget (LAO, 2006). It is not surprising, therefore, that as the state controls larger and larger portions of school revenues, it also has become more influential in the ways school systems operate, taking more control away from local school districts, either through how funds are allocated to schools or through direct legislative actions designed to elicit certain behaviors on the part of school districts. Each of these events and their impact on school governance are discussed next.

Serrano

The first major event was the *Serrano* court case. Originally filed in 1968, the case is the "grandfather" of all equity-based school finance cases filed across the United States since that time. Alleging that the system of funding schools in California violated the equal protection clause of the California constitution, the plaintiffs in *Serrano* were eventually successful in securing a ruling that required substantial improvements in the equity of school revenues in California. Specifically, the court ordered that all property wealth related revenue differences across school districts be reduced to no more than $100 per student in Average Daily Attendance (ADA). This figure is adjusted for inflation and today is approximately $343 per ADA.

The legislative reaction was to use the existing foundation program approach to school funding, but limit the amount of money school districts could raise. Each district was given a revenue limit, which determined its general revenue per ADA. The revenue limit was based on revenue per ADA for the 1970–1971 school year, and allowed to grow at varying rates. Districts with low revenue limits were allowed greater spending growth than were districts with high revenue limits so that over time their general revenue per pupil would be "squeezed" closer together.

The system had a number of loopholes, notably the ability of districts to override the revenue limit. In addition, the varying rates of increase were such that it was estimated it would take more than twenty years to squeeze revenue limits enough to comply with the requirements of *Serrano*. Although new legislation, in the form of Assembly Bill 65, was passed in the 1977 session of the legislature, it was rendered moot by the June 1978 passage of Proposition 13.[3]

Proposition 13

Proposition 13 dramatically reduced local property tax collections, limiting property taxes to 1 percent of assessed value, and placing restrictions on the rate of growth of assessed value notwithstanding the sale of the property. Legislative action to deal with the fiscal crisis created by Proposition 13 led to a system of school finance that is controlled almost entirely by the state. Revenue limits remain in place and have been substantially equalized. Today a statutory Cost of Living Adjustment (COLA) is made each year to the level of revenue limits.

The legislature controls the collection and distribution of property taxes (which are still physically collected and distributed by the counties), making the property tax effectively a state tax. If the property tax allocation assigned to a school district does not equal its revenue limit, the state makes up the difference.[4] EdSource (October 2000) estimated that in fiscal year 2000–2001, 84 percent of school district revenues were controlled by the state either through direct appropriations or allocation of the property tax. The remaining 16 percent was composed of federal funds (9 percent); local miscellaneous funds such as community contributions, interest income, developer fees, and fees from parcel tax elections (5 percent) and the lottery (2 percent). There is nothing that would suggest these proportions had changed by 2006.

Proposition 98

Over time, a number of factors led to a sense that the portion of the state budget devoted to K–12 education was shrinking. Evidence that the portion of the state's general fund spent on K–14 education declined following the establishment of the state lottery and supported the view that state support was declining. In 1988, to end this trend in state resource allocation patterns, the voters approved Proposition 98, which essentially guarantees that a fixed portion of the state's general fund resources will be devoted to education. As modified by Proposition 111 two years later, the system has three tests that assure either the same proportion of the general fund as the previous year or the same amount of revenue adjusted for the cost of living and change in the number of students. The third test allows adjustments to the Proposition 98 level of funding in the event of severe state revenue declines or increases. This guarantee can only be suspended by a two-thirds vote of the California legislature.

Today, the state exerts a tremendous amount of control over how education funds are allocated and used by local school districts. It is this control that ties directly into discussions of educational governance in the Golden State. Finkelstein, Furry, and Huertra (2000) point out that "California's school finance system is centrally controlled. Requests for marginal increases in spending are made through the state legislative process and are not the decisions of local property taxpayers" (p. 47). While some cities have appropriated funds to school districts, and a number of districts have successfully passed parcel taxes—taxes levied in equal amounts on each piece of property, or in some cases on a square foot basis, rather than on the value of that property—to fund their programs, local revenues of this nature amount to less than 5 percent of total K–12 education spending in California. Interestingly, one of the districts that relies on a parcel tax to balance its budget is the same Berkeley district that Professor Guthrie once served.

The school finance system in place in California today appears to have little logic. With the exception of the school accountability legislation passed in 1999, which provides a relatively small amount of revenue linked to student performance, there is no link between finance and other education reform efforts. Because of the *Serrano* court's use of wealth-related spending differences as the standard on which the equity of the system is to be judged, California has determined that revenue differences resulting from other characteristics, such as district type or size, or student needs, are not part of the equity calculation for *Serrano* compliance.

Because the courts required that "wealth related" differences be minimized, efforts to fund programs "outside" the revenue limit have proliferated (Walters, 2006). The most frequent approach is to establish a categorical program that funds a special need or program in districts that meet certain criteria or the students exhibit certain characteristics. While categorical grants are not a bad thing, and are often used to meet the special needs of children (e.g., special education funding), or to address different characteristics of districts (e.g., funds for transportation when per pupil costs are a function of population density and geographical terrain), EdSource (October 2000) estimates that over 130 state and federal categorical programs were in existence for the 2000–2001 school year. Finkelstein, Furry, and Huertra (2000) have stated there may be as many as 150, but point out that because some programs are run by other state agencies, it is nearly impossible to get an accurate count.

More important than the number of categorical programs is the amount of money spent for them. In 2005–2006, over half of the state appropriation for K–12 education was earmarked through categorical programs. If local property taxes are included in the calculation, this represents over one-third of total school spending, or nearly $20 billion. If these funds were all dedicated to meet specific student needs, a factor that would improve the vertical equity of the system, it might be understandable. However, many of the programs are specifically designated for small programs that benefit a small group of students. In short, legislators are able to circumvent the equity requirements of *Serrano* by creating narrow categorical programs that benefit small groups of districts or schools. Additionally, for many programs, once they are established, entry to the program by other districts is restricted. While there has been an effort in recent years to reduce the complexity of categorical grants, and while the two largest categorical programs—special education and class size reduction—are focused more closely on identified student needs, even the efforts to simplify categorical programs have led to additional reporting complexities for school districts.

The precariousness of this dependence on state funding became apparent during the state's recent fiscal crisis wherein newly elected Governor Schwarzenegger struck a deal with the education community to suspend Proposition 98 for one year with a promise to pay back the funds in future years. The next year, when insufficient revenues were available to make good on the promise, the governor simply did not include those funds in his annual budget. While the situation changed for the 2006–2007 fiscal year, due to unexpected increases in state revenue, it is not clear that the governor would have eventually provided that funding in the absence of a vicious political campaign orchestrated and paid for largely by the CTA. In fact, as part of his ballot measure campaign to control California's budgeting and spending, the governor supported Proposition 76, which would have slowed the growth of the Proposition 98 guarantee and given the state more flexibility to suspend the requirements of that guarantee in years when revenues did not meet expenditure expectations—all without providing a local option for additional school revenues (for details on Proposition 76, see Matsusaka & Picus, 2005).

Standards-Based Education and State Control

State control over education does not end with school finance. In fact, the collision of state control over school finance, combined with the growing pressure at all levels for standards-based education and accountability, has led to increased state control over what students learn and how it is taught. Like school finance, this growing control has occurred over a period of more than twenty years and shows little or no sign of abating, despite political rhetoric to the contrary. We now consider the major factors leading to increased state control over schools in general chronological order.

Collective Bargaining

State control over school district programmatic decisions began to grow as the state took over increased responsibility for funding the schools as previously described. The Rodda Act, passed in 1975, gave school district employees the right to collective bargaining with local school districts, ushering in a new reality for school district management. While it did not specifically require that school districts negotiate with organizations representing their employees, the reality today is that all districts have collectively bargained contracts, and the terms of those contracts drive many of the local decisions that are made regarding educational programs. Moreover, contract terms that set class size, establish salary and benefit levels, and control other work conditions, often work at cross-purposes to the establishment of new educational programs that research suggests will lead to improved student performance. Although collective bargaining is not a straightforward example of increased state control, the effect of the Rodda Act in the thirty years since it was passed has been dramatic on the organization and operation of school districts, not only in the classroom, but in the overall relationship between school boards and all nonmanagement employees.

School Reform: Step 1—Senate Bill 813

California was one of the first states to jump into the fray of education reform in response to the release of *A Nation at Risk* in 1983 (National Commission on Excellence, 1983). Senate Bill 813 was heralded for both increased funding, and the explicit trade made by the legislature to provide school districts with more money in exchange for reforms in the education system. Among the many components of SB 813 were incentives to school districts to increase the length of the school year and school day, increased minimum salaries for teachers, and enhanced high school graduation requirements. Picus (1988) argued that the legislature's main tool for influencing local school district behavior through SB 813 was the use of incentives to fund its specific goals. However, Picus also points out that although SB 813 contained an extensive list of reforms and expectations, it "contained virtually no provisions to evaluate the effectiveness of its reforms" (Picus, 1988, p. 44). Since that time, many other reforms have been implemented in California, most with more comprehensive compliance requirements.

Curriculum Frameworks and Content Standards

California was one of the leaders in the establishment of curriculum frameworks and content standards to identify what students should know and be able to do. The California Department of Education's Web site states that content standards "were designed to encourage the highest achievement of every student, by defining the knowledge, concepts, and skills that students should acquire at each grade level."[5] The Department states that curriculum frameworks "are the blueprints for implementing the content standards adopted by the State Board of Education."[6] Together the content standards and curriculum frameworks drive the content that schools are expected to provide for all students. California's standards are generally thought of as among the strongest in the United States—*Education Week*'s widely read Quality Counts publication gives California a B+ for standards and accountability (*Education Week*, 2006).

To further support the state's role in the design of curriculum, California is—and has been for many years—a textbook adoption state. That is, the textbooks used by schools must be approved by the State Board of Education. Textbooks are approved through a nearly three-year process, and new adoptions occur regularly with new texts adopted every six years by subject. The result is additional control at the state level over what is taught in each of the 8,000-plus schools in the state, and often how it is taught.

California's political environment is confounded by the ability of citizens to place initiative measures on the ballot. Propositions 13 and 98 were both initiatives, and over the course of the state's history, many state policies have been put in place via the initiative process. In June 2006, a proposition to mandate—and pay for through income taxes on the highest-income Californians—preschool for three and four year olds was placed on the ballot. Had it passed, it would have created a system that cost an estimated $24 billion to provide universal preschool, including schools for children whose parents are currently paying for preschool themselves.

Other initiatives have impacted what California schools can and can't do. Proposition 227, passed by the voters in 1998, requires all public school instruction in California to be done in English and limits the way English Language Learners are taught to one-year intensive sheltered English immersion programs. This is perhaps the most compelling example of how state policy has limited local decision making and authority.

Accountability and Testing

Today, every school leader and teacher is focused on California's Academic Performance Index (API). Established in 1999, this tool is used to measure student progress under the content standards described earlier. A school receives a raw score of between 200 and 1,000 based on the results of the Standardized Testing and Reporting (STAR) system—a standardized test administered annually in California—and the California High School Exit Exam. The target score for every school is 800, and all schools scoring below the 800 mark are expected to show improvement each year. If they fail to show sufficient improvement, the state intercedes through the Intermediate Intervention/Underperforming Schools Program (II/USP).

The API is further complicated by the fact that schools receive two "rankings" in addition to their raw API score each year. The first indicates the decile score for the school generally, and the second shows its relative decile rank among schools with similar demographic characteristics. Thus, a school whose ranking is a 2/10 has an API score in the second lowest decile, but compared to similar schools is a very high performer. To a large extent, this scoring system seems to confuse the general public, and even many in the education community. However, the API—despite a change in the standardized test used to measure each school's API, and the current controversy over the CAHSEE—still seems to drive much of what is taught in California schools and is the focus of much debate across the state.

In addition to the API, every school must prepare an annual School Accountability Report Card (SARC). One of the requirements of Proposition 98, SARCs have become part of the educational landscape in California. The contents of the SARC are proscribed by the state and are quite comprehensive, dealing with all school activities.

As this discussion shows, the combination of state school finance and education policy has driven control over most important education decisions to the state level. While this shift has turned the focus of school improvement toward improved learning—with an emphasis on the state's curriculum content standards—school districts have often had a difficult time meeting the wide range of state requirements, in part because the state's governance structure lacks clear lines of authority and responsibility. This dysfunctional governance is described in the following section.

California School Governance: Who is in Charge Here?

California presents something of a paradox in deciding what type of governance structure would best support high student achievement.[7] On the one hand, many of the elements of a successful education system are in place; on the other, California schools are hampered by a system that appears to have too many agencies responsible for establishing educational policy, along with a finance structure that not only does not support efforts at educational improvement, but may well hinder such efforts.

In this section, options for governance are presented and discussed. Four distinct issues are considered: options for school governance, or the relationship between the state and schools and school districts; options for the organization of state agencies with responsibility for education; options for school finance; and options for employee relations.

Options for School Governance

It seems that a model of governance that has the state responsible for development of standards and accountability measures, and local schools responsible for the implementation of educational programs that meet those standards, is the approach California has taken to this point. In fact, this approach makes sense from a policy perspective, but the question that remains is what form the relationship between the state and schools should take. The state has to make a fundamental choice between two overarching alternatives. Specifically, will the state establish the standards and leave the implementation up to locals while holding the locals accountable for performance? Or will the state be more explicit in dictating the actions schools and school districts must take in meeting the standards? (The second approach has been used more often in recent years.)

This fundamental distinction in the role of the state must be resolved if the rest of the state's educational governance system is to operate successfully for the benefit of children. As described elsewhere in this volume, current literature and research on the relationship between schools and the state suggest that implementation of state policies be left up to local schools and school districts. The state's role would focus on establishing standards and measuring how well schools are meeting those standards. The actual programs put in place to meet the standards would be designed and implemented locally where, it is argued, knowledge of specific student needs is the greatest.

The Legislative Analyst's Office (LAO), in a 1999 report on the need for a Master Plan (Hill, 1999), suggested creation of a system whereby the state's role was to provide adequate funding for schools, establish a system that offers schools and school districts substantial flexibility in program implementation, and supply information to help teachers, parents, and voters understand what constitutes successful school programs and which schools are successful. The LAO also argued that the state can help improve local control by making sure local school boards have the power to make decisions "in the best interest of students," and by increasing competition within the public school system. Competition, the LAO suggested, could lead to more efficient schools and make them more responsive to parental needs. Finally, the LAO argued that the state could play a major role in mitigating cost shifts between school districts and other governmental agencies.

Local responsibilities under the LAO's model include the power to decide how to structure the relationship between a district and its component schools, and allow districts to determine the best programs for improving student performance and meeting individual student needs.

Options for the Organization of State Agencies

If the governance system is to operate effectively, the mechanisms of state governance must be well organized and specific responsibilities spelled out clearly. Today, at the state level, there is confusion and disagreement over who is responsible for the development of state policy and its implementation, with no fewer than five different players in the mix. Like most states, California has both a chief state school officer and a State Board of Education. In California, as in ten other states, the Superintendent of Public Instruction is an elected official—in California a nonpartisan office—while the State Board of Education is appointed by the governor, subject to approval of the state senate. Current law does not clearly define the roles of the board and the Superintendent of Public Instruction (SPI). The result has been considerable conflict and legal activity since about 1919 (Haberman, 1999).

Recent legal actions between the state board and the SPI include a court ruling in which the court stated that the role of the board was to establish goals for public education, but not be involved in micromanagement, whereas the role of the SPI was to manage the day-to-day operations of the California Department of Education (CDE) and execute board policies. Until recently, there was continuing controversy over whether the state board can hire its own legal counsel and effectively take a position different from that of the SPI in matters pertaining to the operation of the state's education system. Although this conflict has been moderated under the current Superintendent of Public Instruction, it is still a factor in state education policy decisions.

To further complicate matters, in 1991, Governor Wilson, through an executive order, created the position of Secretary for Child Development and Education as part of his cabinet. Although attempts to create the position through statue have failed, Wilson funded it through the Office of Planning and Research, and Governors Davis and Schwarzenegger have retained the position, renaming it Secretary for Education.

During this time, the legislature has continued to enact legislation focused on both school financing and education programs and policy. As demonstrated earlier, as the state's fiscal control grew, so too did programmatic control over schools, particularly those involving categorical funding. Much of the actual implementation of these new programs is left to the California Department of Education, the fifth party in the state governance structure. Despite increasing responsibilities, in the early years of the decade, the department's budget was been reduced by nearly 50 percent, much of which has not been restored.

In 1996, the Constitution Revision Commission's report said that "California has an educational system that provides no real focal point for responsibility, no flexibility for local districts and responsibilities are widely scattered, resulting in no single official or entity being accountable for the state's education system either at the state or local level" (cited in Haberman, 1999, p. 15).

Kirst, Hayward, and Fuller (2000) argued that at the beginning of the decade the governor was the most powerful force in California for determining education policy. Governor Wilson's Class Size Reduction plan is an excellent example of the powerful role played by the governor. Under Governor Grey Davis in 1999, Kirst, Hayward, and Fuller (2000) argue that the governor's power in education policy "soared to unprecedented heights" (p. 89). There is no reason to believe that Governor Schwarzenegger has relinquished any of the influence or power in recent years, despite the efforts of the CTA to undercut his political support following the so-called breaking of the promise to restore Proposition 98 funding in FY 2004.

The result is a system in which no one appears to be in charge, and one that sends often-conflicting messages to the schools. Moreover, despite considerable rhetoric to the contrary, state policy in California is more a series of requirements and mandates than it is a system with clear policy goals and adequate support for schools to meet those goals in the ways they deem most appropriate.

What are the appropriate roles of each of these agencies or individuals? To a large extent, that depends on the answer to the question posed about the role of the state. Assuming that the state elects to increase local control in the future, the LAO argues that any solution to this gridlock at the state level would reduce the role of these agencies and find ways for their functions to complement each other better. The LAO (Hill, 1999) suggests that the Superintendent of Public Instruction (SPI) promote accountability and local control. The SPI would collect and disseminate information about the success of the K–12 education system and serve as in independent advisor to the governor and legislature.

Under the LAO's recommendation, the Secretary of Education's office would have expanded responsibilities, including implementation of state policy and enforcement of existing rules and regulations. The Secretary of Education would remain a cabinet-level appointment, and the LAO argues that by providing this position with authority similar to that of other state agency heads, it would improve lines of authority and accountability to the governor since, unlike the SPI, the position would be appointed and not elected. Many of the current functions of the California Department of Education would be transferred to this executive agency.

Finally, the LAO suggests that the State Board of Education be recast as a long-term policy board, focusing on overall direction of the K–12 education system over time. The board would monitor the implementation and effectiveness of state and federal programs and recommend a comprehensive plan for the administration of K–12 education programs.

The key to resolving the logjam of state agencies and players is to define clearly the role of each. The LAO's recommendations provide role clarification without requiring major constitutional changes. The SPI could remain an elected official. Charged with maintaining system accountability and monitoring local control, the SPI could serve as an advocate for the public without confusing the roles of advocacy with the management of the system, which would now largely be a function of the new executive agency and of the local districts—where more authority would theoretically be located. Moreover, this model would help reduce the existing tension between the State Board of Education and the SPI and their respective roles in the system.

An alternative model would be to make the SPI responsible to the State Board of Education. The SPI could be appointed by the board, and the board could either be appointed by the governor and approved by the legislature, or elected by the public. This model would eliminate the question over lines of authority in terms of the operation of the existing CDE, and allow the board to establish state education policy to be carried out by the SPI. However, this model essentially eliminates the role of the Secretary of Education, and gives the State Board of Education considerable independence from both the governor and the legislature. Since the SPI would not be an elected official in his or her own right, this arrangement would be less problematic for an elected governor, but it would still give the CDE independence not enjoyed by most other state agencies. The level of control exerted by the governor would depend to a large extent on whether the state board members were appointed by the governor or elected by the voters. Even if appointed, the state board and the CDE would enjoy a fair amount of independence from the governor.

The advantage of this option is that there are fewer "players" at the state level. The role of the SPI is essentially that of a manager, and the advocacy role identified by the LAO would most likely be managed by the state board, particularly if it were an elected board. The disadvantage of this model is that the governor exercises less influence over educational policy, which, over time could lead to conflict and the establishment of an office more directly under the governor's control to deal with educational issues. That would lead to the type of confusion that exists today.

Each of these scenarios is silent on the role of the legislature. That is because it was assumed that the state would move to a local control model with relatively limited state involvement beyond the establishment of statewide standards for student performance. If the legislature determines that it would like a larger role in the governance of California schools, the model that relies on a State Board of Education appointed by the governor and approved by the legislature, with the state board appointing the SPI, is probably the solution that best achieves that goal. One alternative that would be available would be to require legislative approval of the SPI as well. Of course, it needs to be remembered that any governance option that eliminates the elected SPI will require a constitutional change.

The Role of the CTA

At discussed earlier, the California Teachers' Association, always a powerful influence on educational policy in the state, conducted a very visible and successful campaign to discredit Governor Schwarzenegger in 2005. Many have credited their campaign—along with those of other public employee unions—with defeating the governor's four ballot measures in November 2005. Collective bargaining—a key issue for the CTA—has always been at the forefront of governance discussions in California. Districts often complain that they are restricted from implementing new programs or spending money for important needs because they are locked into the requirements of their collective bargaining agreement. At the same time, the legislature has occasionally tried to get around the requirements of local bargaining agreements by mandating how new funds will be spent, which explains the large number of categorical programs in existence today.

It seems unlikely that collective bargaining will go away. Thus, any governance system needs to take into account that bargaining at some level will continue. The question is, should it remain with local school districts, or should there be one statewide collective bargaining agreement? In a system of locally controlled schools and school districts, statewide collective bargaining seems out of place. Moreover, the biggest single drawback to a statewide bargaining agreement is the likely establishment of a statewide salary schedule. While a salary schedule may sound like a positive step—particularly in relation to the adequacy funding system previously proposed—in reality there are many drawbacks.

The state of Washington established a statewide salary schedule in the early 1980s as part of its attempt to fund a basic education as required by the Washington State Supreme Court. Over time, it created substantial inequities in teacher compensation based on the substantial differences in the cost of living between the urban areas in the western part of the state and the largely rural areas in the eastern part. Absent a regional cost adjustment, a uniform salary schedule can create a number of problems over time.

But, more important, if the state's goal is to minimize state interference with local decisions, why would it eliminate local collective bargaining? While one might argue that, taken to its logical conclusion, the state should not require collective bargaining at all, but leave that decision up to the local districts, it would be hard at this point in time to take back that right from teachers in local school districts. It might be possible to eliminate some of the statutory employee conditions (e.g., tenure and dismissal requirements), and let local districts and their bargaining units determine the relative trade-offs of each individually, but attempting to take away what is perceived as a local right might prove to be too difficult.

In short, unless the state were to dramatically increase state authority over local decision-making, it seems inappropriate to eliminate the current collective bargaining rights available to school employees. Rather, by making local districts responsible for the performance of their students, establishing a funding system that educators agree is adequate for meeting those standards, and letting local officials determine how those standards will be met, perhaps both sides will come to the bargaining table prepared to find ways to work together to improve student performance.

Conclusion

This chapter has considered the current role of the state in the educational governance of California, with a particular focus on the relationship of the school finance system to programmatic and policy needs of local schools and school districts. It suggests that California faces a two-dimensional problem in improving its educational governance. First, the state needs to create a more rational and streamlined system of state educational governance, and, second, the school finance system needs to be reformed to more closely support the educational needs of children.

It is also important to consider the effectiveness of this high level of state control. On its merits, state control of education is not a bad thing. In fact, as we move toward funding systems based on measures of adequacy rather than equity, establishing certain parameters within which schools and school districts must operate may be an important component to manage the costs of the overall education system—and offer states a way to defend future adequacy suits by suggesting that the problem in underachieving schools is not lack of funds, but the use of those funds for programs or organizational structures that vary substantially from those used to estimate adequate levels of resources.

To the extent that high levels of state control can focus schools on good instruction and high-quality curriculum, influence from above can lead to improved student outcomes. The problem in California—despite highly regarded state curriculum guidelines—is that the overall governance from the state level has become incoherent, forcing local school officials to undertake many actions and activities that are counterproductive to student learning. Therefore, it is not state control per se that is problematic; it is California's lack of a coordinated strategy that has bogged schools down in the morass of high state control.

A number of factors must be considered in development of any new governance or finance structure for California. The most important is Proposition 13. The constitutional restriction on collection of property taxes dramatically eliminated any local control over the level of funding for schools, instead shifting responsibility for that decision to Sacramento. It is unlikely that the provisions of Proposition 13 will be changed in the near term, if ever. Therefore, discussions of educational governance and school finance must be cognizant of the fact that the legislature will always control the vast majority of resources available for schools. Creating a governance structure that recognizes that reality and seeks to find solutions within the tax structure of the state is also important.

Consequently, options for local control of the decision-making apparatus are more limited than they are in many other states. This governance system does not doom a structure that sets state goals and leaves the locals free to implement as they see fit, but it does require that state policy makers take steps to both undo the many categorical grant programs in existence today, and resist the urge in the future to add more.

In summary, California's education system today is the embodiment of state control. If schools are to improve learning at all levels, the governance system needs to shift from one of managing policy implementation through review of inputs, to one of measuring results on the basis of student outcomes, and through establishment of systems that measure the extent to which schools develop and live by a coherent instructional vision, and allocate their resources toward meeting the goals so established. A change of this magnitude would require a substantial paradigm shift for state policymakers—and local school officials who for years have conveniently blamed the state for most, if not all, of their ills—and will require a great deal of debate and careful consideration before it can be fully implemented.

Notes

1. *Serrano v. Priest*, 5 Cal 3d 584, 487 P2d 1241, 96 Cal Rptr 601 (1971) (Serrano I).

2. Proposition 13, passed by the voters in 1978, placed a 1 percent limit on property tax rate and limited the growth in assessed value of all property until it is sold. The impact of the measure has been to dramatically reduce local property tax revenues for all levels of government. Proposition 98, passed by voters in 1988, established a minimum percentage of the state's general fund that had to be devoted to K–14 education.

3. Although never implemented, Assembly Bill 65 was one of the most comprehensive school finance reform packages ever passed by a state. Had it been implemented, it would have substantially increased funding for schools by taking advantage of a large state surplus, and enhanced the equalization aspects of the funding formula both through additional aid to property poor districts and recapture of tax revenues from property wealth school districts.

4. In a few instances, districts receive virtually all, or more than their entire revenue limit funding from property taxes. Because these districts also receive a basic aid grant of $120 per student as provided for by the state constitution, they get more revenue than dictated by their revenue limit and are known as "basic aid districts."

5. http://www.cde.ca.gov/be/st/ss/indexasp; June 4, 2006.

6. http://www.cde.ca.gov/ci/cr/cf/indesasp; June 4, 2006.

7. This section relies heavily on the author's earlier work. See, in particular, Picus, 2001.

References

California Department of Education. (2005). *School accountability report card: Data element definition and sources.* Sacramento: California Department of Education (February). Available: http://www.cde.ca.gov/ta/ac/sa/definitions04.asp; June 4, 2006.

EdSource. (2000, October). *School finance 2000–01: What will $49 billion in education funding buy?* Palo Alto, CA: EdSource.

Education Week (2006). *California State highlights from Quality Counts.* Available: http://www.edweek.org/ew/articles/2006/01/05/17shr.ca.h25.html; June 4, 2006.

Finkelstein, Neil, Furry, William, & Huerta, Luis. (2000). School finance in California: Does history provide a sufficient policy standard? In Elizabeth Burr, Gerald C. Hayward, Bruce Fuller, & Michael W. Kirst (Eds.),

Crucial issues in California cducation 2000: Are the reform pieces fitting together? (pp. 45–78). Berkeley, CA: Policy Analysis for California Education.

Haberman, M. J. (1999, July). *A double-headed system: A history of K–12 governance in California and options for restructuring*. Sacramento: California Research Bureau.

Hill, E. G. (1999, May). *A K–12 master plan*. Sacramento: Office of the Legislative Analyst.

Kirst, M. W., Hayward, G. C., & Fuller, B. (2000). Governance and accountability." In Elizabeth Burr, Gerald C. Hayward, Bruce Fuller, & Michael W. Kirst (Eds.), *Crucial issues in California Education 2000: Are the reform pieces fitting together?* (pp. 79–94). Berkeley: Policy Analysis for California Education.

Legislative Analyst's Office (LAO). (2006). Overview of the 2006–07 May revision. Sacramento: Legislative Analyst. Available: http://www.lao.ca.gov/2006/may_revise/may_revise_051506.html; May 31, 2006.

Matsusaka, J., & Picus, L. O. (2005). *Proposition 76 analysis: Issues related to spending caps and state spending—Insights from research and best practices*. Sacramento: California Policy Institute.

National Commission on Excellence in Education. (1983). *A nation at risk*. Washington, DC: U.S. Government Printing Office.

Picus, L. O. (1988). *The effect of state grant-in-aid policies on local government decision making: The case of California school finance*. Santa Monica: RAND Corporation, P-7492-RGS.

Picus, L. O. (1991). Cadillacs or Chevrolets? The effects of state control on school finance in California. *Journal of Education Finance, 17*(1), 33–59.

Picus, L. O. (1992). An update on California school finance 1992–93: What does the future hold? *Journal of Education Finance, 18*(2), 134–146.

Picus, L. O. (1998, April). California school finance 1998–99: More money for schools, but what will it buy? In D. R. Tetreault (Ed.), *The state of the states and provinces 1998*. Proceedings of the 1998 Annual Meeting of the American Educational Research Association Fiscal Issues, Policy and Education Finance Special Interest Group. San Diego.

Picus, L. O. (1999, April). School funding and education reform in California, 1999. In B. O. Brent (Ed.), *The political economy of education: The state of the states and provinces 1999*. Proceedings of the 1999 Annual Meeting of the American Education Research Association fiscal Issues, Policy, and Educational Finance Special Interest Group. Montreal, Quebec.

Picus, L. O. (2001). Educational governance in California: Defining state and local roles. In J. Sonstelie & P. Richardson (Eds.), *School finance and California's master plan for education*. San Francisco: Public Policy Institute of California.

Picus, L. O. (2004). California school finance 2004–05: Heavy lifting required. *Journal of School Business Management, 16*(2), 10–13.

Walters, D. (2006, May 30). Then was then, now is now and LA has a grip on pork barrel. *Sacramento Bee*, p. A3. Available: http://www.sacbee.com/content/politics/story/14261743p-15075257c.html.

Chapter 3

Kentucky

Tricia Browne-Ferrigno

Educational reform has been ongoing in Kentucky for well over a decade and a half, since passage of the landmark Kentucky Education Reform Act of 1990 (KERA), making the state one of the leaders in comprehensive and systemic change in schools (Foster, 1999; Pankratz & Petrosko, 2000). KERA restructured PreK–12 public education through significant changes in curriculum, governance, and finance and embarked the commonwealth on a demanding pace of school accountability (Kannapel, Aagaard, Coe, & Reeves, 2000; Legislative Research Commission, 1990). This ambitious legislation, however, was not independently initiated by the General Assembly; rather, it was required when the Kentucky Supreme Court dismantled the entire state education system and required the building of a new one (Foster, 1999; Steffy,1993a).

This chapter presents an overview of the redesign of the state education system and its ultimate implementation in schools and classrooms. The state action required extensive collaborative efforts by policymakers and consultants, state education officials and researchers, teachers and administrators, lawyers and citizens, and university-based teacher and leadership educators. Although the various groups did not often cross institutional boundaries to do the work, enactment of KERA marks a major shift from local to state control of public education in Kentucky. It also represents systemic educational change that is an intricate blending of both educational reform and renewal.

Conceptual Distinctions: Reform versus Renewal

Before progressing further, a distinction needs to be made concerning the meanings of two words often used interchangeably in policy and educational literature. According to dictionary definitions (*Random House College Dictionary*, 1999; Webster's *Seventh New Collegiate Dictionary*, 1963), *reform* means to improve by change of form or by removal of defects as measured against some standard of excellence. *Renewal* means to revive or bring back to a condition of freshness and vigor.

American public schooling has long been used as the instrument with which to institute—or at least appear to institute—radical changes in social policy to meet often-conflicting interests of multiple stakeholder groups (Tyack & Cuban, 1995). Such changes have come from forces both outside and inside of education. Advocates for educational reform are most often government officials and policy-makers, business leaders, special interest groups, and school board members. Usually, reform proposals are efforts directed toward correcting perceived short-comings in public schools that cause broader societal or economic problems (Cuban, 1990; House, 1998; Schlechty, 1997). Conversely, advocates for educational renewal are usually administrators, teachers, parents, students, and researchers who work in PreK–12 schools, and occasionally representatives of the local communities where schools are situated. Educational innovation through renewal is perceived as the primary responsibility of those groups that work in schools or that are most closely connected to schools (Fullan, 2004; Glickman, 1998; Goodlad, 1997; Peterson-del Mar, 1994; Smith & O'Day, 1991).

This distinction between *reform* and *renewal* is important in understanding the forces that influenced actions and events leading to passage of KERA and the equity and accountability efforts that are critical components of the systemic initiative. While KERA may be perceived at first glance as a top-down reform policy enacted by state legislators, private citizens and educators agitated for educational innovation and assumed major responsibility for its long-term bottom-up implementation (Conley, 2003; Steffy, 1993b).

Citizen-based Advocacy for Educational Reform

Citizen-based advocacy groups outside the policymaking and implementation framework, what Fuhrman (1994) calls "constituency-bridging groups" (p. 6), can overcome four major stumbling blocks to coherent educational reform: "fragmented organizational structure, election cycles, policy overload, and specialization" (Sexton, 2000, p. 249). Two such groups played critically important roles in Kentucky's efforts to improve its public schools.

From 1980 to 1983, a group of citizens appointed by the Kentucky Council on Higher Education, known as the Committee on Higher Education and Reform, gathered data to complete a report about higher education in the state. It found that:

> Kentucky was last in the nation in the percentage of adults with high school diplomas, second from last in the percentage of adults attending college, last in adult literacy, and depressingly low on other indications of educational performance, including spending. (Sexton, 1995, p. 2)

After completing their state-appointed charge, members of that committee reformed under the guidance of attorney Edward Prichard into an independent organization advocating for citizen action to improve public education. The independent nonpartisan, nonprofit Prichard Committee for Academic Excellence is "perhaps the first and most influential of all state commissions" (Conley, 2003, p. 139). They advocated for change "out of frustration with the indifference of elected officials toward education and because they felt that Kentucky's historic educational deficits would not solve themselves" (Sexton, 2000, p. 245). Their intent was—and has remained—to influence educational innovation through citizen involvement in the policy-development process and public attention on high student academic achievement in public schools (Heine, 2002).

During the mid-1980s, another grassroots advocacy group formed, calling itself the Council for Better Education, and included sixty-six property-poor school districts, seven local school boards, and twenty-two public school students. It filed a class-action suit in the Franklin Circuit Court in 1985 (Steffy, 1993a), asserting that "funding in Kentucky was *inequitable* and *inadequate*—inequitable because some school districts had much more money than others to support education and inadequate because of Kentucky's low level of educational achievement" (Adams, 2000, p. 30). Although only seeking changes in school funding, the council's legal action unexpectedly lead to the Kentucky Supreme Court ruling in June 1989 that "the state's *entire* elementary and secondary school system—not just the school finance system—[was] inefficient and unconstitutional" (p. 34). This sweeping decision applied to "the whole gamut of the common school system in Kentucky" (*Rose v. Council for Better Education*, 1989, p. 215). All three branches of government were involved with rebuilding the state's system of public schools from the ashes of the previous one that was declared "inequitable, inefficient, and inadequate" (Pankratz & Petrosko, 2000, p. 4). The General Assembly was charged with the task of constructing a new public schooling system through appropriate legislation (i.e., organization, control, financing) by the end of the 1990 session (Haselton & Miller, 1999; Steffy, 1993a). Policymakers met the Kentucky Supreme Court deadline for designing a new system of public education by enacting KERA in April 1990.

KERA: Legislative Action to Improve Public Schools

While not emerging or existing in isolation as a state policy action to address educational equity and accountability issues, KERA is unique because its purpose was to "alter the experiences of every school and every student" (Pankratz & Petrosko, 2000, p. 2). The sweeping changes in educational policy emerged through work completed by the Task Force on Education Reform composed of twenty-two individuals. Six members were appointed by then Governor Wilkinson; the House and Senate each selected eight members. The elected

Superintendent of Public Instruction was intentionally excluded from the task force because the Supreme Court ruling effectively abolished the duties of that office when it ruled that the entire system of public education was unconstitutional. During the court cases leading up to the Supreme Court decision, Governor Wilkinson and several legislators disagreed vehemently in public about the type of educational reform needed. The governor

> argued for structural changes that involved moving primary responsibility for education reform from the statehouse to the school site, development of a method by which to hold school personnel accountable for results, and providing a significant financial reward to schools that show progress. (Foster, 1999, p. 9)

Hence, he chose to exclude himself from membership on the task force because he wanted to avoid potential political disruption of the process. Nonetheless, several elements of the transformed system of public education system in Kentucky reflect Governor Wilkinson's vision of a balance between state and local control.

The task force divided into three major committees (i.e., curriculum, governance, finance) and conducted national searches to locate and hire experts to assist them as consultants. Although working independently throughout most of the policy-development process, during the early months of its existence the task force adopted twelve principles to guide the separate and combined work: (1) All students can learn and nearly all at high levels; (2) We know how to successfully teach all students; (3) Curriculum content must reflect high expectations and instructional strategies must be successful ones; (4) Ours must be a performance-based system; (5) Ours must be a system in which school performance results in appropriate consequences; (6) School-based staff should have a major role in shaping instructional strategies; (7) School staff must be equipped with the capacity to make good instructional decisions; (8) Non-essential regulations must be reduced significantly; (9) Schools have responsibility for outreach to home and community; (10) What is tested will heavily influence what is taught; (11) Learning begins early and does not end with high school graduation; (12) There is a need to provide for a measure in independent assessment and enforcement authority (Foster, 1999, p. 20). The task force—and ultimately the entire General Assembly—had only nine months in which to restructure Kentucky's educational system and pass new legislation to support it. Following is a summary of the most significant portions of the comprehensive educational reform policy enacted in April 1990.

KERA-initiated Changes in Curriculum

Through the efforts of the Task Force on Education Reform Curriculum Committee and its consultant David Hornbeck, KERA made five major changes in the area of curriculum, instruction, and assessment. First, schools became responsible for creating challenging learning opportunities for all students by expecting high levels of performance in six broad areas related to core content, problem solving and thinking, and knowledge development and application. Much of this work was done by the governor-appointed Council for School Performance Standards that developed the first set of seventy-five valued outcomes that transformed into core content.

Second, to assure a focus on high levels of student learning, the state department of education was required to develop an assessment system that would make schools accountable for student performance and to provide support for schools needing assistance in achieving their accountability goals. Third, early childhood education was enhanced to include preschool programs for three- and four-year-old children at risk of not learning, and kindergarten through grade 3 were transformed into multiage primary programs.

Fourth, KERA required schools to provide enhanced learning opportunities for at-risk students through the introduction of Extended School Services, which provides academic tutoring and access to social and medical services through greater school–community collaboration. Finally, to achieve these broad goals, the curriculum committee requested additional funding through KERA to expand use of technology in all schools and to provide ongoing inservice professional development of educational practitioners (Darling-Hammond & McLaughlin, 1999; Foster, 1999; Kannapel et al., 2000; Pankratz & Petrosko, 2000).

KERA-initiated Changes in Governance

The Task Force on Education Reform Governance Committee received advice from two consultants, Luvern Cunningham and Lila Caro. Through its recommendations and final enactment of KERA, leadership of the state department of education changed from an elected superintendent of public instruction to an appointed commissioner of education. Further, the commissioner of education was empowered to enforce new anti-nepotism regulations, restructure the state department of education, and take over failing districts and schools if needed. The Office of Education Accountability was created and charged with statewide monitoring compliance of reform efforts and reporting of progress directly to the Kentucky General Assembly (Darling-Hammond & McLaughlin, 1999; Foster, 1999; Pankratz & Petrosko, 2000).

Individual schools gained greater local authority from local boards of education through the mandated installation of site-based management groups having legal authority over school matters (Foster, 1999; Kleckler, Austin, & Burns, 1999). These School-Based Decision-Making (SBDM) Councils are composed of three teachers, two parents, and the principal or a multiple of this configuration that must remain in a three-two-one ratio of representation (Lindle, 1992;

Van Meter, 1991). While teacher and parent members are elected by their peers and serve limited terms, the principal is the only continuing member and usually serves as the chairperson. KERA also empowered SBDM councils to make new principal selections that are binding and to approve hiring of new certified staff recommended by the principal. Superintendents' authority to select principals for the schools in their districts was minimized as a result of this governance change.

KERA also created an autonomous regulatory agency responsible for oversight of the preparation and certification of teachers and administrators, known as the Education Professional Standards Board (EPSB), and empowered it to determine continuing professional development for in service certified school personnel (Pankratz & Petrosko, 2000). Somewhat unique among most state-bureaucratic models, EPSB is managed by educators and now functions independently from the state department of education. In additional to establishing standards of performance for the preparation and practice of public school educator, the board serves as the state accrediting agency for public and private preparation programs in Kentucky, selects certification assessments for teachers and administrators, oversees the mandated first-year induction programs for new teachers and principals, and administers Kentucky's incentive program for National Board for Professional Teaching Standards certification.

KERA-initiated Changes in School Finance

The Task Force on Education Reform Finance Committee selected John Augenblick to assist it in developing new funding procedures to address required equity issues in the legislation. KERA significantly increased school funding through the establishment of the Support Education Excellence in Kentucky (SEEK) formula. The intent of the SEEK formula created by the finance committee was to narrow differences between per-pupil revenues in richer and poorer districts throughout the commonwealth by providing a guaranteed minimum amount of state money to districts for each student. Upward adjustments to the base amount provided by the state are made to each district to compensate for additional costs required to provide special services to children and youth with disabilities or who are perceived of being at risk of not learning and to transport students to schools. KERA also gave districts discretion to collect and use local sources of revenue to increase per-pupil revenue and teachers salaries (Foster, 1999; Pankratz & Petrosko, 2000; Steffy, 1993a).

Governmental Policy Making: Grassroots Implementation

Although the task force held public forums during the months it developed the comprehensive education reform legislation and invited the public and organizations with special interest in education to present position papers, they conducted almost all their work behind closed doors. Because the task force was composed predominately of Democratic legislators, the governor and task force chairs agreed that "all decisions would be by consensus rather than formal vote" (Foster, 1999, p. 16). Further, the group determined that the governor and leaders of the two legislative bodies had private veto over task force decisions to avoid public rifts. Thus, no individual or branch of state government can claim sole credit for enactment of KERA (Harrison & Klotter, 1997). The Prichard Committee for Academic Excellence (1990) continued to advocate for sweeping changes in the education system throughout KERA's development. Governor Wilkerson and members of the General Assembly worked closely together to draft the legislation that was ultimately enacted (Foster, 1999; Steffy, 1993a).

Policymakers created the framework for a new system of public education in Kentucky, but educators at all levels were required to make "drastic changes in nearly every aspect of schooling, all within a short period of time" (Guskey & Oldham, 1996, p. 3). The comprehensive reform initiative required administrators, teachers, and even parents to work collaboratively in developing new core content standards, assessments and portfolio scoring rubrics, and curriculum. Equitable opportunities for learning through increased school funding and accountability of performance outcomes became the goals that drove the work done in schools, districts, and state education offices (Steffy, 1993a). Concurrently with those efforts, citizen-advocacy groups worked to inform the media and general public about the ongoing efforts and results (Prichard Committee for Academic Excellence, 1999; Sexton, 1995, 2000).

Rising State Power: Equity and Accountability

The Kentucky Supreme Court ruling that led to enactment of KERA contained two important charges: the establishment of a system of public schools that ensured equitable opportunities for learning for all children and youth regardless of where they lived, and the creation of a system to monitor performance progress (Guskey & Oldham, 1996). Hence, two outcomes of the comprehensive educational reform legislation and driving forces that first stimulated and later sustained the systemic initiative were equity and accountability.

Equity Achieved through Leveled and Capped Funding Strategies

The landmark United States Supreme Court decision in 1954, *Brown v. Board of Education*, asserted that "all laws concerning or permitting school segregation were in conflict with the Fourteenth Amendment and [ordered] involuntary segregation to cease within a 'reasonable time'" (Pulliam & Van Patten,

1999, p. 202). Despite this political attempt to assure equal opportunity for learning to all children living in America, "savage inequalities" (Kozol, 1991) continued to exist among Kentucky schools, particularly those in rural Appalachian districts. According to the class-action suit filed in 1985 by the Council for Better Education, the 50 percent discrepancy in educational funding between rich and poor districts at that time was estimated to be "more than $23,400 per classroom" (Adams, 2000, p. 31). Discriminatory school funding—economic segregation—emerged as a cause for continued social injustices and inequalities in public schooling that deprived many children and youth from receiving full educational benefits. Hence, equity is defined here as "the attempt to balance the inequality of educational resources and, to some extent, the uneven outcomes of educational progress" (Haselton & Miller, 1999) through evenly shared funds.

Although school-funding litigation has occurred in all fifty states, two cases reviewed by the U.S. Supreme Court are important. In its 1971 *Serrano v. Priest* decision, the California Supreme Court used for the first time "the equal protection guarantee of the Fourteenth Amendment" (Pulliam & Van Patten, 1999, p. 206) as the basis for its discriminatory ruling on the state's system of school funding. The other important finance equity case, *San Antonio Independent School District v. Rodriquez* (1973), used the notion of accident of birth (i.e., students living in property-poor districts versus those living in property-rich districts) as justification for differences in educational resources. The U.S. Supreme Court held that school-funding decisions must be determined at the state level in order to preserve local control of education. Thus, through its landmark decision in *Rose v. Council for Better Education, Inc.* (1989), the Kentucky Supreme Court moved well beyond school funding equity when it "declared the state's public school system unconstitutional" (Foster, 1999, p. 1). The court ruling and reform legislation that followed led to "more effective schools together with equity in taxation to assure a guaranteed minimum level of financial support per pupil for all school districts" (Pulliam & Van Patten, 1999, p. 206).

Redistribution of wealth to remove disparities between the rich and poor districts has long been a challenge in the quest to assure adequacy and equity of school funding (Haselton & Miller, 1999). Thus, the Task Force on Education Reform Finance Committee developed specific objectives concerning the new school finance system to guide its work, including, but not limited to, (1) sensitivity to the disparity of wealth among districts, (2) assurance of consistency across districts in determining property wealth, (3) correction of structural problems in the old system and provision for an adequate base of revenue for all school districts, and (4) flexibility in taxation efforts to balance the requirement for increasing tax bases in the poorest districts and special needs of all districts. Equity in school funding was originally achieved through a four-part system that addressed capital and debt, teacher retirement, other programs, and creation of a new funding formula, perhaps the most important part of the finance legislation incorporated into KERA (Steffy, 1993a).

The Kentucky school-funding formula contains three components. The first is a guaranteed minimum amount for each student called the "base guarantee" (Adams, 2000, p. 35) that provides the same level of per pupil revenue for all districts. The composite base guarantee is formulated upon average daily attendance from the previous academic year and adjusted according to specific district costs (e.g., special services for exceptional or at-risk students attending school, students convalescing in hospitals or at home, or students with limited English proficiency or for transporting students). The adjusted base guarantee of state funding that a district receives for each student is determined by adding the per-pupil base guarantee to monies generated by transportation and special services costs and then dividing that total by the number of students in the district (Haselton & Miller, 1999). Although the state provides this revenue, districts determine how the funds will be used under the provision that all federal regulations are met appropriately (Steffy, 1993a).

Over the years the base guarantee has increased from $2,305 in 1990–1991 to $3,508 in 2006–2007 (Kentucky Department of Education, 2006). The SEEK formula requires every school district to levy a uniform tax ($0.30 per $100 of assessed property value) to guarantee equal tax effort by localities. Funding for public education starts at the local level through taxes on utilities, personal property, or vehicles. The state provides money to districts, as needed, to assure that the basic guarantee for each student is achieved and to minimize disparities between rich and poor districts (Adams, 2000).

Two other components of the funding formula include leveled and capped taxing opportunities that permit districts to generate additional educational revenue. Tier I allows local school boards to raise additional funds up to 15 percent of the adjusted base guarantee. School districts where per pupil wealth is less than 150 percent of the estimated statewide average per pupil wealth receive equalizing funds from the state. Conversely, Tier 2 allows districts to generate additional revenue for schools by levying an additional tax—only with voter approval and subject to recall provisions. However, this school revenue generation is capped at 30 percent of the total amount generated by the adjusted base guarantee and Tier I. The capped amount is an attempt to maintain some control of variation in total funding across all districts (Haselton & Miller, 1999; Knoeppel, 2007). Because school funding is dependent on average daily pupil attendance for the preceding year, the SEEK formula includes incentives for districts to work at ensuring a high base guarantee (Steffy, 1993a).

The KERA model of school funding to increase equity across districts is not unique. Nonetheless, SEEK has made great strides in providing equitable education funding across a state with huge differences between rich and poor districts (Decker, 1999; Kessinger, 1996; Vick, 2002). While not yet a perfect outcome, "Kentucky's school finance system exhibits more equity and educational opportunity today than it did before reform" (Adams, 2000, p. 39). Over the period from 1991 through 1999, the total per pupil revenue has been "reasonably equitably distributed" (Roeder, 2002, p. 3) across all districts, and although local per pupil revenue has increased slowly but steadily, the amount of state contribution has decreased. This trend can be problematic for property-poor districts that do not have a strong tax base, which ultimately can lead to greater inequity and inadequacy. A challenge still facing Kentucky—as well as most other states—is assuring adequacy in funding to achieve all the demands placed on public schools today (Verstegen, 1994: Verstegen & Knoeppel, 1998). And although uniform funding equity and adequacy have not been achieved, the accountability system that emerged from KERA has stimulated improved school and student performances (Haselton & Keedy, 2002; Pankratz & Petrosko, 2000).

Accountability Based on School—Not Just Student—Progress

A comprehensive system of student performance-based assessment and school accountability, originally known as the Kentucky Instructional Results Information System (KIRIS) and changed in 1998 to the Commonwealth Accountability Testing System (CATS), is a direct result of KERA. Today students are tested at the end of each school year in seven content areas, with content focus and assessment type staggered across different grade levels, beginning in grade 3 and continuing through grade 12 (Poggio, 2000). Each student is not assessed each year in all core content areas (e.g., literacy, mathematics), and, thus, tracing annual yearly learning progress for individual students is not possible under the current Kentucky system. Some districts, however, recently initiated voluntary testing programs that assess students' annual yearly progress to meet the requirements in the No Child Left Behind (NCLB) legislation.

The learning goals, known as the Core Content for Assessment, defined specifically what students should know and be able to do in reading, writing, mathematics, science, social studies, arts and humanities, practical living, and vocational studies. A variety of assessments (e.g., multiple-choice questions, open-response questions, on-demand writing, portfolio development) was created to align what is taught with what is tested. Over the years, the core content topics and evaluation methods have been modified and updated to address limitations and inadequacies in the student performance assessment (Poggio, 2000).

CATS is based on an accountability index for each individual school and includes rewards and sanctions determined by attainment of school-wide improvement goals (Van Meter, 1991). Shortly after passage of KERA, all public schools were assigned "individualized *baseline* and *improvement goal* indices based upon [their] past school performance in relation to the 2014 statewide index goal of 100" (Lyons, 2004, p. 1). In other words, all Kentucky public schools are expected to achieve a score of 100 or above by the year 2014. Both cognitive measures (e.g., student scores on standardized tests) and noncognitive measures (e.g., attendance, retention, dropout rate, successful transition following graduation) are used to classify school improvement measured against the state-assigned goals (Foster, 2000; Guskey & Oldham, 1996). Thus, in each biennial accountability cycle, schools are classified three ways (meets goal, progressing, assistance level) based on multiple performance indicators (Kentucky Department of Education [KDE], 2000). While high-performing schools have received recognition for their accomplishments in the form of cash awards, low-performing schools face possible sanctions such as an academic audit, possible state intervention, and technical assistance from a state-assigned trained Highly Skilled Educator (Foster, 2000). As a result of the school accountability system, Kentucky principals have become highly accountable for student learning and visible in the reported school results (Winter & Morgenthal, 2001).

According to Guskey and Oldam (1996), Kentucky's original accountability system, known as KIRIS, was "probably the most thoughtfully designed and carefully constructed" (p. 12) performance-based assessment system in the nation. Yet, it was challenged on the grounds of inadequate reliability by the Kentucky Institute for Research (1995) and restructured into CATS, which attempts to negate potential biasing influences of socioeconomic factors on school performance by individualizing school goals (Ladd, 2001). CATS was designed as an interim target design accountability system, which is based on an underlying assumption that "school achievement targets would be reasonably attainable for a school functioning in an acceptable fashion" (Lyons, 2004, p. 7). Further, because CATS focuses on incremental school improvement, it is supposed to provide accommodation for differences in school population demographics and initial student performances and address school concerns about transitory students and differences in student-grade cohorts.

Because both KIRIS and CATS were designed to provide information about results of specific school improvement efforts implemented by individual schools, the results were never intended for use in comparing schools. Yet, comparisons are made by the media, taxpayers, teachers, and principals when the CATS scores are announced each year. After completing his study in Kentucky about the influence of poverty on school achievement, Lyons (2004) believes that "comparing accountability scores of schools with differential socioeconomic characteristics is unfair to the children, parents, teachers, and principals of high poverty schools" (p. 24). He further asserts,

> School accountability systems are a political means of leveraging improvement through a balance of collaboration for school improvement and consequences for poor performance. Although much attention has been given to the appropriateness of the instruments used to measure school performance, possibly the weakest link in the chain of accountability may be the ways in which results are reported and excellence is defined. In light of the implementation of the NCLB Act, the fact that as of 2002 the CATS accountability system shows

> potential for bias against high poverty schools, with no provision made to communicate completely to the public the performance of each school as compared to similar schools is viewed as unjust to all stakeholders. (Lyons, 2004, p. 24)

Roeder (2002) also expresses concern about performance of high-poverty schools because he found that "resource equity and adequacy appear not to reduce the negative effects of poverty on performance" (p. 3). Further, when comparing two noncognitive measures of school performance (i.e., transition to college and dropout rates), he found significant differences between Appalachian and non-Appalachian districts. Additionally, Haselton and Keedy (2002) noted a widening gap in student performance on state-mandated assessments between plaintiff and nonplaintiff districts involved in *Rose v. Council for Better Education* that suggests equitable funding does not guarantee equal academic performance. Rather, how resources—time, money, human capital—are used to improve schools appears to be extremely important.

Because the Kentucky accountability system is based on *school* performance measures, it has no direct consequences attached to individual *student* performance. Teachers and principals have little direct influence over the most significant portion of their schools' ratings because CATS does not support a diagnostic-prescriptive approach to improving individual student achievement; that is, the current accountability tests cannot be used to assess learning each year and identify specific content needing remediation or accommodation. Yet, despite continuing challenges and unintended consequences of the high-stakes accountability system, most educators and researchers believe that the quality of schools and student learning has improved significantly since enactment of KERA (Foster, 2000; Guskey & Oldham, 1996; KDE, 2000; Pankratz & Petrosko, 2000; Poggio, 2000).

Lessons Learned in Systemic School Reform: New Forces at Work

According to Foster (1999), a member of the Task Force on Education Reform, "redesigning public education" in Kentucky through systemic change has been truly remarkable because of the incredible efforts made by citizen advocates, policymakers, educators, parents, and business leaders. The task was quite difficult at times: No other state's entire system of public education has been declared inequitable, inefficient, and inadequate (*Rose v. Council for Better Education*, 1989) and required to be reconstructed in just nine months. Foster further asserts that the development of KERA and the implementation efforts since 1990 provide an incredible success story, mainly because most components of the initiative remained intact for over a decade.

According to Roeder (2002), after initial years of intense reform implementation, the pace of educational progress in Kentucky has "settled into a pattern of relative stability and incremental change" (p. 30). Any long-standing initiative, however, will eventually encounter slowdowns and stumbling blocks that hinder progress. Examples of counterforces in Kentucky are its pervasive poverty, diminished human capital due to the limited postsecondary education of its citizens, health care needs, and aging population (Smith-Mello, Childress, Watts, & Watkins, 2000). The lessons learned and the new forces at work are presented in the following two sections before closing remarks about why KERA was necessary and needed.

Lessons Learned in Stimulating and Sustaining Innovation

Mobilization to improve public schools in Kentucky emerged from citizen advocacy by the Council for Better Education and later the Prichard Committee for Academic Excellence. Using data collected from all stakeholder groups in the public education enterprise, a highly motivated group of volunteers believed that policymakers alone could not make the necessary fundamental changes needed to improve the quality of public schooling (Sexton, 1995). They became determined to agitate for needed policy reform at the state level. Once educational reform legislation was enacted, they then modified their focus to ensuring that policy was implemented in schools and classrooms by keeping parents, citizens, the business community, and the media informed of progress (Sexton, 2000).

Enactment of KERA changed the roles and responsibilities of school principals. Yet, except for publications by the Prichard Committee (1990), descriptions of a new principalship in this systemic reform initiative are missing in early post-KERA documents. It became apparent, however, that successful schools require effective principal leadership. Thus, in 1998 Kentucky adopted—without modification—the ISLLC *Standards* (Council of Chief State School Officers, 1996) as the blueprint for school administration. Preservice preparation, in-service professional development, and annual administrator evaluation were all revised to align with the *Standards*. Work on transforming the Kentucky principalship from school management into leadership for learning has been ongoing since then (Browne-Ferrigno & Fusarelli, 2005).

Forces Impeding Continuing Innovation

KERA was funded through increased taxes and delayed payments for other needed state-infrastructure improvements. With recent worldwide economic downturns and increasing needs in the areas of health and elder care, Kentucky can no longer continue funding educational reform at targeted levels. Many property-poor districts that have numbers of students enrolled in free and reduced lunch programs struggle to meet the dual school accountability expectations that "all children can learn at high levels" (KERA) by being taught by "high-quality teachers" (NCLB). Rural counties located in the Appalachian mountains of eastern Kentucky continue to be classified as "distressed" (Hilston, 2000) because their three-year average poverty and unemployment rates are at least 1.5 times the nation's average, mainly because the coal mining industry suffered a major decline during the late 1990s. Additionally, many children in this region continue to live under conditions that make them at high risk for not succeeding in school (Annie F. Casey Foundation, 2000). A major stumbling block to universal school improvement is not only educational funding (Roeder, 2002), but also poverty that remains widespread and persistent throughout much of Kentucky (Smith-Mello et al., 2000; U.S. Census Bureau, 2000).

Human capital needed to continue the hard work required for educational renewal based on the tenets of KERA is being depleted. Few educators choose to relocate to low-performing schools or impoverished school districts, and many who have worked tirelessly for years to make incredible improvements in student learning are nearing retirement. Individuals who assumed key implementation roles have moved to other positions within the state or elsewhere. With the remarkably stable population in Kentucky, new entrants into the education profession are often natives who remember KERA from perspectives as students in classrooms where changes were seemingly constant. Now working as teachers and principals, they sometimes do not understand how their current practices link to continued implementation of KERA, especially since NCLB has made new accountability demands on them. Institutional memory about the reasons for the comprehensive reform and human energy for sustaining the necessary continuous renewal are dissipating. Furthermore, principals and teachers today often seem more concerned about complying with policy directives rather than viewing them as external change forces (Fullan, 1993, 1999) to which they should respond creatively in order to assure student learning (Fullan, 2003).

Carefully coordinated reform through top-down legislation and renewal through extensive bottom-up implementation is a key factor in the long-term success of KERA. Changes, revisions, and updates to the original legislation and its spin-off statutes, administrative regulations, and district policies have been necessary to meet unexpected challenges and address new circumstances. Policy analysts, historians, and researchers have written about the incredible longevity of this systemic change initiative. Unfortunately, however, in the past two years, important components of KERA have come under scrutiny and challenge. One influence has been federal policies linking Title I funding to evidence of annual yearly progress of *student* performance, which is inconsistent with the KERA-initiated accountability system based on biennial *school* performance. Finding solutions to reconcile the discrepancies in achievement measures is proving to be costly and conflict generating. Another major influence has been recent changes in political-party representation in the executive and legislative branches of government that have renewed long existing, pronounced political and partisan differences. In striving to fulfill his campaign promise of a balanced state budget, the first Republican governor elected to that office in thirty years has authorized major cuts to the education budget. Because mostly Democrats served on the Task Force on Education Reform that designed KERA, these cuts are proving to be quite controversial. Kentucky is a state where heated political partisanship is historically ingrained and currently thriving.

Necessary State Action for Needed Change

Rising state control over local school decisions may cause concern to many individuals, particularly those working in states where education is highly valued and excellence is being achieved based on various measures of success. Kentucky, however, desperately needed a policy-instigated catalyst to address its dismal national rankings back in 1983 when it was "described as a Third World country with the nation's most uneducated work force" (Prichard Committee for Academic Excellence, 1999, p. 4). National rankings among states indicate Kentucky has made improvements—some significant—in educational measures of achievement (Quality Counts, 2002).

Significant work is still needed to transform Kentucky public education into one that invites more business and industry to invest in the Commonwealth, a critically needed step in helping the Commonwealth increase its economic vitality in order to meet mounting social needs (Smith-Mello et al., 2000). Education is not valued in Kentucky. For example, during the 2000 national census, 74 percent of those residing in Kentucky indicated they were born there and had completed high school, but only 17 percent of local residents aged twenty-five years or older at that time reported having earned a postsecondary degree. In 1999, the annual per capita income for Kentucky residents was $18,100, which is significantly lower than the national average of $22,000. Furthermore, 15 percent of Kentuckians lived below the poverty level at that time (U.S. Census Bureau, 2000).

Is there compelling justification for state control over public education when opportunity for learning is inequitable and inadequate? Concerned Kentucky citizens representing more than one-third of the school districts sought equitable funding through court action. The Kentucky Supreme Court found the need for state action to improve public education and compelled policymakers to take appropriate action. Although certainly not a comprehensive solution to all of Kentucky's problems, KERA remains an exemplary model of coherent policymaking integration (Fuhrman, 1994).

References

Adams, J. E., Jr. (2000). Resource equity and educational resources. In R. S. Pankratz & J. M. Petrosko (Eds.), *All children can learn: Lessons from the Kentucky reform experience* (pp. 29–45). San Francisco: Jossey-Bass.

Annie E. Casey Foundation. (2000). *Kentucky kids count.* Louisville: Kentucky Youth Associates.

Browne-Ferrigno, T., & Fusarelli, B. C. (2005). The Kentucky principalship: Model of school leadership reconfigured by ISLLC Standards and reform policy implementation. *Leadership and Policy in Schools, 4*(2), 127–156.

Conley, D. T. (2003). *Who governs our schools? Changing roles and responsibilities.* New York: Teachers College Press.

Council of Chief State School Officers. (1996). *The Interstate School Leaders Licensure Consortium: Standards for school leaders.* Washington, DC: Author.

Cuban, L. (1990). Reforming again, again, and again. *Educational Researcher, 19*(1), 3–13.

Darling-Hammond, L., & McLaughlin, M. W. (Eds.). (1999). *Teaching as a learning profession: Handbook of policy and practice.* San Francisco: Jossey-Bass.

Decker, J. T. (1999). An examination of Kentucky school districts' instructional per pupil expenditures and academic performance at the eighth grade level in mathematics and reading (Doctoral dissertation, University of Kentucky). *Dissertation Abstracts Online,* 60, 11A.

Foster, J. D. (1999). *Redesigning public education: The Kentucky experience.* Lexington, KY: Diversified Services.

Foster, J. D. (2000). A new vision for public schooling. In R. S. Pankratz & J. M. Petrosko (Eds.), *All children can learn: Lessons from the Kentucky reform experience* (pp. 46–67). San Francisco: Jossey-Bass.

Fuhrman, S. (1994). *Politics and systemic education reform* (Policy Brief). Philadelphia: Consortium for Policy Research in Education.

Fullan, M. (1993). *Change forces: Probing the depths of educational reform.* Bristol, PA: Falmer Press.

Fullan, M. (1999). *Change forces: The sequel.* Philadelphia: Falmer Press.

Fullan, M. (2003). *The moral imperative of school leadership.* Thousand Oaks, CA: Corwin Press.

Fullan, M. (2004). *Leadership and sustainability: System thinkers in action.* Thousand Oaks, CA: Corwin Press.

Glickman, C. D. (1998). *Revolutionizing America's schools.* San Francisco: Jossey-Bass.

Goodlad, J. I. (1997). *In praise of education.* New York: Teachers College Press.

Guskey, T. R., & Oldham, B. R. (1996, April). *Despite the best intentions: Inconsistencies among components in Kentucky's systemic reform.* Paper presented at the annual meeting of the American Education Research Association, New York, NY.

Harrison, L. W., & Klotter, J. C. (1997). *A new history of Kentucky.* Lexington: University Press of Kentucky.

Haselton, W. B., & Keedy, J. L. (2002, April). *The Kentucky Education Reform Act: A comparison of equity and adequacy outcomes in Kentucky between plaintiff and non-plaintiff schools districts.* Paper presented at the annual meeting of the American Education Research Association, New Orleans, LA.

Haselton, W. B., & Miller, S. K. (1999, April). *Support Education Excellence in Kentucky (SEEK): Impact on student outcomes.* Paper presented at the Conference of the Center of Excellence for Research and Policy on Basic Skills, Nashville, TN.

Heine, C. (2002). *Kentucky school updates: A parent/citizen guide for 2002–04.* Lexington, KY: Prichard Committee for Academic Excellence.

Hilston, J. (2000, November 26). Online graphic: Distressed counties in Appalachia, 2000. *PG News.* Retrieved October 20, 2003, from http://post-gazette.com/headlines/

House, E. R. (1998). *Schools for sale: Why free market policies won't improve American's schools, and what will.* New York: Teachers College Press.

Kannapel, P. J., Aagaard, L., Coe, P., & Reeves, C. A. (2000). *Elementary change: moving toward systemic school reform in rural Kentucky.* Charleston, WV: AEL.

Kentucky Department of Education. (2000). *Results matter: A decade of difference in Kentucky school 1990–2000.* Frankfort, KY: Author.

Kentucky Department of Education. (2006, July 28). *2006–07 SEEK Forecast.* Retrieved August September 10, 2006 from http://www.education.ky.gov/KDE/Administrative+Resources/Finance+and+Funding/School+Finance/SEEK.htm

Kentucky Education Reform Act, Kentucky Revised Statute, KRS 160.345 (1990).

Kentucky Institute for Education Research. (1995). *A review of research on the Kentucky Education Reform Act (KERA).* Frankfort, KY: Author.

Kessinger, M. W. (1996). School districts' per pupil expenditures and performance in mathematics and reading at the twelfth-grade level as measured by the Kentucky Instructional Results Information System assessment program (Doctoral dissertation, University of Kentucky). *Dissertation Abstracts Online,* 57, 06A.

Kleckler, B. G., Austin, J. L., & Burns, L. T. (1999, April). *An in-depth analysis of decisions made by Kentucky's School-Based Decision-Making Councils.* Paper presented at the annual meetings of the American Educational Research Association, Montreal, Quebec.

Knoeppel, R. C. (2007, Spring). Resource adequacy, equity, and the right to learn: Access to a quality teacher in Kentucky. *Journal of Education Finance, 32*(4), 422–442.

Kozol, J. (1991). *Savage inequalities: Children in America's schools.* New York: Crown.

Ladd, H. F. (2001). School-based educational accountability systems: The promise and pitfalls. *National Tax Journal, 54*(2), 385–400.

Legislative Research Commission. (1990). *A guide to the Kentucky Education Reform Act of 1990.* Frankfort, KY: Author.

Lindle, J. C. (1992). *Developing school based decision making capacities in Kentucky: Communication satisfaction after the pilot year.* (ERIC Document Reproduction Service No. ED 378 667).

Lyons, R. (2004, August 5). The influence of socioeconomic factors on Kentucky's public school accountability system: Does poverty impact school effectiveness? *Education Policy Analysis Archives, 12*(37). Retrieved August 8, 2004, from http://epaa.asu.edu/epaa/v12n37/

Pankratz, R. S., & Petrosko, J. M. (Eds.). (2000). All *children can learn: Lessons from the Kentucky reform experience.* San Francisco: Jossey-Bass.

Peterson-del Mar, D. (1994). *School-site councils.* Eugene, OR: ERIC Clearinghouse on Educational Management, University of Oregon. [ERIC ED 369 154].

Poggio, J. P. (2000). Statewide performance assessment and school accountability. In R. S. Pankratz & J. M. Petrosko (Eds.), *All children can learn: Lessons from the Kentucky reform experience* (pp. 75–97). San Francisco: Jossey-Bass.

Prichard Committee for Academic Excellence. (1990). *The path to a larger life: Creating Kentucky's educational future* (2nd ed.). Lexington, KY: Author.

Prichard Committee for Academic Excellence. (1999). *Gaining ground: Hard work and high expectations for Kentucky schools.* Lexington, KY: Author.

Pulliam, J. D., & Van Patten, J. J. (1999). *History of education in America* (7th ed.). Upper Saddle River, NJ: Merrill.

Quality Counts. (2002). *Education Week, 21*(17), 94–169.

Random House college dictionary. (1999). New York: Random House.

Roeder, P. W. (2002). *School district performance in Kentucky (1993–2001): Do teaching and financial resources moderate the negative effects of poverty?* [ERIC Document ED 469 136].

Rose v. Council for Better Education, 60 Ky. 1289, 790 S.W.2d 186 (Ky. 1989).

San Antonio School District v. Rodriguez, 411 U.S.1 (1972).

Schlechty, P. C. (1997). *Inventing better schools: An action plan for educational reform.* San Francisco: Jossey-Bass.

Serrano v. Priest, 487 P.2d 1241 (1971).

Sexton, R. F. (1995, April). *Building citizen and parent support for school reform: The Prichard Committee experience.* Paper presented at the annual meeting of the American Education Research Association, San Francisco.

Sexton, R. F. (2000). Engaging parents and citizens in school reform. In R. S. Pankratz & J. M. Petrosko (Eds.), *All children can learn: Lessons from the Kentucky reform experience* (pp. 244–262). San Francisco: Jossey-Bass.

Smith-Mello, M., Childress, M. T., Watts, A., & Watkins, J. F. (2000). *Challenges for the new century: Trends that will influence Kentucky's future.* Frankfort, KY: Kentucky Long-Term Policy Research Center.

Smith, M. S., & O'Day, J. (1991). Systemic school reform. In S. H. Fuhrman & B. Male (Eds.), *The politics of curriculum and testing* (pp. 233–267). London: Falmer Press.

Steffy, B. E. (1993a). *The Kentucky Education Reform Act: Lessons for America.* Lancaster, PA: Technomics.

Steffy, B. E. (1993b). Top-down—bottom-up: Systemic change in Kentucky. *Educational Leadership, 51*(1), 42–44.

Tyack, D., & Cuban, L. (1995). *Tinkering toward utopia: A century of public school reform.* Cambridge: Harvard University Press.

U.S. Census Bureau. (2000). *Kentucky quickfacts from the US Census bureau.* Retrieved August 16, 2004, from http://quickfacts.census.gov/qfd/states/21000.html.

Van Meter, E. J. (1991). The Kentucky mandate: School-based decision making. *NASSP Bulletin, 75*(532), 52–62.

Vick, B. H. (2002). An exploration of potential relationships between levels of allocated instructional funds and student achievement in a systemic reform state (Doctoral dissertation, University of Kentucky). *Dissertation Abstracts Online,* 63, 02A.

Verstegen, D. A. (1994). The new wave of school finance litigation. *Phi Delta Kappan, 76*(3), 243–250.

Verstegen, D. A., & Knoeppel, R. C. (1998). Equal education under the law: School finance reform and the courts. *Journal of Law & Politics, 14*(3), 555–589.

Webster's seventh new collegiate dictionary. (1963). Springfield, MA: Merriam.

Winter, P. A., & Morgenthal, J. R. (2001, November). *The impact of school achievement on principal recruitment in a reform environment.* Paper presented at the annual meeting of the University Council for Educational Administration, Cincinnati.

Chapter 4

New Jersey

Bruce S. Cooper and Philip H. Nisonoff

Urbanism, State Control, and School Spending

New Jersey is a prototypic, if not an ideal case of the rising power of the state in public education policy, finance, choice, and control for several reasons. First, New Jersey is considered the most "urbanized" and densely populated state in the United States, with an average of 1,134 residents per square mile. It has major, large urban areas that lie close to other cities outside New Jersey: cities like Newark and Jersey City near New York City in the northern end of the state, and Camden, New Jersey, in the south around Philadelphia, all surrounded by growing, densely populated suburban areas. Salmore and Salmore (1993, p. 6) noted, "The issues that drive New Jersey politics today, and that have transformed its politics and government, grow directly out of the population dispersion. . . . New Jersey politics [is] dominated by [urban and suburban] interests."

Second, New Jersey spends more per pupil for public education on average at $12,027 than any other state (just behind the District of Columbia at $13,455 in 2003, and above New York with $11,326 per pupil). This high spending level is not only related to the high cost of living, but New Jersey also has experienced intense legal efforts to improve school equity, and greater state spending, controls, and policymaking—leading the northeastern United States, and perhaps the nation, in state regulation and controls of schools.

Third, the role of the state of New Jersey in funding schools has increased steadily—again making it a prime example of the "rising state" in education. State spending accounts for 80 to 90 percent of school expenditures in the thirty most impoverished school districts, all but eliminating the power of the local school district in policymaking and influence.

And finally, related to its urbanization, location, size, and spending, New Jersey has a high proportion of poor students (as measured by Title 1 eligibility—

i.e., free and reduced lunch students) and children of color in its schools. New Jersey also faces problems of low student academic achievement and the impact of parental choice (with charter schools and transfer rights under NCLB). In fact, the poor academic achievement of the segregated urban districts compelled the New Jersey Supreme Court to identify the poorest thirty school districts as special-needs districts—known as *Abbott* districts. Thus, education has risen in state political importance, further underlining the centrality of New Jersey as an example of the relationship between equity, funding, policy, bureaucracy, and control of education.

Few issues have affected New Jersey politics like school finance and many of the state's attempts to reform poor schools were the result of State Supreme Court rulings on public school finance. In 1970, a lawsuit was filed against then-Governor William T. Cahill on behalf of a twelve-year-old boy from Jersey City named Kenneth Robinson. The school funding suit was one of the first of its kind and was largely engineered by the Jersey City school district. Robinson argued that financing schools through the use of property-tax revenues discriminated against property-poor districts and that the resulting spending disparities produced substantial achievement gaps between students in poor schools and those in property rich districts. In *Robinson v. Cahill*, the New Jersey Supreme Court declared the state school funding formula unconstitutional. New Jersey subsequently passed an income tax to finance its schools. *Robinson v. Cahill* and the resulting power struggle set the tone for debate over funding New Jersey's poor schools for over thirty years, as poor districts repeatedly went to the state supreme court to seek additional money.

As Howe (1996) explains in his analysis of the aftermath of the *Abbott* cases,

> New Jersey is a useful case for several reasons. First, it has been among the most active states in the post-*Serrano* era with four [now six] major court rulings since 1973, beginning with *Robinson v. Cahill*, 62 N.J. 473 (1973). Also, the fate of Democratic Governor James J. Florio became intertwined with efforts to increase taxes and extend greater inter-district equity. . . . With a Democratic majority in both houses of the New Jersey Legislature, Florio was able in just six moths to resolve a recession-induced budget deficit inherited from the previous administration of Governor Thomas Kean, legislate a redistribution of state resources for a more equitable finance base among school districts, and raise the necessary funds by restructuring the teacher pension systems, and by increasing state sales and upper-level income taxes increases. (pp. 17–18)

Although Florio was successful in restructuring the state's school finances, it hurt him politically and he was unable to maintain his governor's post. He lost reelection to a relatively unknown, conservative Republican, Governor Christine Todd Whitman. Education policy, equity, and school funding were in part the undoing of Florio's governorship and illustrate the political power of education politics.

Rising State Funding and Control Framework

New Jersey thus illustrates the interlocking steps in the rise of state legal and political activity, spending, controls, activities, and bureaucratic development, and provides a dynamic example (since 1973) of how power shifts in a complex, state-controlled educational system like the one in the United States. Using the case of New Jersey, this chapter illustrates each of five "phases" and their interactions in the state's gradual accumulation of power, starting with the important equity lawsuit, *Robinson v. Cahill* (1973), then followed by a string of other equity suits, *Abbott v. Burke* (1983, 1986, 1989, 1991, and 1994). The following phases are discussed in detail in subsequent sections of this chapter.

Phase 1: Intrastate equity cases lead to greater state spending. Constitutional challenges (*Robinson v. Cahill,* 1973) to the state's funding structure result in a need to correct interdistrict equalities and the state increases taxes (New Jersey pushed through a state income tax for the first time in its history).

Phase 2: Increased state spending leads to increased state regulation of schools. New Jersey was one of the first states to establish standards in spending and programs—part of a move toward a move activist state role in education.

Phase 3: More state control leads to a standard curriculum and testing. New Jersey establishes extensive Core Content Curriculum Standards and testing.

Phase 4: More state regulation leads to more state accountability. New Jersey takes over failing school districts like Newark and Paterson when these *Abbott* districts failed to meet the state standards.

Phase 5: New Jersey became more involved in local budgeting. Passage in 2003 of S-1701 all but destroys "local control" and responsiveness.

Phase 6: Costs rise, until the state can no longer afford the price tag and cutbacks occur. Finally, the cost of equalizing spending reaches a point where the state cannot afford it and the New Jersey high court allows more local spending, less state responsibility, greater inequality. But the legacy of greater state control and accountability remains.

The expansion of the state's role came over time, incrementally since the early 1970s, but in closely interrelated stages. In the following sections the phases are discussed in detail.

Phase 1: State's Rising Role in School Finance Equity

In 1973, the New Jersey high court ruled in *Robinson v. Cahill* and again later in six subsequent related rulings in *Abbott v. Burke* (1983, 1986, 1989, 1991, 1994, and 1998), and other versions of the decision in the 1990s and 2000s, that the poorer districts in the state were being inequitably funded under the state's constitution requirement for providing a "thorough and efficient education" for all children. In *Robinson* the court noted the inability of local communities, with their varying property tax bases, to meet the increasing needs related to local poverty and found that New Jersey's dependence on local property taxes denied students of a thorough and efficient education (Lehne, 1978).

After a long, heated battle and the high court's closing down of all the state's public schools in July 1976, the New Jersey legislature finally passed the first broad-based state income tax to support school funding. New Jersey's legislature then passed equity legislation, the Quality of Education Act. It is important to understand that in New Jersey, and other states, the stimulant for greater state spending, regulation, and control came from the judiciary, as is often the case when political pressures to maintain the status quo are too great for the governor or legislature to take decisive, redistributive actions. Prior to *Robinson*, New Jersey had no state income tax—an efficient, effective way to raise money for schools, but an unpopular initiative with voters.

In fact, after the *Robinson* decision in 1973, it took another three years and the unprecedented closing of the entire school system by the state high court to force the legislature to pass an income tax policy. A justice of the state's high court had predicted the need for a state income tax to fund equalization when he stated: "The court did not say that you had to have an income tax, but anyone with an ounce of sense would know that the only possible solution to the problem was the adoption of a state income tax or something worse, such as an increased sales tax or statewide property taxes" (Lehne, 1978, p. 52).

In July 1976—following weeks of hearings, commission reports, and numerous amendments to give cash breaks to renters, homestead property tax reductions, revenue sharing, and tax credits, and the forced closing of all public schools—the New Jersey state legislature passed a broad-based state income tax, with much of the receipts going to equalize funding in the state's poorest public school districts. The results were dramatic for the poorest districts, with state aid jumping from 20 percent of local spending in 1970, for example, in Jersey City to 58 percent in 1976 after the new *Robinson* program was implemented. In 2003, 89 percent of the city's school spending was from state aid—indicating the long-term cumulative effects of the court ruling on the role of the state in local education.

Under Governor James Florio in the 1980s, funding increased to New Jersey's poorest districts, a reaction to the state court's expectations and made possible through increased state taxation. However, because the urban school districts had the greatest need for equalization funding, the effect of Governor Florio's plan, in the minds of voters, was a *redistribution* of wealth from the more affluent suburbs to the urban core.

The equity pressures, focused and intensified by the court cases, led to a major shift in the role of the state. Prior to the cases, the state mainly funded districts using a distributive policy—getting funds for special designated programs and foundation efforts. After *Robinson* and *Abbott*, the state was required to use *redistributive* funding (Lowi, 1969), attempting to give the greatest help to the poorest districts (the thirty so-called *Abbott* districts).

Phase 2: More State Spending, More State Regulation

Following closely on the heels of state equity funding for education came a series of new policies and school regulations. Lehne (1978) had noted this new state activism when he explained: "Increased legislative capacity and enhanced autonomy in the conduct of public policy were already slowly developing in New Jersey politics at the time of the *Robinson* decision, but that ruling highlighted fundamental issues at a critical time and thereby accelerated the transitions that were then occurring" (p. 187). Just after the enactment of broad-based state income tax policy in 1976 came a string of education regulations, culminating in the Education Excellence Act. New Jersey then led the nation in establishing comprehensive statewide educational standards (State Core Curriculum Content Standards or SCCCSs and the Quality of Education Act) that attempted to align cross-grade requirements and standards to local curriculum and teaching, to local tests, and more uniform consequences for failure.

Phase 3: More State Control, Greater Centralization

It was somehow logical that once the state of New Jersey set the standards and provided the money (particularly for low-income districts which were the target of the *Robinson* decision), the state would centralize its control over local school districts.

In 1996, State Commissioner Leo Klaghotz announced that "The Core Curriculum Content Standards (CCCS) represent an historic initiative for New Jersey . . . providing all children in the state with a full and broad educational program at the elementary, middle and high school levels" (Memo from Commissioner, May 24, 1996, p. 1). These state standards, alignment, and testing were directly linked to the New Jersey Constitution and its guarantee of a "thorough and efficient" education for all, the same language that had been used in the *Robinson* case to force equitability in school spending back in 1973. In the introduction to the new state policy, the language is quite clear: "Ours is a state with a 120-year-old constitutional guarantees that regardless of residency, its children will receive a 'Thorough and Efficient' education" (p. 1).

CCCS is a practical way of defining the term "thorough" from the Constitution. Worried that the CCCS would become a rigid, prescribed "curriculum" and not a set of "standards" that freed schools to reach those standards in ways that worked best for them, the guidelines explained that they "define the *results* expected but do not limit district strategies for *how* to ensure that their students achieve these expectations" (p. 1).

Another key concept of these state standards is the comprehensiveness of their subjects and areas of teaching and learning. While NCLB is mainly concentrating (thus far) on language arts (reading and writing) and mathematics, the New Jersey state standards hit *eight* separate areas, ranging from "Workplace Readiness" as the broadest, through arts, health and physical education, to language arts (reading and writing), mathematics, science, social studies, and world (foreign) languages. The power and force of these eight separate CCCS standards lie with their clear statement of expectations, which are then threaded from the first grade through the twelfth, being interpreted for the age-grade and appropriateness of the students' maturity and social/academic development.

Take two examples from two of the eight areas: Under Health and Physical Education, Standard 2.1 is *"All students will learn health and disease prevention concepts and health-enhancing behaviors."* Then, for each grade/age level, a set of "cumulative progress indicators" are provided, such as fourth graders will be able to "Describe a healthy child and identify factors that contribute to good health." These expectations are then raised for eighth graders to describing "a healthy adolescent" with illnesses and injuries common to this age group (twelve to fourteen years old), which is then raised to a "healthy adult" by age eighteen (in the twelfth grade).

In an academic area, for example, the standards are presented and then related to students of all grade levels. In mathematics, for example, Standard 4.4 reads, *"All students will develop reasoning ability and will become self-reliant, independent mathematical thinkers,"* which is age-related: for example, fourth grade students will "Make educated guesses and test them for correctness," which evolves into a twelfth-grade skill, to "Formulate counter-examples to disprove an argument."

The power of the state, then, based on the New Jersey State Constitution, has moved from spending equity to regulations that present curricular standards in eight areas, across all grades. In turn, the state established tests originally at three benchmark grades levels (fourth, eighth, and eleventh) to determine whether the CCCS's levels were being attained, thrusting the state education department firmly into the learning and testing of all students. By 2003, the CCCS had grown more comprehensive and textured, as shown in these examples from health and physical education. Besides the standards, a set of "strands" had come from the education department, across six areas: Wellness, Integrated Skills, Drugs and Medicines (e.g., addiction), Human Relations and Sexuality, Motor Skills Development, and Fitness. Again, these six foci are applied to each of the standards, giving greater definition to the state's role in what's taught in each content area.

Clearly, the power of the state in what children are taught, and to what level, in the 1990s and 2000s, is flowing from the role of the state in equalizing spending and regulating education. Over a ten-year period, based on a broad foundation of subjects and standards, the state has elaborated on what's to be taught, to which grade levels, and to what standards.

Phase 4: More Regulation, More Accountability

With greater state regulation and accountability, it follows that the State Department of Education would be tempted to "take over" failing school districts. And so the state did take control. On July 3, 1983, for example, New Jersey's state education department declared Newark's schools to be "failing," dismissed the sitting elected board of education and its choice of a superintendent, selected a Special Master to oversee the district, and finally appointed a "state superintendent" to run the district. While New Jersey began these actions in the 1980s in Jersey City, Newark, Paterson, Camden, and elsewhere, these designations have now become more common under federal mandates imposed by No Child Left Behind (NCLB).

New Jersey's equity cases (*Robinson v. Cahill* and *Abbot v. Burke*)—accompanied by the growth in state-controlled bureaucracy and accountability—put a heavier burden on local property owners. The state is at the forefront of property taxes for the support of education and other function. As Hester (2004) explained, "In New Jersey, the property tax finances *42 percent* of government . . . while the national average is but *29 percent*. New Jersey property owners and tenants paid $17.2 billion in property taxes last year" (Hester, 2004, p. 10).

CAPITAL BUDGET PLAN AND THE STATE ROLE. A dramatic example of the net effects might be the implementation of the state's capital funding plan, designed to help poor districts to improve their buildings and construct new schools to reduce school overcrowding and increase safety and comfort. The state, in keeping with its new role in school funding, passed an $8 billion act to underwrite school renovations and construction. To make the new law more politically palatable, however, the state set aside some of these funds ($2.6 billion) for school construction in middle-class districts, while earmarking most of the money for buildings in the thirty poorest districts, the so-called *Abbott* districts (those covered by the original *Robinson v. Cahill* case in 1973). More spending, however, come with more state control. To regulate the aggressive school construction program authorized under the Educational School Facilities and Financing Act of 2000, the state created a new agency, the New Jersey School Construction Corporation, with its sole mission to administer the $8.6 billion construction initiative with an *annual budget* of $39.6 million.

While the money was made available to support school building construction, there were various regulations and controls for poorer districts. Whereas the more affluent districts submitted requests for grants from the building fund that were met immediately, the *Abbott* districts were so bound up in paperwork and controls that three years passed before any building construction was begun.

The thirty urban districts found that state construction funds alone were not enough; in additional, poorer district found: (1) That they had little or no available land to construct new schools, requiring the costly, time-consuming efforts to demolish existing schools or other public and private buildings to have room for new construction; (2) That some of the "free" land was contaminated with pesticides and other chemicals from nearby refineries, waste disposal and dumping, and manufacturing plants, making the sites unfit for building school; (3) That the land development and building review processes in the cities were so complex, onerous, and slow-moving that few building projects got approved or schools built; and, (4) That the demands for full-time prekindergarten and other special programs had so overloaded the building capacity of *Abbott* districts that they often had to lease space from private groups and agencies or outsource the children to private, religious, and other child-care providers, often eating up the little new space that was created.

STATE EDUCATIONAL CHOICE INITIATIVES. New Jersey, as did thirty other states, experimented with charter schools and other "choice initiatives," as devices for offering parents (and their children) greater opportunity and mobility, further bringing the state into the school policy arena. In New Jersey, the state, not the districts, opened and funded individual "public" charter schools. First, in 1996, the state enacted the Charter School Program Act, allowing charter schools (schools formed by founders with a specific mission) to operate with public funding. As of 2006, New Jersey had approved fifty-five charter schools and more were on the way.

Second, in 1999, the state passed the Inter-district Public School Choice Act, a five-year pilot program permitting one "choice district" per county to accept students from other school districts without cost to parents or resident district. In the 2002–2003 school year, only 461 students statewide had transferred out of their "home district" and had enrolled in a nearby "choice school." By the 2004–2005 school year, the enrollment of choice students grew to 795 students.

Phase 5: More State Fiscal Regulation, Less Local Control

The net effect of the equity decision and its aftermath is a state system more "tightly coupled" to local districts and classrooms—and the concomitant loss of local actions and autonomy. Perhaps the most telling policy illustrating the growth of state power in school management and finance in New Jersey was the passage of S-1701 (A-99), a "universally despised" law that thrusts the state directly into the life of local school districts. It has several major requirements that many districts are seeing as highly restrictive and repugnant.

1. *Reduction of Statewide Spending "Caps" or Growth Limits:* This new capping (restrictions on the ability of local communities to raise funds) comes on top of the earlier 1996 regulations that attempted to slow down increases in school spending among wealthier districts, thus limiting the percentage that local communities could increase their school budgets. These 1996 regulations, developed to implement the Comprehensive Improvement Educational Finance Act (CIEFA), had failed to curb the ballooning of property tax values and tax income because the legislature enabled the executive branch to ignore the formulas designed to increase state support based on student populations and demographics.

Costs to local school districts—occurring from rising student enrollments, more expensive union salary settlements, health insurance, utilities, and special education service—had mushroomed, while state revenues were decreasing. Although 100 percent state funding for the thirty Abbott districts had been ensured by the courts, the vast majority of school districts had been forced to accept the balance of shrinking state revenues and increase property taxes to maintain their local school programs. The court rulings and subsequent legislation, whose aim was to decrease spending disparities between rich and poor districts, created a new class of underserved students, those in middle-income, but not wealthy, school districts. Wealthy districts and the special needs districts spend at a relatively high levels and all other New Jersey districts operate with fewer resources.

The Comprehensive Improvement Educational Finance Act (CEIFA) had stipulated a series of Statutory Growth Limitation Adjustments (SGLAs), as well as the ability for local school districts to override or augment budget with local approval. This new law, S-1701, reduces the number of "adjustments" and changes that local voters can override—thus restricting local control and increasing state control—by, for example, preventing local districts from eliminating the funding of existing programs, and only allowing additional funding referenda for new initiatives. As the *Star Ledger* explains: "The law also revised spending caps for school districts. Next year, districts will be limited to increasing budgets by no more than 2.5 percent. Previously, districts could increase budgets annually by 3 percent. The law also clamps down on the common practice of transferring funds within a budget, requiring state approval first" (Drobness, September 14, 2004, p. 2). All the "frills" may go, including art and music and co-curricular activities and sports, as it is permissible to cut existing programs to remain "under cap." It's a case of "leveling down" rather than working to raise up uniformly school quality.

The effect was intended to slow down the spending on existing programs, thus equalizing across districts. The real outcome, however, "will result in property-tax hikes by 2006, inadequate supervision of classroom instruction, and reduction of education programs and staff" (see the joint white paper published by NJ Association of School Administrators, NJ Association of School Business Officials, NJ School Boards Association, NJ Education Association, NJPSA, and GSCS).

2. *Reduction and Restriction of the Local School District Surplus:* Another effect of S-1701 is to drastically reduce and restrict the uses of school district surplus and transfers of available balances in voter-approved budgets, including unanticipated revenues. In the past, before S-1701, New Jersey school districts enjoyed some control over their budget surpluses and available fund balances, enabling them to respond to emergencies, or new curricular initiatives, and thus preparing them to respond to unanticipated district needs in a timely, efficient manner. Now, however, districts are forced to appeal to the State Commissioner every time they need to appropriate funds for emergencies from available surpluses or transfer funds to meet new challenges.

The requirement for the reduction of school district surplus, which will be 2 percent of the local budget (down from a range of 3 percent–6 percent), will likely result in record numbers of school district deficit spending because of the many unanticipated costs (e.g., special education, facilities emergencies, health benefit costs) that districts encounter. In addition, school bond ratings may be lowered. Whereas in the past, school districts had adequate control and flexibility by advanced and emergency planning, now the state has such a tight noose around the necks of districts that they cannot readily meet changing and emergency conditions.

Superintendents may lose their jobs as newspapers carry stories of budget deficits resulting from the confluence of emergencies and the inability to have flexible financial responses. As local deficits increase, the state may have to step in with additional funding, thus increasing state control still further. The most significant effect for most school districts came in the 2006–2007 school year when the temporary tax relief provided by the surplus reduction was no longer available, and property tax dollars will be raised significantly statewide before school districts add anything to their budgets.

3. *Caps on Administrative Costs:* The architects of S-1701 also sought to divert attention and cement public support for the drastic measures by emphasizing the intent to restrict administrative spending in their administrative cost per pupil. The emphasis and strict limits came as surprise to most school districts and administrators for two reasons. First, with the gradual and unending ascension of state control and NCLB initiatives, new administrative reporting requirements were continuously increased. Whom did the state expect to manage and prepare these reports? Second, as enrollments have grown and budgets have become more restricted, administrative expenses have been one of the last areas boards of education have sought to increase. In fact, New Jersey had increased the number of school administrators only 0.10 percent from 1989 through 2003 while student enrollments increased 27.1 percent during the same time frame.

In addition, New Jersey ranked only twenty-first among the fifty states in the percentage of school expenditures going toward administration. (NJDOE, 2004). S1701 will limit districts administrative cost per pupil in the 2006–2007 school to no more than the lower of their prior year amount or that of a regional average. Critics note that this regulation places many school districts in the position of being punished for their prior good deeds. If a school district has done an exemplary job of keeping administrative costs down, they are held to their own tighter standard.

4. *Requires State Commissioner's Approval to Make Line-Item Transfers:* Perhaps the most significant example of the erosion of local control, S-1701 now impedes a local school board from making simple budgetary decisions in response to district program needs. The state, in effect, does not trust locally elected school boards to make budgetary line-item transfers and so has relegated this responsibility to state bureaucrats. This rigidity means that in emergencies (e.g., damage to a school building, sudden increase in enrollments) the district has no local funds, and has to appeal to the state for help, on a case-by-case basis.

5. *Restricts Local Districts Ability to Fund Capital Reserve Accounts:* Capital reserve accounts, funded through tax levy or board-approved transfer of surplus, were designed to assist school districts in planning for capital improvements. By saving during years of fiscal prosperity, a district could prevent large property tax increases when capital projects become unavoidable. S-1701 now restricts the school board's ability to fund these accounts, which could result in districts deferring building maintenance and repairs.

6. *Restricts Additional Spending Proposals:* These "second ballot questions" enable school communities with voter approval to exceed their budget caps for specific programs; now these overrides require the approval of the county superintendent and thus limit the types of programs placed on the ballots. The net effect is that local school boards are limited in prioritizing those programs, which should or should not be included in their base budgets.

Thus, the control of the state has grown, from providing funding for Abbott districts that were spending below the state norms, to increased involvement in the curriculum, program, staffing and spending for education and capital improvement of all districts. So, while the state in the 1970s and 1980s had become active in school equity (court cases and curriculum regulation) that mainly affected the poorest districts and children, now the hand of the state has reached into every school system, and curtails the authority of the school board, superintendent, and community to raise, allocate, and spend money, including funds from local property taxes.

Since its passage in 2004, a backlash has occurred, with petitions circulating that urge the law's repeal because S-1701, in the document's words, "endangers children's safety in changing bus routes, reduces budget surpluses to fiscally irresponsible levels, diminishes a school community's authority and flexibility, prevents districts from dealing with annual double-digit increases in fixed costs (e.g., utilities, insurance, health care), and will result in increased costs an property tax spikes reducing instructional staff, programs and facilities." As one newspaper reported, superintendents in New Jersey fear that districts will lose programs, extracurricular services, and the quality of education will be "severely diminished" with fewer staff.

Phase 6: Rising Costs, Declining State Revenues

Facing a $4 billion dollar budget shortfall, newly elected Governor Jon Corzine (a Democrat) petitioned the court in April 2006 to freeze state funding for New Jersey's Abbott districts, a situation that the suburban communities had been accustomed to for over five years. The unprecedented measure, approved by the Supreme Court in May 2006, reversed a decades-long trend and set the stage for other measures, including the reduction in the number of Abbott districts that are sheltered under the protection of the courts orders for full funding. The New Jersey governor was quoted in the *Philadelphia Inquirer* on May 1, 2006: "I don't know that without changes in outcomes we should be keeping our feet on the accelerator. We are saying we want to know what's going on with the dollars we're spending, and we want some time to review how we distribute aid." Corzine proceeded to order forensic fiscal audits of four Abbott districts, including Camden, Paterson, Jersey City, and Newark.

In March 2006, New Jersey's State Commission of Investigation (SCI), an investigative arm of the state legislature, released a scathing report entitled "Taxpayers Beware: What You Don't Know Can Cost You." The report was the culmination of an extensive review of selective New Jersey school administrators' "questionable and hidden compensation" packages. As the executive summary states,

> The Commission examined employment contracts and compensation arrangements between public school administrators and boards of education and found a range of questionable and excessive practices that, collectively, cost unsuspecting New Jersey taxpayers millions of dollars. Lucrative provisions of these privately negotiated deals enable superintendents and others at the top tier of public school administration to receive compensation and benefits often well beyond the reach of any other class of public-service employees. Moreover, it is not unusual for these arrangements to be structured such that they continue to benefit recipients with costly and, in some cases, irregular pensions and perquisites well into retirement.

Although the report did not determine that boards of educations or administrators had broken the law, it sought to alarm the public by revealing a few administrators' extraordinary contracts. For example, the total compensation package for the superintendent of the Toms River School district was $347,462 versus his reported salary of $210,750. The impact of the report on state policymakers was significant; in the weeks following the report, a legislative "frenzy" ensued with bills posted that sought further to impose state control over local school district practices to once again, unprecedented levels.

These bills proposed both increased oversight and disclosure of public school district financial affairs and employment practices, limited compensation benefits for school district administrators, and other measures to protect the public from the newly perceived abuse of taxpayers' dollars. The public is awaiting solutions to overreliance on property taxes, but the legislature and governor have few options since the state is taxed out, and the governor has moved to return half of the new taxes for local relief.

Conclusion

The case of New Jersey is highly informative, showing the steady, and in some ways inevitable, progression from (1) the actions of the state court to enforce greater equity; (2) a rising percent of spending by the state, which reaches nearly 90 percent in some Abbott districts; (3) greater controls, and standard-setting, leading to overpowering state limitations on the responsiveness and autonomy of local school districts; and (4) the financial strain on the state reaching a point where the state treasury does not, or cannot generate the revenues to continue to fund New Jersey schools in an equitable fashion. Add on to these developments the strong hand of the U.S. government in No Child Left Behind, also forcing more centralized state control over the teaching-learning-testing process, and the result is a strengthening of state control over schools and school districts.

Recently, however, the State of New Jersey is showing signs of reconsidering this high level of state funding and control. In part, the reversal results, first, from the staggering costs of funding the Abbott districts, and, second, from the changing levels of spending in some of these districts since 1975 when the process began. As an article in the Newark *Star Ledger* explained, "A legislative analysis of the State Education Commissioner has found nearly half of the current group of 31 school districts could fall off the list. Most of those 13 districts would be the smaller ones, but also include two of the state's largest, Jersey City and Elizabeth" (Mooney, May 19, 2005, p. A1).

A major reason for disqualifications of Abbott districts, according to former state commissioner of education William Librera, was a change in the economic status of districts, since the original *Robinson* decision was based on poverty and the inequalities in spending across New Jersey school districts. In the last fifteen years, for example, Hoboken, just across the Hudson River from New York City, "has since seen its economy improve with the housing boom" (2005, p. A-1), raising it from second poorest district in the state to the second from the top of the thirty-one districts—thus threatening its status as an Abbott district and a recipient of extra state equity funding.

These local socioeconomic changes run up against the original Abbott criteria of the equity case: (a) at least 40 percent of the students would be poor enough to qualify for the free/reduced-lunch program; (b) property taxes would be at least 30 percent above the state's average—meaning that the district is taxing itself higher and producing less results because of low property values; (c) a 3 percent below average per-capita tax base; and (d) lower test scores, higher dropout rates, and fewer course offerings.

Should thirteen or so districts in New Jersey no longer qualify, the $1.6 billion of state support would be phased out over four years, reversing the trends for the last thirty-one years in state funding and support under state court mandates. Already, as one would predict, these affected Abbott districts are banding together to take the state to court (again), although it is unclear that they will win their cases. Thus, we can conclude that the rising power of the state does have a ceiling. For, even in New Jersey, state control and resources are not infinite, although the haggling over control may well be.

Are we are on the cusp of a major paradigm shift in the control structure of schools in New Jersey (and perhaps elsewhere as well)? A number of models of school governance have emerged in New Jersey. The models of state school politics are changing, from the federalist, "loosely coupled" concepts (Weick, 1976) that local leaders know best and that schools should be run by those closest to the children and community, to newer paradigms of more standardized state and federal interventions, ones that rest on the assumption that it's perhaps better to have less local autonomy and greater local equity and adequacy. These "trade-offs" are still be negotiated in a state with strong state government and a history of local school governance.

As early as 1976, a survey of state school board members by Campbell and Mazzoni (1976) found that legislatures were beginning to "interfere" in the operation of schools. Others, too, have concentrated on interaction between interest groups, levels, and changes. In New Jersey, we see phases or waves of reform and change—from *Robinson v. Cahill* to statewide standards, to state takeovers, to testing and regulation of local budgets and decision-making—that overlap and recur. This "wave theory" links later reform initiatives to earlier ones (Cuban, 1990).

As Marshall and Gerstl-Pepin (2005) explain: "Each state has its own set of power struggles and definitions of the meaning and purpose of public education. These struggles are linked to strategic policy shifts and specific cultural meaning systems and idiosyncrasies" (p. 156). Simply explained by Cuban (1990), "if society has an itch, schools get scratched." The constituencies are important (Cooper, Fusarelli, & Randall, 2004), but so are the dynamics of the waves of change, pressures from one reform that lead to another.

The models of government control over education keep evolving, but one thing is clear: The states have become more powerful. In New Jersey, we see pressure toward full state funding and control at the forefront, with small elements of the decentralized (e.g., charter schools) and interdistrict transfers, as follows.

1. *Full State Funding, Full State Control:* A number of Abbott districts in New Jersey are close to being fully state funded and, consequently, they have experienced growing state control. The Passaic Public Schools, for example, report that 91 percent of their $120 million budget is supplied by the state. While several urban Abbott districts were actually taken over by the state, which replaced the superintendent and school board with appointees, other districts are still managed on a day-to-day basis by a locally elected school board, which appointed the local superintendent; the major decisions by the districts are still greatly constrained by the power of the state, which controls their budget levels, surpluses, ability to raise taxes, and so on.

2. *Radical Decentralization:* Running counter to the "big state" model is a move in the opposite direction—the freeing up of schools to be more autonomous and self-managing. Charter schools are now common in the New Jersey, many of which serve the inner-city students in the very districts that the state is controlling. Perhaps, pulling schools from under the thumb of both the district and the state might free them up to better serve the poorest, minority children, although many of these schools are struggling to survive, given that their operating budgets are considerably smaller than the Abbott districts that now spend between $15,000 and $11,000 per student.

Furthermore, charter schools receive no state start-up funding (hence making it difficult to find facilities that are adequate and affordable). Since public schools in many districts are crowded (particularly when the state required preschool and kindergarten without providing adequate funds to house these programs), the chances of charter schools finding housing become more complicated.

3. *Greater Intradistrict Choice and Flexibility:* The third model is perhaps the most likely, as NCLB offers greater choice to districts, and the states are more willing to allow students to transfer out of failing schools, in failing districts. Intradistrict choice may hold promise for helping schools to improve and for families to have greater opportunity to change schools (and even to move children into nearby districts). How this choice option will affect Abbott districts is not yet known. A number of urban districts (Atlanta, Detroit) are seeing the decline in student enrollment, making it difficult to plan and finance reforms.

It is clear that a "perfect storm" has hit New Jersey in the first decade of this new century. Rising property taxes, increasing special education costs, increasing public school enrollments, increasing court rulings, and decreasing state revenues have forced the state to find ways of reducing state support of public schools. While decreasing funding may result in reduction of control in the Abbott school districts, the arm of the state will continue to rise above the remaining six hundred-plus suburban districts. Governor Corzine, in a statement about education, said,

> I am . . . committed to holding public, local and school officials accountable for their efforts. The budget that I have recently proposed is fiscally stringent, and necessarily so. I have called upon state officials at all levels to reduce expenditures and to find ways to do more with less. They have been fully responsive to this call. I expect nothing less from local municipal and school officials. To this end, I am committed to a review of the entire school funding system—one that will meet the needs of all students, including those in the Abbott districts. Ultimately, a new school funding formula needs to be developed that will ensure that State and local resources are applied not only in an equitable manner, but in such a way to maximize the potential of all students to achieve success. Our focus must be to get resources to the children, rather than to the districts. All disadvantaged students, no matter which district they attend, must have the benefit of sufficient fiscal resources to meet their needs. I believe with hard work and knowledgeable debate all of these goals can be met and a funding formula created that will be acceptable to all. (Corzine, 2006)

In conclusion, New Jersey illustrates the bumpy road toward state power and control, and the dynamics of waves of change. It also shows what happens when the state "takes over" and radically reduces the autonomy of school districts, removing their fiscal and governmental flexibility and limiting their ability to react to changes and emergencies. Where will state control end? How can No Child Left Behind, and other laws, hold local district leadership accountable without at the same time handcuffing them?

We see little evidence that the rising of the power of the state in New Jersey has made a significant difference in either equalizing educational opportunity or improving the state's overall performance. Spending is on the rise, to a point where the governor had closed down the state offices to force a higher sales tax (6 percent to 7 percent), just as the New Jersey high court had closed the schools thirty years ago (1976) that forced the legislature to enact a 1.76 percent state income tax. We find that the original *Robinson* case has amazingly equalized the poorest districts with many of the wealthiest, while shortchanging the lower-middle and middle-income districts that benefited neither from the state's largesse nor high local property wealth and income.

We definitely see the state as "in the face" of local districts, starting with Core Content Curriculum Standards, affecting first through twelfth grades for each subject: that is, moving to testing at most grades levels; restricting new school construction; and affecting district financial discretion. We conclude that New Jersey is a prime example of what can happen when the state takes over.

References

Campbell, R. F., & Mazzoni, T. L., Jr. (1976). *State policy making for the public schools*. Berkeley: McCutchan.

Cooper, B. S., Fusarelli, L. D., & Randall, E. V. (2004). *Better policies, better schools*. Boston: Allyn and Bacon.

Corzine, J. (2006). Governor's Statement Regarding Education Funding. Retrieved August 1, 2006, from http://www.nj.gov/governor/news/news/proved/20060407.html.

Cuban, L. (1990). Reforming again, again, again. *Educational Researcher 19,* 3–13.

Drobness, T. (2004, September 14). Legislators get an earful over state's school spending. *Star-Ledger*, p. 2.

Hester, T. (2004, August 27). 14 of 15 members appointed to tax convention task force. *Newark Star-Ledger*, p. 10.

Howe, W. P. (1996). The quest for education equity in New Jersey. In Bruce S. Cooper & Sheree T. Speakman (Eds.), *Optimizing education resources. Advances in education productivity* (pp. 17–43). Greenwich, CT: JAI Press.

Lehne, R. (1978). *The quest for justice: The politics of school finance reform*. New York: Longman.

Lowi, T. (1969). *The end of liberalism: Ideology, policy and the crisis of public authority*. New York: W.W. Norton.

Marshall, C., & Gerstl-Pepin, C. (2005). *Re-framing educational politics for social justice*. Boston: Pearson.

Salmore, S., & Salmore, B. (1993). The transformation of state electoral politics. In C. Van Horn (Ed.), *The state of the states*. Washington, DC: Congressional Quarterly Press.

Weick, K. E. (1976). Educational organizations as loosely coupled systems. *Administrative Science Quarterly 21,* 1–18.

Chapter 5

New York

Sandra Vergari

New York State Activism in Education Policy

New York State is home to one of the nation's largest and most diverse populations.[1] The state has one of the highest tax rates and some of the most extensive public policy programs in the United States. Many interests at the local level want the state to either cut mandates or provide more revenue (Stonecash, 2001a, 2001b). As discussed in this chapter, the state has recently adopted various reform policies for K–12 public education. In a trend of greater centralization of power over public education, New York state policymakers had embraced several features of the No Child Left Behind Act of 2001 (NCLB) even before the adoption of the sweeping federal law. Most notably, recent state mandates have focused on enhancing equity and accountability in public education.

I begin the chapter with a review of public education governance and recent education statistics. I then turn to five key areas of state activity, beginning with an examination of policies pertaining to learning standards and assessments. Second, I discuss new certification requirements for teachers and school leaders, followed by a review of state policy on school violence and character education. Fourth, I examine shared decision-making and charter schools, two policies—one largely symbolic and the other precedent setting—that challenge traditional school district power arrangements. Finally, I discuss dynamics pertaining to a long-standing school finance court case and conclude the chapter.

Education Governance

Article 11 of the New York State Constitution requires the state legislature to "provide for the maintenance and support of a system of free common schools, wherein all the children of this state may be educated." New York was among the first states to establish a strong state role in education when the legislature established the Board of Regents in 1784 (Schneier, 2001). The Regents set overall education policy for the state. There are sixteen Regents, one from each of the state's twelve judicial districts and four at-large members. Regents are appointed by the state legislature and do not receive a salary for their service.[2] The Regents elect a chancellor who chairs the monthly meetings and appoints members of committees.

The Regents also appoint the commissioner of education, who leads the state education department. The commissioner and the education department implement policies adopted by the Regents. Commissioners of education have enjoyed substantial power in the education policy arena, including quasi-judicial power to review appeals of actions by local school boards and other education officials (Ward, 2002).

During the past two hundred years, the most important role of the Regents has been oversight of curriculum, instruction, and student assessment (Ward, 2002). Compared to other state boards of education, the New York State Board of Regents is noteworthy for the scope of its powers and its independence from executive control. Across the nation, governors frequently seek to be champions of education reform policy and the independence of the Regents and commissioner of education from gubernatorial control has been a source of frustration for New York State governors (Schneier, 2001; Ward, 2002).

New York State Education Numbers

There are about 2.8 million K–12 public school students, 700 public school districts, and 4,000 public schools in the state.[3] The public school system employs more than 220,000 classroom teachers and 40,000 professional staff.[4] Between 1992–1993 and 2002–2003, total public school expenditures in the state increased $15.17 billion (67.2 percent) and state funding increased $8.36 billion (94.8 percent). Over the last two decades, state funding as a percentage of total public school expenditures ranged from a low of 38 percent in 1993–1994 to a high of 48 percent in 2001–2002.[5] In 2003–2004 and 2004–2005, the state provided about 44.3 percent and 44.7 percent of total public school expenditures, respectively (NYS Education Department, 2005).

State Learning Standards and Assessments

New York has been a national leader in the establishment of policies regarding student learning standards and assessments.[6] The policies discussed below reflect concerns about accountability and equity among students and public schools.

Standards and Tests

New York has a long history of state-mandated testing in education. In 1864, the Regents required public examinations of all students who sought admission to private or public high schools. In 1877, the state legislature authorized the Regents to administer examinations for high school graduation and college admission. High schools were required to use Regents exams in order to qualify for funding from the state Literature Fund (established in 1801). The Regents exams were accompanied by curricula that were outlined in published syllabi and teachers' guides. In 1906, in a shift toward local control, high schools were permitted to issue local diplomas to students who had not passed Regents exams (Folts, 1996).

As of 1984, the Regents required high school graduates to demonstrate basic competence in English, math, science, global studies, and U.S. history and government. In order to receive a high school diploma, students could choose to pass local exams (in place since 1978) or more challenging Regents exams. Students choosing the local exams received a local diploma, while students passing the Regents exams earned the more prestigious Regents diploma (Folts, 1996; Ward, 2002).

In 1996, the Regents adopted new learning standards for each grade level and more rigorous requirements for high school graduation. In 1997, 23 percent of graduates from high-needs districts and 53 percent of students in the rest of the state received Regents diplomas (NYS Board of Regents & Education Department, 1998). According to the NYS Education Department (2004b, para. 2), the learning standards promote equity: "students may expect an intellectually powerful education no matter where they live."

Under the new state rules, the option to meet school district standards and earn a local diploma was discontinued for general education students. Regents exams are now required for high school graduation.[7] Students entering ninth grade in September 2001 or later must pass Regents exams in English, math, science, global history, and U.S. history in order to receive a Regents diploma. State tests in English and math have been required for fourth and eighth grade students since 1999. In 2006, the state testing program expanded to include grades 3–8 as mandated by NCLB.[8]

In addition to the Regents-mandated learning standards, state lawmakers have adopted numerous curricular mandates. A 1994 amendment to the education law, for example, requires instruction in patriotism, citizenship, and human rights issues with particular attention to genocide, slavery, and the Holocaust. A 1996 education law requires instruction about Ireland's Great Irish Famine in 1845–1850. Moreover, a 2000 law, discussed later in the chapter, requires character education in K–12 public schools.

Academic Intervention Services

New York is one of nineteen states to require remediation for students who fail state exams; however, unlike fifteen states, it does not provide funding specifically for this remediation (*Education Week*, 2006). The state Academic Intervention Services (AIS) mandate took effect in 2000. Districts were required to develop AIS plans and to review the plans every two years. Academic intervention services are supposed to help students achieve state standards in English and math in grades K–12, and the social studies and science standards in grades 4–12.

Students in need of AIS are identified based on their state test scores and other district procedures. The services include academic instruction that supplements regular classroom instruction and support services that address barriers to academic success. Support services might deal with student problems in such areas as attendance, nutrition, health, and family. Schools are required to provide AIS no later than the beginning of the semester after a student has been identified in need of AIS. School districts are to use their own funds for AIS or apply for state and federal grants that are appropriate for one or more AIS components (see Kadamus, 2000).

All districts are required to develop and implement AIS plans, and all students in need of extra assistance in order to meet state learning standards are supposed to receive it. In a study of AIS policy implementation, Killeen and Sipple (2005) observed a swift and high degree of district compliance. They also identified two areas of local divergence from state guidelines. First, while the state requires that AIS teachers be certified in the AIS subjects they instruct, more than 50 percent of districts indicated that they relied on special education staff to provide AIS instruction.[9] Second, according to state rules, "all" students scoring below level 3 on the state exams "are eligible" to receive AIS (Kadamus, 2000).[10] Yet Killeen and Sipple (2005) report that 15 percent of AIS-eligible students in New York City did not receive AIS; and, outside of the largest five districts in the state, 5 percent of those eligible did not receive AIS.

Reasons for lack of AIS for eligible students include district capacity deficiencies, scheduling problems, student absenteeism, and student refusal to participate.[11] Districts with large numbers of students eligible for AIS in multiple subjects face formidable constraints on their ability to lengthen the school day, build more classrooms, or require that students stay after school or attend Saturday classes (Killeen & Sipple, 2005). Thus, while intended to boost equity by offering extra assistance to lagging students, AIS policy implementation and student access to AIS depend on district will and capacity.

School Accountability

The state holds not only students but also schools accountable for meeting state standards. Two types of school accountability policy are school report cards and the state registration review process.

REPORT CARDS. The state education department has published annual school report card data since 1997. The report cards embody a form of transparency in public education that has the potential to produce greater accountability. The report cards provide data on student performance on state tests, and permit the public to draw comparisons between schools and districts. Report card data receive a good deal of publicity; they are published in newspapers, school district newsletters and Web sites, and on the state education department Web site.

SURR. Schools that are farthest from meeting state standards may be placed on the state list of "schools under registration review" (SURR), a process established in 1989. Such schools must adopt and implement corrective action plans. Schools under registration review receive technical assistance from both the state and their respective districts. If improvements do not occur, SURR schools are subject to state takeover or closure. Between 1989 and 2006, 280 schools had been placed on the SURR list, and 189 of these had been removed from the list due to improving academic performance. Forty-seven schools that did not meet their performance targets were closed. As of January 2006, there were sixty-one schools on the SURR list and forty of these were in New York City (NYS Education Department 2006d, p. 1).

Analysis

The state limited the freedom of local school districts and teachers by adopting detailed learning standards and more rigorous graduation requirements. While some analysts lament what they perceive to be an unfortunate focus on "teaching to the test," others note that the state standards ensure greater equity and accountability across school districts. If the exams measure skills and knowledge that experts and society indicate should be measured, then teaching to the test should not be controversial. Moreover, school districts are free to extend student instruction beyond the state standards. State exams required for graduation also hold all students accountable for meeting learning standards. The AIS mandate addresses equity concerns by requiring extra assistance to students struggling to meet state standards. Finally, school report cards that shine light on student performance across schools and the SURR process promote accountability in public education.

State Mandates for Teachers and School Leaders

In addition to equity and accountability policies focused on students and schools, state policymakers have recently adopted reforms pertaining to teachers and school leaders.

Teacher Certification

In 2000, the Regents issued a number of new mandates pertaining to teacher certification. The Regents invoked both the equity and accountability values in their proclamation that "no longer will children have teachers with uneven levels of knowledge and skill" (NYS Regents & Education Department, 1998, p. 14). The Regents decided that, by September 2003, all New York State public school teachers must be certified. As of February 2004, teachers seeking permanent certification (now called "professional certification") must complete an approved teacher education program, earn a bachelor's and master's degree, pass two general teacher tests and a content specialty test in the subject area to be taught, and complete three years of teaching, including a year of "mentored" teaching.[12]

An initial teaching certificate requires a bachelor's degree. In the past, candidates for permanent teacher certification were permitted five years in which to complete a required master's degree. The 2000 regulations narrowed that time frame by two years, requiring recipients of the initial certificate to obtain the master's degree within three years in order to qualify for the professional certificate.[13] However, prospective teachers, school leaders, directors of teacher preparation programs, and education interest groups lobbied state education officials for a change in the policy. Teachers working full-time in their first teaching positions reportedly struggled to find time to complete coursework for the master's degree in three years; officials were informed that "teachers' graduate education programs are often richer and more beneficial" when teachers have had classroom experience (Duncan-Poitier, 2005, p. 1). In January 2005, the Regents responded by returning the term of the initial certificate to five years, permitting teachers more time to earn the master's degree required for professional certification.

PROFESSIONAL DEVELOPMENT. Prior to the 2000 reforms, permanent teaching certificates did not expire. Under the new state rules, professional certificates are maintained via completion of 175 hours of professional development every five years.[14] State policymakers left decisions regarding professional development content, delivery, and providers to school districts. Each district is required to have a professional development plan that specifies its goals, strategies, and evaluation standards for professional development, including specification of a mentoring program for first-year teachers.

The regulations offer significant leeway to districts and teachers. For example, the state does not require that any portion of the 175 hours be completed annually. Moreover, with district permission, teachers may fulfill 100 percent of the 175 hours by providing mentoring services. The state education department offers a broad list of suggested activities on its Web site, but emphasizes that authority to assess appropriateness of activities for fulfillment of the professional development requirement rests solely with school districts (NYS Education Department, 2006a).

TEACHER EDUCATION PROGRAMS. The Regents mandated that teacher education programs achieve accreditation, and that 80 percent of their graduates pass one or more teacher certification exams. New York is one of twenty-nine states that publish pass rates or rankings of teacher education providers (*Education Week,* 2006).

SCHOOL LEADERSHIP CERTIFICATION. Public school leaders in New York must also be state certified. The state now awards three types of school leadership certificates: school building leader, school district leader, and school district business leader. In 1998, the Regents and Commissioner of Education Mills formed a "Blue Ribbon Panel on School Leadership."[15] State school leadership regulations were subsequently amended in 2003.[16] The Regents specified nine characteristics that comprise "Essential Knowledge and Skills for Effective School Leadership."[17] These characteristics form the basis on which school leaders are to be recruited, trained, assessed, and certified (Kadamus & Duncan-Poitier, 2002). School leadership programs in forty-nine colleges and universities across the state revised their school leadership programs (a total of 116 programs) in order to meet the new state standards by September 2004 (Duncan-Poitier, 2005).

Requirements for the initial certificate as a school building leader include a master's degree, completion of an approved school leadership program, and three years of experience in classroom teaching or pupil personnel service.[18] The initial certificate is valid for five years. A candidate for the professional certificate must have at least three years of educational leadership experience, including at least one year as a school building leader. Prospective school district leaders and school district business leaders earn professional certificates that require sixty credit hours of graduate study, including a master's degree; completion of an approved preparation program; and, for school district leaders, three years of classroom teaching or education leadership or pupil personnel service experience. Each of the professional certificates remains valid as long as the professional development requirement (discussed later) is fulfilled every five years.

INTERNSHIP OF 600 HOURS. The state effectively doubled its existing internship requirement in 2003, mandating that prospective school leaders now complete a fifteen-week, full-time internship.[19] Proponents of the expanded mandate avow that it will enhance the skills and knowledge of school leader candidates. Others note that internships are typically unpaid and the lengthier internship requirement, combined with other certification rules, could discourage potential entrants to the school leadership ranks.

SCHOOL LEADERSHIP EXAMS. Prior to 2003, the state did not have specific mandates regarding school leadership competencies or assessments for school leaders. Under the new regulations, a prospective school leader must develop knowledge and skills specific to the certification title and pass a new state exam designed to measure these qualities. Student success rates on the exams are also intended to measure school leadership program effectiveness (Duncan-Poitier, 2005). Oddly, in order to comply with the 2003 regulations, school leadership programs had to design their new curricula prior to receiving information from the state on the contents of the school leadership exams. As of July 2006, the state education department was still developing the exams. Therefore, the Regents waived the exam requirement for certification candidates who complete school leadership programs prior to the availability of the state exam.

SCHOOL LEADERSHIP PROGRAMS. Formerly, the state provided no specific guidance on admissions criteria for school leadership preparation programs. The new regulations guide such programs to recruit historically underrepresented candidates and applicants with demonstrated leadership potential, collaborate with school districts, ensure candidate mentoring by college faculty and school leaders, and deliver competency-based curricula. Similar to teacher education, the state previously had few accountability measures in place for school leadership programs. Under the new rules, school leadership programs must be accredited and their students' performance on the state school leadership exams is to be evaluated during program reviews.

PROFESSIONAL DEVELOPMENT. As in the case of teacher certification, state policymakers adopted new professional development requirements for school leaders. In the past, school leadership certificates were permanent. In 2006, the Regents mandated that holders of professional certificates in school leadership who are regularly employed by a school district complete 175 hours of professional development every five years.

Analysis

Prior to adopting the teacher certification reforms, state policymakers explained that "higher standards for students require higher standards for teachers" (NYS Regents & Education Department, 1998, p. 12) They observed an uneven quality across teacher preparation programs and avowed that "only by holding all programs to high standards will we ensure that all teachers are prepared to teach to high standards" (ibid., p. 18). Thus, the new state mandates are intended to yield greater accountability in teacher preparation and evaluation processes, and greater equity in teacher quality across schools.

Prior to the school leadership reforms, Lankford, O'Connell, and Wyckoff (2003) surveyed almost 2,900 individuals under age fifty who were state-certified in school leadership but not yet in leadership posts. While 90 percent of the respondents claimed to be well prepared to assume leadership positions, 60 percent of these indicated that they wanted additional training in school finance and facilities management, and 30 percent wanted more training in staff supervision and program evaluation prior to assuming leadership roles. These data support Regents claims that prospective school leaders would benefit from improvements in school leadership program curricula.

For both teachers and school leaders, the Regents changed the wording of certificate titles from "permanent" to "professional" and mandated new professional development requirements. These changes reflect efforts to ensure that teachers and school leaders are accorded the expectations and standing commensurate with professional status in other sectors. Overall, the certification regulations leave little room for variation across districts, leaders, and teachers. However, they do permit substantial local discretion in the areas of mentoring and professional development.

School Violence and Character Education

In addition to education reform policies adopted by the Regents, education commissioner, and state education department, the governor and state legislature have engaged in education policymaking. As discussed below, school violence has been a key subject of recent lawmaking.

In January 1999, Governor George E. Pataki announced creation of a statewide Task Force on School Violence to be chaired by Lieutenant Governor Mary O. Donahue. In April 1999, Pataki released his Project SAVE (Safe Schools Against Violence in Education) plan and charged the task force with building on that plan. The task force released its recommendations for ensuring school safety in October 1999. Shortly thereafter, New York State's Safe Schools Against Violence in Education Act, dubbed "Project SAVE," was signed into law in July and took effect in November 2000.

This law requires school districts to implement measures aimed at maintaining safe, secure schools. Each district must adopt a district-wide school safety plan in addition to school building safety plans. Boards of education are required to appoint school safety teams to develop, review, and update their district wide plans annually.[20] Districts must also adopt codes of conduct regarding students, school personnel, and visitors on school property (including school buses) and at school-sponsored events. Project SAVE also includes provisions for students who assault teachers and for suspensions.[21]

Teacher and school leader certification candidates must complete two hours of training in school violence prevention and intervention, and school districts must include such training in their professional development plans. School districts are also required to file annual reports to the commissioner of education regarding violent and disruptive incidents, and a summary of the information is to be included in district report cards.

Weak Implementation of District Reporting Requirement

Each year, the education department is required to review the data on violent and disruptive incidents submitted by school districts, decide whether any schools should be designated as persistently dangerous, and publish a list of the state's most dangerous schools. According to a state comptroller's audit released in May 2006, some school districts were underreporting violent incidents, and the state education department had not done enough to address misreporting problems and identify schools with serious violence problems. The audit focused on 2003–2004 and districts outside of New York City. In visits to a representative sample of high schools, auditors found that, in a majority of the schools, at least one-third of violent and disruptive incidents in school records were not reported to the education department. In one high school, 780 of 924 documented incidents (84 percent) in 2003–2004 were not reported to the state. Of these 780, two were sexual offenses, eleven involved weapon use, and one involved weapon possession.

The audit concludes that annual school violence reports prepared by the state education department do not indicate the full seriousness of the situation to state policymakers (NYS Comptroller, 2006). On the same day that the audit results were announced, Commissioner of Education Mills announced corrective actions the education department would implement in response to fourteen recommendations of the comptroller (see NYS Education Department, 2006b).

Character Education

Project SAVE also requires character education in public schools. The legislature directed the Regents to ensure that instruction in grades K–12 includes:

> a component on civility, citizenship, and character education. Such component shall instruct students on the principles of honesty, tolerance, personal responsibility, respect for others, observance of laws and rules, courtesy, dignity and other traits which will enhance the quality of their experiences in, and contributions to, the community. The regents shall determine how to incorporate such component in existing curricula and the commissioner shall promulgate any regulations needed to carry out such determination of the regents. (Education Law of NYS, §801-a)

A September 2001 state guidance memo to districts notes that the state learning standards "for social studies and for health, physical education, and family and consumer sciences include many of the elements listed in the Project SAVE curricular requirements" (Kadamus, 2001, para. 3).[22] This suggests that at least part of the character education legislation had already been addressed in state policy.

The guidance encourages school districts to analyze their existing efforts in providing instruction in civility, citizenship, and character education. "Through this process, districts can build upon established practices to strengthen curriculum and staff development in these areas" (Kadamus, 2001, para. 4). Finally, the memo offers a list of resources to assist school districts in complying with the requirements of the law. The list contains a broad array of references, including social studies syllabi, teachers' guides on the U.S. Supreme Court and law, more than a dozen character education programs used by districts across the state, literature on sports and character education, and character education resources from ten different states.

Analysis

The state education department and school districts have not implemented some elements of Project SAVE as robustly as supporters of the law would prefer. Districts have not fully and accurately reported violent and disruptive incidents to the state because the reporting guidelines have not always been understood and accepted by district officials, and districts might be reluctant to report such incidents publicly (NYS Comptroller, 2006).

The character education mandate reflects the equity value in that it seems to require the provision of character education across all districts. However, the state legislature and Regents did not attach any accountability measures to the mandate. State lawmakers left implementation details to the Regents. The Regents refrained from adopting specific regulations and instead offered districts a range of ideas on how they might approach the legislation. The aforementioned guidance from the education department is wide-ranging and largely devoid of concrete requirements. Thus, the character education policy appears to be mostly symbolic, and districts have responded to the mandate with varying levels of enthusiasm and activity.

Structural Challenges to Traditional School District Power

In addition to reforms pertaining to learning, teaching, leadership, and school safety, the state has approved changes in processes by which local decisions may be made for public schools. As discussed below, at the beginning of the 1990s, the education commissioner mandated a new form of decision-making structure for public schools. At the close of the 1990s, state lawmakers took a giant leap further and approved a charter school law.

Shared Decision-Making

In 1992, the education commissioner required that, by February 1994, each school district adopt a shared decision-making plan that permitted teachers and parents to participate with administrators and school board members in school-based planning and shared decision-making. The plans were to address six components, including educational issues that would be subject to "cooperative planning and shared decision making at the building level by teachers, parents, administrators and at the discretion of the board of education . . . other parties such as students, school district support staff, and community members" (Regulations of Commissioner of Education, Part 100.11). The plans were also supposed to specify "the means by which all parties will be held accountable for the decisions which they share in making" (ibid.).

School districts are required to conduct biennial reviews of their shared decision-making plans and to submit biennial reports to the state education department. The department then produces biennial state reports summarizing the results of the district reports. The regulation has engendered a number of appeals to the education commissioner regarding alleged violations. Biennial state reports on the policy offer little indication that genuine site-based decision-making is occurring across the state or that shared decision-making teams enjoy power to make key school decisions. As discussed next, charter schools, on the other hand, enjoy site-based decision-making power.

Charter Schools

A charter school is a publicly funded, nonsectarian school of choice that operates free from many of the regulations under which traditional public schools operate. Unless partnerships are formed with one or more school districts, charter schools operate independently from school district boards and superintendents. For example, a charter school can enter contracts without having to secure school district approval.

New York State adopted a charter school law in 1998. In 1999, Governor Pataki proclaimed boldly that "creation of charter schools represents the single greatest improvement in education in state history" (Office of the Governor, 1999, p. 1). With this law, the state permitted a direct and potentially powerful challenge to the school district monopoly over public education delivery. When a student chooses to attend a charter school rather than a traditional public school, the per pupil funding follows the student to the charter school.

The 1998 Charter Schools Act permits one hundred newly created charter schools.[23] There is no limit on the number of conversion charter schools formed from previously existing public schools. Charter schools that are newly created (rather than converted from existing public schools) do not need school district approval to operate.[24] In 2005–2006, seventy-nine charter schools were in operation, serving over 21,000 students; forty-seven of these schools were in New York City (Center for Education Reform, 2006; NY Charter Schools Association, 2006).[25]

Many charter schools are too young to yield reliable longitudinal data rather than snapshot data on school performance. To date, the overall performance of charter schools in the state appears mixed. Students in some charter schools have performed very well on state tests while students in other charter schools have not; a couple of charter schools have been assigned probationary status; and five operating charter schools have been required to close.

Analysis

Shared decision-making has been implemented unevenly in the state. The state is not well positioned to provide careful monitoring and enforcement of the mandate. When it comes to core issues of schooling and budgeting, school leaders and district boards may be reluctant to share decision-making power with other stakeholders.[26] Thus, the shared decision-making mandate appears to be a weak state policy.

The more consequential charter school law embodies principles of equity as well as accountability. Where charter schools are available, students from families that cannot afford the tuition expense of private schools (preferred by some families for various reasons) or residence in areas with good schools are not limited to the public school to which they are assigned. The accountability provisions of the charter school reform are twofold. First, charter schools are supposed to be held accountable by their public authorizers and can be closed for failure. Second, charter school competition is supposed to spur greater accountability on the part of traditional public schools.

In adopting a charter school law, state lawmakers embraced the concept of local power in education, albeit not school district power. They bypassed school districts and authorized even greater decentralization of power to the school building and family levels. Nonetheless, the law retains state power in the area of learning standards since charter schools are accountable for meeting those standards. Thus, while charter schools may vary in terms of how education is delivered, the equity value is preserved in that charter school students must meet the same state standards as other public school students.[27]

School Finance

Concerns about equity and accountability are salient features of school finance politics. Across the nation, including in New York, when legislatures and governors do not meet organized demand for school finance reform, interest groups often appeal to the state judiciary to compel state action.[28]

Each school district in the state spends at least the national average per pupil on education. Moreover, New York ranks third in the nation in per pupil spending (*Education Week*, 2006).[29] Nonetheless, the state's school finance system has been characterized by many as archaic and grossly inequitable. The Campaign for Fiscal Equity (CFE) is a coalition of public education advocates who are participants in a nationwide movement pushing for "adequacy" in school finance. The self-declared main goal of CFE is "to ensure that each student in New York City has adequate resources and the opportunity for a sound basic education" (Campaign for Fiscal Equity, 2006, FAQs, para. 2).

Campaign for Fiscal Equity, Inc. v. State of New York

In 1993, CFE initiated a lawsuit in which it asserted that New York state had failed to provide a sound, basic education to New York City public school students and that the city's public schools were underfunded.[30] The state's motion to dismiss the case was granted. However, in 1995, the state's highest court, the Court of Appeals, ruled that CFE had a valid cause of action and could pursue its constitutional challenge to the state school finance system. In 1999, *Campaign for Fiscal Equity, Inc. v. State of New York* was heard by the state Supreme Court (a trial court); in January 2001, the court ruled in favor of CFE. The court declared that the state had violated the Education Article of the state constitution for failing to ensure that New York City schools received funding necessary to provide their students with a sound, basic education. The court ordered the state to reform the school finance system for the city by September 15, 2001.

A series of back-and-forth appeals on the part of the state and CFE followed over the next five years.[31] In March 2006, the Appellate Division of the Supreme Court ruled against the state and ordered the state legislature to provide New York City schools $4.7 to $5.63 billion for operations and $9.2 billion for facilities by April 1, 2006.[32] As of July 2006, the saga continued. The CFE appealed to the judiciary to order the state to comply with the March 2006 ruling, and the case was scheduled to be heard by the Court of Appeals in October 2006.

Analysis

The CFE has focused its rhetoric and actions on its notions of equity and adequacy. The meaning of school finance "adequacy" is, of course, a matter of great debate. Hanushek (2004, para. 12) notes that while some advocates have attempted to define "adequacy" scientifically, "this pseudo-science neglects two fundamental issues." He asserts that "data on the currently inefficient use of funds cannot possibly tell us what would be required" if resources were used more effectively and efficiently; second, determining public funding on schools "is a political decision, vested with legislatures and governors. It is not a scientific decision" (ibid.).

The CFE saga shows that political controversies are not always resolved swiftly by turning to the courts. Some state legislators and governors do not appreciate being told what to do by the judiciary. Indeed, the state senate majority leader referred to the court order to pay billions of dollars to New York City schools as "lunacy" (Lovett & Andreatta, 2006, p. 2).[33] The equity focus of school finance reform typically engenders unease among lawmakers who represent wealthy districts for fear that they will have to deliver less to their constituents in order to deliver more to high-needs districts. The CFE case, with its focus on New York City, also highlights competition for state funds on the part of the city and upstate New York.

In 2006, an election year with a budget surplus that state lawmakers were eager to spend in order to gain favor with voters, lawmakers approved $1.8 billion in new funding for school facilities in New York City in 2006–2007.[34] The state also authorized $9.4 billion in bonds for school construction in New York City, half of which will be backed with a pledge of state building aid. This $11.2 billion school facilities package fulfills the aforementioned court order to provide billions in new facilities dollars to city schools. However, the $420 million state operating aid increase for New York City schools in 2006–2007 did not meet the court order.

The CFE effort has largely neglected the principle of accountability. The case also raises questions about the wisdom of "throwing money at schools" as an easy "answer" to a wide-ranging, complicated series of problems that explain uneven opportunities and outcomes among public education students.[35] Moreover, if the state is to assume a greater role in funding public schools, it would makes sense for state lawmakers to demand increased accountability from schools in return for those state tax dollars. Hanushek (2004) thus predicts that a greater state role in funding would lead to greater state centralization of education policymaking and a decline in school district power.

Conclusion

As in other states, New York policymakers determined that long-standing local power over public education had not yielded satisfactory outcomes. The active state role in New York has led to more rigorous requirements for all public school students, teachers, and leaders; the delivery of extra supports to lagging students; a new type of public school called a charter school; stepped-up attention to school safety issues; and large increases in funding for school facilities and other needs. Substantial state power over education promotes both accountability and equity in the school system, although there is variance in implementation quality across policies.

Effective implementation of state policies by school districts requires both state pressure (to focus attention) and support (to enable implementation). Moreover, enthusiastic compliance with the spirit of a policy cannot be compelled (McLaughlin, 1987). When implementation of state accountability policies is robust, the policies advance equity. When implementation is weak or uneven—due to state or school district approaches to a policy—the impact in terms of enhancing equity is lower than could otherwise be the case (see Malen, 2003; Sipple & Killeen, 2004).

Cibulka (1999) identifies six approaches to accountability in education: information (performance data), executive leadership, bureaucratic oversight, rewards for performance, contracting, and markets. With the exception of direct rewards for performance, these approaches are embodied in the policies discussed in this chapter.

First, the learning standards, report cards, and SURR process yield important performance data by which to assess public schools. Comparative report card data might also spur grassroots political action aimed at ensuring greater equity in student opportunities to meet state standards. Second, changes in certification requirements for teachers and school leaders, the shared decision-making mandate, and charter schools reflect concerns about educational leadership as a key accountability issue. Third, New York has adopted many bureaucratic compliance measures for public education. As noted in this chapter, school districts must develop plans or reports for academic intervention services, professional development, shared decision-making, and Project SAVE. Indeed, a recent analysis found that school districts are required to file seventy-five plans, applications, and reports annually to the state (NYS Education Department, 2003). Fourth, the accountability approaches of contracting and markets are embodied in the charter school reform. Moreover, the publication of school report card data creates potential for a market dynamic in public education. Public education consumers now have ready access to authoritative, standardized data that may shape educational choices.

Multiple factors contribute to school and student outcomes, and limited extant data on various components of state education policy. Thus, in many cases, it is difficult to link particular outcomes to particular state policies. For example, the state permitted the existence of one hundred new charter schools, yet there is a lack of systematic data on whether school districts have gained knowledge from charter schools and whether charters have spurred improvements in traditional public schools. Nor are there data indicating whether student character has improved since the adoption of the character education mandate.

In the area of state learning standards and assessments, it is useful to examine whether student achievement has improved since the most recent reforms were adopted. Recent aggregate data indicate improved student achievement on standardized tests in elementary English and in elementary and middle school math, including significant gains among black, Hispanic, and low-income students. However, there has been a lack of progress in middle school English, and the four-year high school graduation rate in 2005 was only 64 percent (*Education Week*, 2006; NYS Board of Regents & Education Department, 2005).

While the state has established numerous objectives to be fulfilled locally, school districts have not been reduced to mere administrative arms. State enforcement of reforms such as shared decision-making and character education is weak. In the interest of promoting both equity and accountability, the state is enforcing and supporting a number of mandates pertaining to the core of schooling. Nonetheless, school districts continue to enjoy a significant level of discretion in selecting the means by which to fulfill many of the state objectives.

Moreover, districts with the capacity and will to extend their efforts beyond state minimum requirements are free to do so. Despite this local leeway, there is now a precedent of a strong state role in education. This centralizing trend in education policy, reinforced by the requirements of the federal No Child Left Behind Act of 2001, is likely to continue.

Notes

1. Special thanks to Bonnie Fusarelli, Bruce Cooper, and Ray O'Connell for helpful comments on previous drafts of this chapter. The New York State population of about nineteen million ranks third in the nation, after California and Texas.

2. The Regents are reimbursed for travel and related expenses connected to official duties.

3. New York has more than 470,000 students in nonpublic schools, nearly 15 percent of total state enrollment (NYS Education Department, 2005).

4. In 2004–2004, New York ranked third in the nation for teacher salaries. The average teacher salary was $55,181, an increase of 4.1 percent from 2002 to 2003. The median salary in 2003–2004 was $55,050 (American Federation of Teachers, 2005b; NYS Education Department, 2005).

5. Some of the increase in the state share since 1997–1998 is due to property tax relief reimbursed to school districts by the state under the "STAR" program.

6. A 2004 national analysis identified New York as the only state to have "clear and specific standards" in English, math, science, and social studies/history at the elementary, middle, and high school levels and to have tests aligned with the standards (*Education Week*, 2004, p. 144). In 2005, New York was among seven states classified as having standards that are clear, specific, and grounded in content at the three school levels (*Education Week*, 2006; American Federation of Teachers, 2005a).

7. Students with disabilities must sit for Regents exams. If they do not pass a required Regents exam, they may fulfill this graduation requirement by passing a Regents Competency Test in the subject. Under the state's "safety net" for students with disabilities, such students receive a local high school diploma rather than the Regents diploma. In districts that have adopted the "low-pass" option, students with disabilities who pass Regents exams with scores of 55–64 may receive a local diploma.

8. In 2005, New York was not among eight states that required passage of statewide exams for grade promotion (*Education Week*, 2006).

9. Not all special education teachers are subject-area certified. Killeen and Sipple (2005) suggest two possible interpretations of the noncompliance:

(1) district rejection of this element of state policy, and (2) district judgment that special educators are best equipped to provide AIS to students in need.

10. The performance levels range from 1 to 4. State regulations indicate that districts should use multiple measures to assess the intensity of AIS to be delivered to students.

11. Students cannot be compelled to participate in AIS (Killeen & Sipple, 2005).

12. The content specialty test was not required previously. In the past, two general teacher tests were required and teachers could receive permanent certification after two years in the classroom.

13. A one-year extension could be obtained to complete graduate coursework for the professional certificate, provided that the candidate had completed twenty-four semester hours of study by the end of the three-year period.

14. Professional development (PD) activity accrues according to hours spent in an activity. Each semester hour of college credit equals fifteen hours of PD, and each quarter hour of credit equals ten hours of PD (NYS Education Department, 2006c).

15. In 2000, the panel issued three recommendations: (1) creation of an environment where school leaders succeed in improving student achievement, (2) provision of quality preparation for school leaders, and (3) expansion of the scope and incentives for recruiting, developing, and retaining effective school leaders (NYS Board of Regents & Education Department, 2003).

16. Follow-up amendments were adopted in 2006.

17. The nine characteristics are: (1) Leaders know and understand what it means and what it takes to be a leader, (2) Leaders have a vision for schools that they constantly share and promote, (3) Leaders communicate clearly and effectively, (4) Leaders collaborate and cooperate with others, (5) Leaders persevere and take the "long view," (6) Leaders support, develop, and nurture staff, (7) Leaders hold themselves and others responsible and accountable, (8) Leaders never stop learning and honing their skills, and (9) Leaders have the courage to take informed risks.

18. This chapter does not discuss limited alternative routes to school leadership certification.

19. An equivalent leadership experience is permitted; students may complete the 600-hour internship over the course of more than fifteen weeks. The new regulations encourage internships that occur throughout the school leadership studies rather than culmination experiences at the end of studies.

20. At least one public hearing and a thirty-day public comment period must occur prior to adoption of a district-wide school safety plan.

21. Assaults on teachers were changed from Class A misdemeanor to Class D felony. The law also empowers principals to suspend students without specific school board delegation of that authority; districts must include in their codes of conduct minimum suspension periods for violent or repeatedly disruptive students.

22. For example, Kadamus (2001, para. 3) notes that "Social Studies Standard 5, Civics, Citizenship, and Government focuses on basic civic values such as justice, honesty, self-discipline, due process, equality, majority rule with respect for minority rights, and respect for self, others, and property. This standard also emphasizes . . . rights, roles, and responsibilities of citizenship. . . . The one-half unit social studies requirement, participation in government, reinforces these concepts and provides a culminating learning experience for students as they prepare to assume the roles of citizens in our society."

23. The cap of one hundred charters was reached in early 2006, and there were heated political battles over raising it; as of July 2006, the cap remained. Four entities can approve charter school applications. The Regents and Board of Trustees of the State University of New York (SUNY) can authorize new charter schools; a local board of education can approve charter schools to be operated within district boundaries; and the New York City schools chancellor can approve applications for charter schools within the city school district. The Regents formally issue all charters and cannot veto a SUNY decision to issue a charter. SUNY is eligible to authorize fifty charter schools; the Regents, school boards, and New York City schools chancellor may approve fifty new charter schools (see Vergari, 2002).

24. Conversion charter schools must be approved by the relevant school district board or, in New York City, by the schools chancellor. There were six such schools in 2005–2006, five in New York City and one in Buffalo.

25. Eighteen additional charter schools were scheduled to open in 2006–2007.

26. On shared decision-making initiatives, see Wohlstetter, Mohrman, and Robertson (1997) and Leighwood and Menzies (1998).

27. For a discussion of how equity might be enhanced more broadly through centralized educational standards and financing combined with decentralized school governance, see McDermott (1999).

28. According to the U.S. Supreme Court ruling in *San Antonio Independent School District v. Rodriguez*, 1973, education is not a fundamental right under the U.S. Constitution. Subsequently, state courts have been key settings for school finance cases.

29. Expenditures are highest in the District of Columbia; New Jersey is the first-ranked state. Average per pupil spending in New York in 2003 was $10,665 (*Education Week*, 2006).

30. In *Levittown v. Nyquist*, 1982, the New York Court of Appeals established that the state Constitution entitles students to a "sound basic education."

31. The state appealed the 2001 decision and won in 2002 when the Appellate Division of the state Supreme Court rejected the ruling of the trial court. Predictably, CFE appealed this decision. In 2003, the Court of Appeals reversed the 2002 Supreme Court ruling and ordered the state to reform the school finance system by July 30, 2004. The state did not meet the Court of Appeals deadline. In August 2004, three court-appointed referees were directed to submit a state compliance plan to the court by November 30, 2004. In November 2004, the referees delivered six recommendations, most notably that the state provide New York City schools with funding increases in the billions. In 2005, Supreme Court Justice Leland DeGrasse affirmed the recommendations and ordered the legislature and governor to provide New York City schools an additional $5.63 billion for operating expenses (phased in over four years) and $9.2 billion for facilities (phased in over five years). Predictably, the state appealed the 2005 ruling.

32. Amounts to be phased in over time, see note 33.

33. Bruno stated: "The judge in his lunacy said 'you have to.' I'm sorry, that is lunacy" (Lovett & Andreatta, 2006, p. 2).

34. The school facilities program also includes $800 million for school construction elsewhere in the state. The new school facilities funding for New York City is in addition to $500 million in existing school building aid to the city.

35. Such problems include school factors such as leadership and teacher quality. They also include formidable personal, family, and community challenges faced by students that are well beyond the purview of schools to alter substantially.

References

American Federation of Teachers. (2005a). State-by-state analysis. Retrieved August 1, 2006 from http://www.aft.org/topics/sbr/states.htm.

American Federation of Teachers. (2005b). Survey and analysis of teacher salary trends, 2004. Washington, DC: Author.

Campaign for Fiscal Equity. (2006). FAQs. Retrieved August 1, 2006, from http://www.cfequity.org.

Center for Education Reform. (2006). National charter school data at a glance. Washington, DC: Author.

Cibulka, J. G. (1999). Moving toward an accountable system of K–12 education. In G. J. Cizek (Ed.), *Handbook of educational policy* (pp. 183–211). San Diego: Academic Press.

Duncan-Poitier, Johanna. (2005). CEO memo #05-02—Two important teaching policy changes. Albany: New York State Education Department.

Education Week. (2004). Quality counts 2004; Count me in: Special education in an era of standards. *Education Week 23*(17).

Education Week. (2006). Quality counts at 10; A decade of standards based education. *Education Week 25*(17).

Folts, J. D. (1996). *History of the university of the state of New York and the state education department, 1784–1996*. Albany: New York State Education Department.

Hanushek, E. (2004). Who could be against 'adequate' school funding? *The Education Gadfly 4*(24). Retrieved August 1, 2006, from http://www.fordham institute.org/institute/gadfly/issue.cfm?id=153#1869.

Kadamus, J. A. (2000). Guidelines for implementing academic intervention services. Memo. Albany: New York State Education Department.

Kadamus, J. A. (2001). Project SAVE, Safe Schools Against Violence in Education Act: Instruction in civility, citizenship, and character education. Memo. Albany: New York State Education Department.

Kadamus, J. A. (2003). Schools under registration review. Memo. Albany: New York State Education Department.

Kadamus, J. A., & Duncan-Poitier, J. (2002). Creating a framework for the preparation of schools [sic] leaders. Memo, 10 April. Albany: New York State Education Department.

Killeen, K. M., & Sipple, J. W. (2005, March 6). Mandating supplemental intervention services: Is New York State doing enough to help all students succeed? *Education Policy Analysis Archives 13*(19). Retrieved August 1, 2006, from http://epaa.asu.edu.

Lankford, R. H., O'Connell, R. W., & Wyckoff, J. H. (2003). *Our next generation: school leadership in New York State*. Albany: New York State Education Department.

Leithwood, K., & Menzies, T. (1998). Forms and effects of school-based management: A review. *Educational Policy 12*(3), 325–346.

Lovett, K., & Andreatta, D. (2006, February 28). $7.4B school aid bonkers: Bruno. *New York Post*, p. 2.

Malen, B. (2003). Tightening the grip? The impact of state activism on local school systems. *Educational Policy 17*(2), 195–216.

McDermott, Kathryn A. (1999). *Controlling public education: Localism versus equity*. Lawrence: University Press of Kansas.

McLaughlin, M. W. (1987). Learning from experience: Lessons from policy implementation. *Educational Evaluation and Policy Analysis 9*(2), 171–178.

New York Charter Schools Association. (2006). *Charter schools in New York State*. Albany: Author.

New York State Board of Regents & Education Department. (1998). *New York's commitment to teaching to higher standards*. Albany: Author.

New York State Board of Regents & Education Department. (2003). *Growing tomorrow's leaders today: Preparing effective school leaders in New York State*. Albany: Author.

New York State Board of Regents & Education Department. (2005). *New York: The state of learning*. Albany: Author.

New York State Comptroller. (2006). *Reporting of violent and disruptive incidents by public schools*. Audit report 2005-S-38. Albany: Author.

New York State Education Department. (2003). *A proposal on planning and reporting by New York State school districts for the strategic use of school resources for school improvement*. Albany: Author.

New York State Education Department. (2004a). *Education statistics for New York State*. Albany: Author.

New York State Education Department. (2004b). *New York State learning standards*. Albany: Author. Retrieved August 1, 2006, from http://www.emsc.nysed.gov/ciai/describe.html.

New York State Education Department. (2005). *Education statistics for New York State*. Albany: Author.

New York State Education Department. (2006a). *175 hour professional development requirement*. Albany: Author. Retrieved August 1, 2006, from http://www.highered.nysed.gov/tcert/resteachers/175.htm#3.

New York State Education Department. (2006b, May 22). *Commissioner Mills announces actions to improve school district reporting of violent incidents*. Press release. Albany: Author.

New York State Education Department. (2006c). *FAQs about NYS certification: Professional development*. Albany: Author.

New York State Education Department. (2006d, January 20). *Fifteen schools placed on SURR list, three removed in New York City*. Press release. Albany: Author.

Office of the Governor of New York. (1999, June 15). *Governor Pataki applauds approval of first charter schools*. Press release. Albany: Author.

Regulations of Commissioner of Education. (n.d.). Albany: New York State Education Department.

Schneier, E. (2001). The politics of local education. In J. M. Stonecash (Ed.), *Governing New York State* (4th Ed.) (pp. 215–240). Albany: State University of New York Press.

Schneier, E., & Murtaugh, J. B. (2001). *New York politics: A tale of two states.* Armonk, NY: M. E. Sharpe.

Sipple, J. W., & Killeen, K. M. (2004). Context, capacity, and concern: A district-level analysis of the implementation of standards-based reform in New York State. *Educational Policy 18*(3), 456–490.

Stonecash, J. M. (2001a). Introduction. In J. M. Stonecash (Ed.), *Governing New York State* (4th Ed.) (pp. 1–2). Albany: State University of New York Press.

Stonecash, J. M. (2001b). Introduction to part I: Political conflicts and their representation. In J. M. Stonecash (Ed.), *Governing New York State* (4th Ed.) (pp. 5–6). Albany: State University of New York Press.

Vergari, S. (2002). New York State: Over 100 applications in year one. In S. Vergari (Ed.), The *charter school landscape* (pp. 230–252) Pittsburgh: University of Pittsburgh Press.

Ward, R. B. (2002). *New York state government: What it does, how it works?* Albany: Rockefeller Institute Press.

Wohlstetter, P., Mohrman, S. A., & Robertson, P. J. (1997). Successful school-based management: A lesson for restructuring urban schools. In D. Ravitch & J. P. Viterriti (Eds.), New *schools for a new century: The redesign of urban education* (pp. 201–225). New Haven: Yale University Press.

Chapter 6

Texas

Brendan D. Maxcy, Andrea K. Rorrer, and Enrique Aleman, Jr.

The State of the State of Texas: An Account of the Shifting Balance of Power between State and School

In this chapter, we take up the case of Texas. We recount the developmental dynamics of a dramatic scaling up of state power vis-à-vis local education authorities in the state. This transformation occurs over twenty years through the convergence of an expanding accountability system and a reconfiguration of the state's school funding system. The Texas system has garnered substantial interest over the past decade, due in part to reports of its relative effectiveness (see Grissmer & Flanagan, 1998; McNeil & Valenzuela, 1998; Scheurich, Skrla, & Johnson, 2000), to its emergence as an issue in the 2000 campaign (e.g., Haney, 2000; Klein, Hamilton, McCaffrey, & Stecher, 2000), and to the influence of Texas elites on national educational policy, including the two recent secretaries of education. Given this extensive literature, the reader might ask, "What will one more visit to Texas reveal?"

Why Mess with Texas?

The reauthorization of the Elementary and Secondary Education Act in 2001—commonly referred to as No Child Left Behind (NCLB)—imposed new federal and state mandates and enhanced existing mandates for schools promoting achievement for all students. To a large degree, NCLB leveraged potent new administrative tools and logics piloted at the state level in the prior decade, notably the widespread adoption of "new" performance accountability systems to spur reform in the 1990s (Cibulka & Derlin, 1998; Fuhrman, 1999). These systems—

displacing relations of internal accountability with new systems of external accountability (Adams & Kirst, 1999)—provided states new levels of institutional capacity to promote school- and district-level reform through more tightly coupled policies (Fusarelli, 2002; Rorrer, 2001). While state policy systems of this type may have provide some legitimacy for changes in district and school practice (Rorrer, 2003), they also may have "a strong effect by narrowing the conversations . . . within districts and across educators to discussion and action related to the new curriculum and assessment standards" (Sipple, Kileen, & Monk, 2004, p. 161).

As discussed later, the Texas legislature enacted an external system of accountability of this variety over the past twenty-five years, substantially "tightening the grip" (Malen, 2003, p. 195) on local districts. To many, NCLB appeared to be a national-level scale up of so-called Texas-style accountability (Valenzuela, 2005). This characterization was reinforced by the invocation of the Texas model by candidate Bush in the 2000 campaign and by the articulation of his early educational treatise (Bush, 2001) offered as the cornerstone of his reform agenda. Obvious commonalities with NCLB notwithstanding, our effort to trace the history of the transformation may temper the polarized characterizations of NCLB as a national scale-up of a state-level pilot.

In a brief recounting of a series of finance and administrative reforms offered below, we find: (1) a dramatic and rapid consolidation of power over education among state-level actors in a state where local control has historically bordered on civic religion; and (2) paradoxical consent for the consolidation offered as a check on state power. We argue that while Texas holds substantial illustrative value regarding a growing state presence in education, the case "must be viewed in light of several circumstances that we believe may be unique, if only in degree, to the state of Texas" (Farr & Trachtenberg, 1999, p. 616).[1] Thus, our discussion addresses some of the unique features of the state's rise in power.

To support this argument, the chapter unfolds in the following way. Finding one-dimensional accounts of the consolidation of power in Texas unconvincing, we argue for an accounting of the interplay of historical conditions, agency, and ideology. Taking this approach, we begin by recounting the enactment of an increasingly comprehensive, coherent, and interacting slate of accountability and school finance policies. Next, we then introduce Douglass North's work on institutional development and change to examine the growth of institutional capacity to govern education in Texas. Then, we apply this framework—which foregrounds the roles of entrepreneurial organization, path dependence, and ideology—taking special note of the reconfiguration of finance and accountability systems over the past twenty-five years. We conclude with a discussion of further and alternative analyses, drawing on critical policy studies, critical race theory, and postcolonial theory that may yield insights into the growth in the state's institutional capacity and into the production of consent among Texans.

Framing the Rise of the State

This account finds a steep rise in state power over the delivery of public education. The tightened grip is reflected in: (a) explicit articulation, monitoring, and enforcement of curriculum delivery; (b) new constraints on raising local funds, mandates to redistribute wealth-based revenues; and (c) increasing levels of prescription by state actors regarding the terms of efficient use of resources to maintain and operate schools. How can we account for this rise in light of the general historical institutional weakness of state education agencies in the United States (Timar, 1997) and apparent institutional incompetence to reform systems to align with public demands (Cibulka, 1996; Timar & Kirp, 1987)? As curious, how did this rise occur in Texas, a state with an aversion to a powerful central state and affinity for local control?

Elite-Focused Accounts

In a state of colorful and (in)famous politicos and power brokers, from Davey Crockett and Sam Houston, to Ma and Pa Rainey, to Lyndon B. Johnson, Sam Rayburn, Ann Richards, and Tom Delay, it is tempting to turn to one-dimensional, elite-centered accounts of the rise in state power. On one hand, the rise of the state might be understood from the perspective of Galbraith's (1956, 1958) *counterveiling power* by a *progressive elite*, restabilizing a society that was disintegrating due to erosion of the self-regulating mechanisms of the market all the while free market conditions give way in an era of large firms and big labor. As champion of the citizen-client, the progressive elite induces an affluent society to redistribute its excess resources, redirecting it from narrow self-interests toward an expansive, collectivist vision—a greater society, so to speak. In the case of Texas, this theme might be inferred from depictions of state accountability policies as "levers for social justice" (see Skrla, Scheurich, Johnson, & Koschoreck, 2001), or castings of the school finance system as a populist Robin Hood challenging injustice by redistributing funds from the haves to the have-nots.

An alternative account, similarly one-dimensional, is best summed up in the late president Reagan's quip, "Government isn't the solution. Government is the problem." Opponents of a centralized power, such as Milton Friedman (1962; 1977; 1980) or Fredrick Hayek (1988/2000; 1994), argue the growth of state power under the Keynsian vision holding sway in the mid-twentieth century interfered with the self-regulating mechanisms of the market. Drunk with power and deluded regarding its comprehensive planning capacities, the arrogant progressive elite of these accounts has "gummed up the works" in presuming to steer society from the center. That is society's central problem—pun intended—and, as such, it cannot be resolved by vesting more power with the state, but by wresting control from it. In contrast to portrayals of state as champion, this theme may appear at the fore in denunciations of Texas-style accountability as a "design for mediocrity" (see Patterson, 1997), or alternately as an insidious tool of cultural subtraction exacerbating historic inequities for students of poverty and students of color (see Valenzuela, 2005). Similarly, antistate rhetoric may seem to pervade negative portrayals of the state finance system as a common thief masquerading as a champion of the poor (for discussion of the school finance rhetoric, see Alemán, 2006).

Multidimensional Accounts

Though powerful elites traditionally take center stage in historical accounts, other actors have increasingly moved to the forefront in social histories since the 1960s. An associated reconceptualization of power figures prominently in social historical studies by Hobsbawm, Thompson, Williams, and others (Gunn, 2006, para. 1).

> Social history proposed a substantial extension to the understanding and expression of power; it was no longer seen as restricted to institutions of government and state, but operative in multiple sites: in the workplace, on the streets, in the home . . . political history was radically expanded by looking beyond parties and organized movements to the political cultures rooted in the labour process and structures of popular belief. . . . At its roots, social history challenged a traditional version of power as a smooth, one-way process; it represented the past as replete with checks, resistances, dissonances.

Gunn suggests the move from uni- to multidimensional views of power significantly enriched historical accounts. Taking this cue, we move away from one-dimensional views of power to account for the state's rise that overplay the capacity of elites to hold sway in political decision-making. In the case of state intervention in educational delivery, we take note of work in the mid-1970s on state legitimation crises by Jurgen Habermas (1975; 1979). *Legitimation Crisis* (Habermas, 1975) draws attention to the maintenance of state legitimacy demanded for effective societal steering and troubled by inherent and lurking class conflicts arising in late capitalism. His analysis points to the complex interplay of state (political) and market (economic) systems involved in steering late capitalist societies—and brings into focus the Scylla and Charybdis about which we must navigate in tracing the rise of state power in Texas.

On the one hand, we seek to avoid deterministic accounts, which overdraw parallels between biological and social evolution. The heroic portrayal of progressive elites noted earlier appears so, using as its foil an "absent presence" (Ball, 1994) of an impending destabilization stemming from opposed class-interests of capitalist society. In essence, it employs an inevitability that never arrives as a compelling rationale for the disposition of systems of governance directed by its progressive elite on behalf of an undisciplined working class. This account underplays the ongoing transformation of social relations stemming from individual agency in adapting to and adapting societal structures in situ (Bourdieu & Wacquant, 1992; Foucault, 1980; Giddens, 1979), which must remain central to our accounts of the development and implementation of accountability structures (Rorrer, 2001; Rorrer & Skrla, 2005).

On the other hand, we are wary of counterstories that largely discount the role the state plays and has played in forming the opportunity structure around which social organization occurs. Some market-valorizing stories scrupulously avoid reference to the development of the welfare state to attenuate a motivation crisis as the market lost credibility as a fair arbiter of life opportunity (Habermas, 1975). Other stories may valorize precapitalist society and underplay the social welfare generated in market societies functioning with modern forms of government (Foucault, 1980). As with the earlier heroic portrayals, the assertion that scaling back state activity would lead directly to preferable societal outcomes—greater productivity, increased levels of justice, and enhanced democracy—is utopian.

The accounts are ideologically counterposed, but similarly lopsided, privileging the economic moment at the expense of others in the ensemble of forces—social, cultural, and political processes—steering society (Hall, 1996). Making sense of the state's rise and how its rule is legitimized with various groups demands some account of how its ruling ideas effectively connect through practical thinking and common sense with particular constellations of social forces. "In that sense, ideological struggle is part of the general social struggle for mastery and leadership—in short for hegemony" (Hall, 1996, p. 43). In the following discussion, we attempt to provide an understanding of "the effective coupling of dominant ideas *to* the historical bloc which has acquired hegemonic power in a particular period" (Hall, 1996, p. 44). That is, rather than suggesting that dominant groups impose the logics of action in some determinative sense, we seek to show how these logics appeal to the actors' common sense regarding achievement, fair play, and the proper conduct of government in promoting both.

In a Foucauldian sense, we hold that the changing nature of the state derives from changes in the practices of government—activity guiding or shaping the conduct of others—not from essential properties and propensities of the state (Gordon, 1991). Toward that end, the following section recounts a series of policies altering the funding and administration of Texas schools over the past twenty years—policy changes that constitute a substantial local to center shift in power. The subsequent discussion makes sense of the developmental dynamics of the power shift and the production of consent underpinning its legitimation. A number of alternative approaches are available to account for the rise of institutional capacity in Texas. We construct an account around elements

Douglass North (1990) outlined in *Institutions, Institutional Change and Economic Performance* to explain institutional development and change through rational choice of actors. In its attention to the roles of agency, opportunity, and ideology in shaping and reshaping institutions, we find it offers a promising if incomplete framework for this case.

Recounting the Rise of the State

In this section, we trace the changing character of the Texas educational system from its highly fragmented origins to its present, relatively tightly coupled form. Revisiting the early system, we note preference for local control in the aftermath of Reconstruction contributing to creation of a deliberately fragmented system and generating egregious inequities among communities. A low level of institutional capacity to reform the system gave way from the 1970s to 1990s with the reconfiguration of accountability and school finance systems. The fusion of these with a court decision in 1995 sets the stage for a dramatic shift in state–local power relations over the past decade.

Early Years to 1970: Low Institutional Capacity and High Funding Inequity Administering a Fragmented System of Schools

A number of factors—geographic, demographic, sociocultural, political, and economic—contributed to the development of a highly fragmented school system operating under a weak state education agency. The geographic scale of the state with a widely dispersed population did not foster centralized control. Still, a preference for local control of schooling may be expressed in the number of independent school districts (ISDs)[2] that were incorporated following the rural high school bill of 1911. Authorizing county boards to create rural high schools at local expense, the bill prompted a surge in the number of districts from 526 in 1910 to 6,953 in 1936 (TEA, 2004). While the state board district pursued consolidation based on findings from an adequacy study commissioned in 1936, consolidation met steady resistance a the local level (Texas Education Agency, 2004b). The Gilmer-Aiken reforms[3] passed in 1949 led to a reduction in districts from 4,500 to 2,900, the number leveling out at just over 1,000 in the late 1990s. Today, the number has risen again to 1,227 districts, with approximately 200 new charter districts.

Central control is complicated by the interplay of race, class, and culture figuring prominently in the state's political struggles (Davidson, 1990; Key, 1949). For instance, a number of culturally and linguistically distinct groups—American Indian, Mexican, Anglo-American, and German among these—were settled or settling in Texas as the public school system formed in the nineteenth and twentieth centuries. Aggregation of, and competition among, differing visions did not yield a simple, integrated state-level vision of the means and ends of public schooling. Further, state constitutional framers granted the state government limited power to impose such a vision, if one were to emerge. Working in the aftermath of Reconstruction, "the group that met mirrored statewide sentiment for retrenchment, economy and disestablishment of the centralized state government" (Walker & Casey, 1996, pp. 4–5). Even if an integrated educational vision were to emerge, a general antipathy toward central control imbued in the state ethos and written into the state constitution would undermine its administration by state actors.

During the twentieth century, the state's traditional–individualistic political culture (see Elazar, 1994) combined with shifting economic and political fortunes to further complicate state administration. Taking its place in an economy dominated by agricultural concerns, an ascendant oil industry contributed to a more diverse though volatile economy, the growth of new population centers, and a rapid expansion, but uneven distribution of wealth (Green, 1979). The latter, according to Green, fueled efforts in the 1940s and 1950s of an influential new oil elite[4] to challenge any regulatory or potentially redistributive state policies as socialist machinations. These power brokers gained popular support by tapping into anticommunist sentiments of the period and the general distaste for central authority previously noted. The result was a particularly weak central state as evidenced by a 1969 study ranking Texas forty-second in the adoption of innovative policies to address statewide problems (Nimmo & Odden, 1971, cited in Green, 1979).

The Gilmer-Aiken laws of 1949 bolstered central control to a degree by substantially reconfiguring the state administrative structure and school funding system. In addition to establishing the foundation program for funding discussed below, the laws replaced the appointed nine-member State Board of Education with an elected twenty-one-member board and established the Texas Education Agency (TEA) directed by an appointed commissioner of education. The shift from an elected state superintendent to appointed commissioner provided a degree of administrative continuity. Pointing to an "unwritten law of political tenure" undermined long-term planning, Eby (2004) noted that state superintendents typically

> secured more permanent and lucrative positions and resigned before the expiration of their second term. Without assurance of tenure beyond two years no administration could set up a long-range plan for the improvement of the school system. . . . When the superintendent did attempt to perpetuate his tenure beyond the usual time he was obliged by the very nature of the case to bow continuously to political expediency; long-range planning for the improvement of the school system was impossible. (p. 58)

Ten individuals served in the office between 1885 and 1920. Since Gilmer-Aiken, twelve individuals served in the retitled role of commissioner of education, reflecting a modest increase in tenure and capacity for longer term planning.

FUNDING THE FRAGMENTED SYSTEM OF SCHOOLS. As noted, the constitutional framework and subsequent legislation led to a fragmented system and weak central control. The finance system further undermined state power vis-à-vis local districts. Required by the constitution to maintain a system of free public schooling, the Texas legislature was provided little constitutional direction regarding financing such a system (Farr & Trachtenberg, 1999). In line with the noted antipathy to central control, the constitutional framers established independent local taxing authority for education and omitted reference to the statewide ad valorem tax used to support schools for the prior three decades. In these elements, the constitution laid the cornerstones of a system characterized by extreme interdistrict inequity noted in the majority opinion offered later in the 1973 *Rodriguez* decision discussed later in this section.

Like many states, the legislature's decision to depend heavily on local property taxes to finance schools led to wide disparities in available funds among Texas districts. A foundation program emerging from the Gilmer-Aiken proposals in 1947–1949 sought to ensure some minimal level of educational opportunity through a state–local partnership (Hobby & Walker, 1991). Under the legislation, a foundation level of school funding was provided through equalized local tax effort and supplemented by the state to compensate for variation in local tax bases. Under the program, local districts could raise additional revenues to enrich educational opportunities. Revenues provided through the state–local partnership failed to provide districts adequate funds to meet the state's own minimum standards for accreditation (Farr & Trachtenberg, 1999). "Local supplementation of state monies [to meet requirements for teacher-student ratio, infrastructure, and special programs], therefore, was an absolute necessity" (p. 614). Given wide variations in local property wealth, the result was dramatic disparities between district funding levels and wide gaps in educational opportunity afforded the states' students.[5]

By the 1970s, the state of Texas appeared limited in its capacity to direct schooling from the center, much like its U.S. counterparts (Timar, 1997). This lack of capacity is hardly surprising in a state system navigating substantial race, class, and cultural divisions, composed of a large number and wide variety of districts, and working within constitutional provisions and an administrative structure limiting authority to regulate or to raise and redistribute revenues. In light of these factors, the surprise is the rise of a regulative state taken over the ensuing three decades. As discussed below, a substantial reconfiguration of the state-school relations from the late 1970s to the mid-1990s dramatically changed the relative balance of power.

1970 to 1995: Growing Institutional Capacity and Higher Levels of Finance Equity, Challenging Funding Inequity

Subject to ongoing contestation and tinkering, the essential structures of Texas school finance began to change rapidly toward the close of the 1960s. Coalescing in and around Edgewood ISD in San Antonio, efforts to infuse equity into the provision of education in the state would have important consequences for the state and the nation. This section sketches a brief account of precipitating events, reviews the *Rodriguez* decision, and closes with a state court opinion offered in 1995 that would set the stage for a dramatic change in the state–local balance of power in the subsequent decade.

RODRIGUEZ V. SAN ANTONIO ISD. With school revenues dependent on local property wealth, frustration with interdistrict inequity mounted in the 1960s. Advocates and interest groups organized at the local level and political parties had pressed with limited success for funding equity.[6] One group representing parents from Edgewood ISD, the Concerned Parents Association (CPA), initially sought district consolidation to balance property wealth and alleviate the financial burden on any one district. Jose Cardenas, then-superintendent of Edgewood ISD, expressed reservations, concerned that the strategy would yield a single, large, but poor district (Cardenas, 1997). CPA opted to challenge the school finance system in federal court, filing suit in 1968 against San Antonio ISD, Edgewood ISD, and five other Bexar County districts.

Aided by the Mexican American Legal Defense and Education Fund (MALDEF) and the Intercultural Development Research Association (IDRA), the plaintiffs argued that the quality of education afforded students in property-poor districts patronized by largely Mexican American families was exceptionally low. Working from the decision in *Brown v. Board of Education* fourteen years earlier, *Rodriguez et al. v. San Antonio ISD* (*Rodriguez v. San Antonio ISD*, 1973) argued that the Texas school finance system failed to provide equal protection for low-income and minority students as a class as guaranteed by the Fourteenth Amendment to the U.S. Constitution. The federal court agreed, finding in favor of the plaintiffs and declaring the state system unconstitutional in December 1971. Consistent with the findings in *Serrano I* (*Serrano v. Priest*, 1971), the court found the state's method of relying on local property wealth discriminated against children living in poor school districts (Farr & Trachtenberg, 1999).

In 1973, the U.S. Supreme Court reversed the decision on appeal. Writing for the majority, Justice Powell stated that the system met the legal standard of "a rational relationship to legitimate state purposes" (p. 16) and was therefore constitutional despite the "imperfections" and "defects" of the system the state "virtually concedes . . . could not withstand the strict judicial scrutiny" (p. 4). Noting an absence of evidence of discrimination against or absolute deprivation of education for a definable category of "poor" people by the system, the Court also stated that wealth was not a "suspect class" as required for a strict scrutiny test appropriate when state actions interfered with a fundamental right or operated to disadvantage a suspect class. Further, education, in the court's opinion, was not a fundamental right explicitly or implicitly protected by the federal Constitution and thus not subject to the equal protection clause. In finding the state system of public school finance an inappropriate candidate for strict judicial scrutiny, the *Rodriguez* decision effectively closed the door of the federal courts to school finance litigation (Ladd & Hansen, 1999).

THE EDGEWOOD CASES. While the *Rodriguez* decision removed the immediate threat to the Texas finance system, the justices noted high levels of inequity and urged the state legislature to address the inherent interdistrict inequities caused by the system's reliance on local property tax. From 1975 to 1984, the legislature attempted to amend the finance system to stave off impending court challenges, (Walker & Casey, 1996). House Bill 72 in 1984 was a milestone in finance equity in Texas (and a major event in the state's move toward performance accountability, as discussed below).[7] Despite reforms increasing the overall equity in the system, attorneys representing property-poor districts challenged the system in the state courts in 1984 in *Edgewood v. Kirby*. Upholding a lower court ruling and overturning a ruling on appeal, the Texas high court rendered a unanimous ruling in 1989, finding the system violated the "efficiency" provision of the education clause of the state constitution.

The system remained in flux from 1989 to 1993 as the legislature rewrote the state's educational code to bring school finance into accord with court opinion regarding equitable and efficient system rendered in *Edgewood v. Kirby* (*Edgewood II*, 1991) and *Carrolton-Farmers Branch ISD v. Edgewood ISD* (*Edgewood III*, 1992). According to a variety of measures, legislation enacted from 1989 to 1993 resulted in a greater degree of equity among Texas school districts (Alemán & Brownson, 2001). In 1993, the 73rd legislature passed a bill meeting the courts directive that districts making similar tax efforts raise similar revenues.[8] A controversial feature of the plan, dubbed "Robin Hood" for its redistributive character, was a provision for state "recapture" of district property wealth exceeding $280,000[9] per student[10] through one of several district-determined options. In 1995, the system was found to meet the state's constitutional obligation for "suitable provision for the support and maintenance of an efficient system of public free schools" (*Edgewood IV*, 1995).

The system remained in good standing until November 2005 when it was again overturned by the high court in *Neeley v. West Orange Cove*. Of interest here, given the documented aversion to the state raising and redistributing revenues, the new powers accorded the state are a marked departure. Further, as discussed below, a reinterpretation of the term "efficient" in the 1995 decision underpins a dramatic change in state–school power relations—particularly in a state where the tradition of local control bordered on state religion.

EXPANDING ADMINISTRATIVE CONTROL: THE INSTITUTION OF PERFORMANCE ACCOUNTABILITY. Historically, equitable educational opportunity and corresponding levels of achievement have been discouragingly absent in Texas, similar to a number of other states (Shirley, 1997; Valencia, 2000). As previously discussed, a host of factors led to a highly fragmented system operating under the auspices of a state agency with limited power or control. In an effort to respond to pressure to improve the system from various sectors—those pressing for finance reform noted above, an increasingly active and organized business lobby (Luce, 1995; Texas Business and Education Coalition, 2001), and elements of the state's "educational establishment" including associations of teachers, administrators, and school boards—the Texas legislature enacted a series of accountability reforms between 1979 and 1999. The end result was an increasingly comprehensive system of external accountability for local education agencies administered by the Texas Education Agency (TEA).

STATEWIDE ASSESSMENTS, PERFORMANCE REPORTING, AND ACCREDITATION. Undergoing a number of expansions and intensifications, the Texas system features formalization of the state curriculum and aligned assessments, specification of student- and school-level performance outcomes with associated standards and stakes for each, and a public reporting system providing demographic, programmatic, staffing, and performance information. In these ways the system is consistent with national trends, reflected in a heavy emphasis on high-stakes student performance testing and public comparisons of school performance (Elmore, Abelman, & Fuhrman, 1996; Fuhrman, 1999). As discussed in the following section, the steady expansion of the accountability regime between 1979 and 1995, outlined in this section, sets the stage for a dramatic intensification of state control in the last decade.

ASSESSMENTS. Senate Bill 350 in 1979 enacted the Texas Assessment of Basic Skills (TABS), a statewide criterion referenced tests for grades 3, 5, and 9 in reading, writing, and mathematics based on new learning objectives created by committees of Texas educators (TEA, 1999, p.1). Two years later, House Bill 246 called for articulation of a statewide curriculum for each subject and for all grades, which became known as the Essential Elements.

In July 1984, House Bill 72 expanded monitoring of student and school performance as it increased funding for property-poor districts. The omnibus bill instituted: (a) the Texas Educational Assessment of Minimum Skills (TEAMS) assessments administered annually in odd-numbered grades in English/Language Arts and mathematics beginning in 1985; (b) an exit-level examination for graduation starting with the class of 1987; and (c) annual district performance reports. TEAMS was notable for two reasons: (1) for the first time the test, as a graduation requirement, carried stakes for students, and (2) the test marked a shift to an emphasis of student performance as the basis of accountability (Texas Education Agency, 2000).

Reforms enacted by the 71st legislature, in special session in the summer of 1990, led to major changes to the Texas accountability system. A third assessment system replaced the TEAMS. The Texas Assessment of Academic Skills (TAAS) increased the scope and rigor of the assessments. TAAS was also accompanied by increased failure rates in the early administrations—an impact visited disproportionately on students eligible for free and reduced lunch, and students of color (Haney, 2000; Valencia & Villareal, 2005). The disparity in passing rates closed in subsequent years, but assessment of the underlying achievement gap was the subject of extensive debate (Grissmer & Flanagan, 1998; Haney, 2000; Klein et al., 2000).

PERFORMANCE REPORTING. The 1990 legislation also laid out the basic structures of integrated accountability system incorporating: (1) an explicitly defined curricular framework; (2) an aligned assessment and associated consequences; and (3) a public information system (Texas Education Agency, 1996). Through expanded reporting of student performance information, the state sought to raise the stakes for schools as well as for students. A statewide information management system—the Public Education Information Management System (PEIMS)—became fully operational in 1987.

In 1990, Senate Bill 417 instituted new monitoring provisions for schools and districts, establishing performance indicators for each school and an annual review of school districts to assess compliance with accreditation criteria. To provide "parents . . . better information about how their children's schools compare to other schools [so that] they will pressure weak schools to improve" (Texas Education Agency, 1996, p. 8), the state replaced the annual performance reports with the expanded Academic Excellence Indicator System (AEIS) reports in 1990. Beginning in 1992–1993, district and campus results on the newly instituted TAAS were disaggregated by race/ethnicity categories and socioeconomic status and publicized through AEIS.[11] Information released through the annual AEIS reports continued to expand and currently offers state-, region-, district-, and campus-level information compiled by district offices on student performance, school staffing, student enrollment, and program delivery.

ACCREDITATION. Ostensibly, the developing system sought to foster student and school accountability through an expansive performance indicator system including overall ratings for schools and districts and meting out rewards and sanctions. The progression in assessment and performance reporting set the stage for the enactment of a more coherent and powerful accountability regime through a 1993 rewrite of the Texas Education Code as it related to assessment, accreditation, performance reporting, and accountability. Under the Texas public school accountability system, the 73rd legislature expanded the power of the state to accredit school districts and rate school performance based on student performance, annual TAAS passing rates, as well as dropout and attendance rates beginning in 1993–1994.[12] A notable feature of the system was the coupling of school and district ratings to the performance of the lowest achieving of several racial/ethnic and socioeconomic student groups. Texas was one of the first states to invoke pressure through its campus and district rating system to close performance gaps between student groups in this manner.

In addition to these notable changes in administrative authority, Senate Bill 1 in 1995 called for a new state curriculum to replace the Essential Elements. The Texas Essential Knowledge and Skills (TEKS) were adopted in 1997. SB 1 also resulted in an expansive rewrite of the Texas Education Code, distilling and bringing some clarity to an administrative framework that had expanded rapidly in the prior fifteen years. Over this period, we note a dramatic rise in central control over education through (a) articulation of an official curriculum, (b) new authority to assess and credential student learning, and (c) new authority to credential schools and districts and to monitor, rate, and report school and district performance. The educational system operating under this accountability regime contrasts starkly with the highly fragmented system it replaced.

1995–2005: The Convergence of Finance and Texas-style Accountability

As noted, HB 72 of 1984—enacted in the wake of the *Rodriguez* decision and under the specter of the impending *Edgewood* litigation—marked a significant uptake in state activism in redistributing local revenues and establishing external forms of accountability. Growing intertwinement of the accountability and finance systems during the 1980s and 1990s allowed the state to further "tighten the grip" (Malen, 2003) over local schools in sharp contrast to the decentralized system set in place by constitutional framers in 1876, pursued by oil elites of the mid-twentieth century, perennially frustrating to progressive educational reformers from Elisha Pease in 1850 to Gilmer and Aiken in 1947, and scrupulously avoided by Supreme Court justices treading carefully around the tradition of local control in *Rodriguez*.

CONNECTING EQUITY AND EFFICIENCY IN SCHOOL FINANCE. In *Neeley v. West Orange Cove* (*Neeley v. WOC*, 2005), the Texas Supreme Court ruled the state's school finance system unconstitutional. The court charged the legislature with redesigning the finance system outlined in 1993's SB 7. When it met constitutional muster a decade earlier, this system ended a long-running struggle over the provision of public education beginning in earnest with the filing of *Rodriguez v. San Antonio ISD* in federal court in 1968. Much of this struggle occurred in four state-level school finance cases (*Edgewood –IV*, discussed earlier) from 1984 to 1995. The court arguments focused heavily on the term "efficient" in Article VII of the state constitution:

> A general diffusion of knowledge being essential to the preservation of the liberties and rights of the people, it shall be the duty of the Legislature of the State to establish and make suitable provision for the support and maintenance of an efficient system of public free schools.

To a large degree, collectivist notions of equity ascended relative to the tradition of local control in the decisions in these cases and challenges that followed. Dismissing a case concerning erosion of local discretion in 2001, the district court found,

> As a result of *Edgewood*, resources for education wrongfully set aside by the state for the few have been shared with the many. . . . On our oath to uphold the constitution, the judiciary should never retreat from defense of the great principle of equal educational opportunity. (p. 16)

However, the opinion also noted, "The public school finance system that ultimately emerged from the struggle to achieve this principle is as ugly as the principle is grand." Apparently, those warts became too unsightly to bear four years later.

REVISITING EDGEWOOD I, REDEFINING EFFICIENCY, AND RECONFIGURING STATE–LOCAL RELATIONS. The 2005 ruling by the Texas Supreme Court found the funding system violated Article VIII—a constitutional prohibition of an ad valorem ("statewide") property tax—by effectively eliminating any meaningful discretion of local districts in setting rates. However, the high court overturned a lower court finding that the system violated the efficiency standard of Article VII. In its opinion, the court cited three efficiency standards: financial efficiency, adequacy, and suitability. Traced to the intent of the framers, the financial efficiency standard relating tax revenues and tax effort was established in *Edgewood I*,

> Efficiency . . . does not allow concentrations of resources in property-rich school districts that are taxing low when property-poor districts that are taxing high cannot generate sufficient revenues to meet even minimum standards. There must be a direct and close correlation between a district's tax effort and the educational resources available to it. (*Edgewood I*, 1989, p. 9)

The adequacy standard was of more recent vintage, deriving from a substantial shift in the court's characterization of efficiency articulated by former justice and current U.S. senator, John Cornyn (R-TX). In a minority opinion in *Edgewood III* (*Edgewood III*, 1992, p. 35), Cornyn asserted that the earlier *Edgewood* decisions implied an additional legislative obligation "to articulate the requirements of an efficient school system in terms of educational results, not just in terms of funding" (p. 36). Putting forward an adequacy standard, he argued,

> An "efficient" education requires more than elimination of gross disparities in funding; it requires the inculcation of an essential level of learning by which each child in Texas is enabled to live a full and productive life in an increasingly complex world. (p. 35)

From 1993 and 1995, the legislature enacted an articulated state-level performance monitoring system as discussed above. Offering the majority opinion on SB 7 in 1995, Cornyn noted,

> In addition to reforming the financing system, Senate Bill 7 makes significant educational reforms in . . . the Texas Education Code. . . . [T]he Legislature defines the contours of its constitutional duty to provide a 'general diffusion of knowledge' by articulating seven public education goals [which] emphasize academic achievement. . . . To ensure that all districts are able to meet these goals, the Legislature has established a system of student assessment and school district accreditation . . . and districts that chronically fail to maintain accreditation standards are subject to penalties. (*Edgewood IV*, 1995, p. 6)

As a result, "The accountability regime set forth," the Court found, "meets the Legislature's constitutional obligation to provide suitably for a general diffusion of knowledge" (p. 8).

Cornyn's contentions "were radical departures from prior court pronouncements" (Farr & Trachtenberg, 1999, p. 670). With this ruling, the "adequate" level of public dollars provided through the school finance system was explicitly tied to the state's specification of minimally acceptable academic performance in the foundation curriculum monitored through the performance accountability system. As noted, the performance accountability system is explicitly designed to direct "action" and thus time and resources toward the outcomes associated with the indicators (and away from other outcomes). With the shift to adequacy in the argument, a potentially troublesome equity claim on the state was reconstituted as a problem of efficient administration. As discussed below, this shift dramatically altered the state–school power balance, allowing the state the power to define its reach and tighten its grip. We now take up how this occurred over the subsequent decade, beginning with an intensification of standards.

Changing Administrative Practices: Intensified Oversight

Theorizing the art of government, Foucault suggests that the changing nature of the state as an institution "is a function of the changes in practices of government, rather than the converse" (Gordon, 1991, p. 4). In the wake of the fusion of the finance and accountability systems, we note a series of concerted and interrelated practices on the part of state actors to shape and guide activity across Texas schools.

EXPANSION AND INTENSIFICATION OF STANDARDS AND STAKES. In 1999, the 76th Texas legislature passed Senate Bill 103 mandating the most substantial changes to the state educational assessment system since 1990. The bill provided for an expansion and intensification of the current state assessment program in the 2002–2003 academic year. Creating a new assessment system, the Texas Assessment of Knowledge and Skills (TAKS), the bill affected student testing from third grade to high school. A primary focus was to increase the rigor and breadth of the current exit examinations.[13]

The TAKS exit-level requirements represented a substantial increase in rigor over the TAAS standards for students slated to graduate in the 2004–2005 school year.[14] Collected in the spring of 2002, field test data from the TAKS exit exam in mathematics suggested sharp declines in passing rates.[15] To soften the impact, the State Board of Education adopted a three-year phase-in period for the standard in November 2002 (Texas Education Agency, 2002a). Under this plan, the introduced standard was two standard errors of measure (SEM) below the recommended standard and rose to the recommended standard over two years. Despite the phase-in and the potential increase of scores in the "live" administration,[16] TEA projections clearly indicated that the exit-exam failure rates would increase dramatically for all students and for low-income, black, and Hispanic student groups in particular.[17]

In a related bill, the 76th legislature enacted the Student Success Initiative (SSI), tying grade advancement to tested performance as part of the TAKS assessment program, introduced high stakes testing to the grade school. The legislation phased in the requirements with a grade three reading test beginning in 2002–2003, reading and mathematics tests at grade five beginning in 2004–2005, and reading and mathematics tests at grade eight beginning in 2007–2008. A centerpiece in a campaign opposing the "soft bigotry of low expectations" SSI received a strong push by then-governor George W. Bush. Opponents raised concerns based on research that grade retention: (1) demonstrated little or no positive impact and often negative impacts on achievement; (2) consistently resulted in a disparate impact on low-income and nonwhite students; and (3) was a strong predictor of dropping out of school (Valencia & Villareal, 2005). Raising assessment standards and introducing high stakes attached to performance in the early grades significantly tightened the state's tether on local education authorities, particularly as the state reduced its share in funding.

DRAWING DOWN THE STATE SHARE. Several factors encouraged Texas districts to run leaner operations in the late 1990s. Primary among these was erosion in the state share of funding. At the same time that the legislature was increasing academic standards and stakes for students, it was also drawing down the state share of school funding, dropping it from just below 50 percent in the mid-1990s to 38 percent in 2003. The system increasingly drew on local funds to make up the difference. During the 1990s, annual growth in property values swelled the revenue streams available to many Texas districts. As the state's economic boom receded in the late 1990s, the stream slowed, requiring additional tax effort to balance budgets. Tax rates in many districts began to approach the state-defined maximum allowable rate of $1.50 on the maintenance and operations tax rate established with SB 7 in 1993.

This deliberate capacity reduction was a key factor in the *West Orange Cove* plaintiffs filing suit, and the subsequent finding for the plaintiffs. The plaintiffs argued that the state was unfairly increasing expectations for local districts while shifting the funding burden to local property taxes. The district court found the system was "out of capacity" as districts' use of available funds rose from 83 percent in 1993 to 97 percent in 2003.

> Because the State has not adjusted the funding formulas to keep pace with rising costs, districts have to rely increasingly on the local property tax and are pushed to the $1.50 statutory cap on local maintenance and operations property tax rates. Once districts reach that legislatively determined ceiling, they have nowhere to turn (other than budget cuts) to address inflation, increases in uncontrollable costs, the cost of attaining higher levels of student performance, and the costs of enrollment growth. (FOF 104 in *WOC v. Neeley*, 2005, p. 26)

Commenting on the case, the governor located the problem in efficiency, not capacity, arguing that "it is possible for the Legislature to implement new reforms that will improve student success without necessarily spending additional dollars" (Staff, 2005). Appealing the lower court ruling, attorneys for the state argued that while districts may be approaching the revenue ceiling, administrators retain discretion over spending,

> The State commends school districts for striving to provide the best education possible to the State's children. Nevertheless, the State cannot be held to have created an unconstitutional state property tax in the absence of evidence that *state requirements*, and not *districts' choices*, have resulted in the districts' assessment of tax at the maximum rate. A necessary element of the districts' proof must be that districts are taxing exclusively—or almost exclusively—to comply with *state* requirements, *i.e.*, items over which the districts have no choice. Because the [plaintiff] Districts failed to establish that preliminary element,

> the districts have not proved that the State so controls the levy of tax that they have no meaningful discretion. (Appellate Brief, 2005 p. 99)

The state argument suggests that some administrative choices may be commendable, but gratuitous. In court, the State's attorneys pressed district superintendents on this issue, inquiring specifically into district fund balances and discretionary spending (*Neeley v. WOC*, 2005).

If such arguments were once largely rhetorical, the accountability regime and finance system provide the state dramatic new power to enforce efficient operations. As discussed, the state legislature and board sanctioned creation of an official curriculum designed under the direction of elite groups of educators. The state agency monitors delivery through assessments designed under contract to private corporations. Schools and districts are accredited by the agency based on these assessments and those underperforming are discredited with highly visible ratings and public information system. Both can dramatically influence a community's ability to attract and to raise taxes from residents. Moreover, the imposed cap for maintenance and operations taxes along with the right to recapture and redistribute revenues deriving from unevenly distributed property wealth, empower the state to tighten the reins by drawing down state revenues relative to those from local sources—which it does.[18] In short, the state attorney's arguments notwithstanding, in the opinion of the *West Orange Cove* plaintiff's, the state supreme court and the authors, the state–school balance of power has shifted dramatically in favor of the former. In the following section, we consider this dramatic swing in institutional capacity through Douglass North's path-dependent institutional change.

Discussion

North's Theory of Institutional Development and Change

For North (1990), "the central puzzle of human history is to account for the widely different paths of historical change" (p. 6). As with choice-based approaches generally, North begins with the assumption that individuals organize to transact exchanges of goods and services to maximize wealth, income, or other objectives. North takes up Coase's (1937) observation that institutions matter when costs are incurred in transactions. North argues that contrary to neoclassical assumptions of free transactions, costs are incurred in negotiating, monitoring, and enforcing contracts associated with exchanges. Institutions, which are more and less formal conventions, emerge according to North to reduce costs by reducing uncertainty and inducing stability. In doing so, they create an environment that encourages growth in the volume of transactions. Given the potential benefits accruing to an educated community and the costs associated with organizing schools, formal and informal "rules of the game" may evolve within and among communities to encourage educational investment and to guide and shape the development of schools.

North attributes the long-term performance of national economies to the development of particular institutional arrangements—arrangements that are more or less conducive to economic growth. His central assertion is that the lack of convergence of productive institutional arrangements over time—at variance with neoclassical assumptions that efficiency pressures would encourage isomorphism—points to the path-dependent nature of institutional development. That is, development is subject to increasing returns along particular paths, whereby critical choices that might appear routine, inconsequential, and arbitrary may lead to major long-term consequences as activity responds to and reinforces certain choices.

If North's theory accounts for the development and performance of economic institutions, typically assumed to have some self-regulatory mechanisms, Paul Pierson (2000; 2004) argues that path dependence is likely more determinative in the development and performance of political institutions. Pierson distinguishes politics from economics for its "preoccupation with the provision of public goods" (p. 257)—for example, the delivery of public education. He argues the collective nature of the activity, development of change-resistant institutions, potential for political authority to magnify power asymmetries, and inherent ambiguity in political processes, all intensify increasing returns contributing to path dependence.

For North, *institutions* are those evolving formal and informal routines, customs and conventions, that facilitate transactions by inducing stability, reducing uncertainty, and thereby encouraging economic growth. Institutions—the "rules of the game"—are explicitly distinguished from *organizations*—the "players" (1990, p. 4). Organizational play consists of purposive activity "to maximize wealth, income or other objectives defined by opportunities afforded by the institutional framework of society" (p. 73). Though occurring within, this activity may also be directed at the institutional framework. Exploring the case of Texas, we note strategic efforts by state and local actors to transform those "rules of the game" in ways that serve their interests—pursuit of funding equity for some and administrative efficiency for others.

The purposive character of this organization is animated by *entrepreneurialism*, steering activity toward profitable opportunity and thus served by knowledge of the operating environment and willingness (and ability) to assume risk (and sustain losses) in investing. Because success in entrepreneurialism depends on savvy scanning of the environment access to information and ability to process information become crucial.[19] Here, North's identification of the central role of *ideas and ideology* in an entrepreneurial organization and, as discussed below, in institutional change is relevant. North identifies ideology as "the subjective perceptions (models, theories) all people possess to explain the world around them . . . the *theories* individuals construct are *colored* by normative views of how the world should be organized" (p. 23). Probing the developmental dynamics of the power shift in Texas, we note interplay of ideologies appealing variously to different social groups in rise of new ruling ideas constituting the change in power relations.

Finally, North suggests that *path-dependent* processes may result in relatively subtle and arbitrary choices and may lead to substantial long-term consequences as these choices are reinforced by subsequent organizational activity and institutional development. As noted earlier, post-Reconstruction attitudes to central government have had an ongoing influence on the organization (or disorganization) of Texas schooling. Here we see that the rise of state's power in education derives in part from certain critical choices and decisions that may well have been otherwise. In the following discussion, we will employ key elements North's framework—entrepreneurial organization, path dependence, and ideology—to understand the rapid rise in institutional capacity in Texas over the past two decades.

READING THE DEVELOPMENTAL DYNAMICS IN TEXAS THROUGH NORTH'S FRAMEWORK INDUCING INCREMENTAL INSTITUTIONAL CHANGE BY AN ENTREPRENEURIAL ORGANIZATION. Typically, institutions provide "rules of the game" that both constrain and facilitate organizational activity. However, entrepreneurs may elect to induce incremental institutional change if profitable opportunities are afforded to do so,

> The (economic or political) entrepreneurs may devote their talents or tacit knowledge to ferreting out profitable margins, estimating the likelihood of success, and risking the organization's resources . . . to the degree that there are large payoffs to influencing the rules and their enforcement. (North, 1990, p. 87)

For example, we might understand the efforts of the Concerned Parents Association of Edgewood ISD, led by Jose Cardenas and leveraging the talent and knowledge of MALDEF and IDRA, as entrepreneurialism directed to a high-risk, high-return strategy of pursuing court action against the state. The maldistribution of property wealth created conditions whereby a change in rules might net additional revenues for property-poor districts, but an unsuccessful challenge may close off later opportunities (as occurred in *Rodriguez*).

The lower court finding for the plaintiffs in the *Rodriguez* suit, and the high court's encouragement to address the problems of the finance system, enhanced the climate for institutional reform. Still, as is clear in the series of cases from 1968 to 1995, the sustained challenge to the state finance system demanded a formidable organization with access to substantial resources and directed by savvy strategists with clear understandings of the legal opportunities presented by the legal and constitutional framework. In addition to the legal expertise, Farr and Trachtenberg (1999) note Cardenas's assistance in creating the Equity Center in 1982, an IDRA spin-off directed by Craig Foster, to concentrate on the detailed analysis of facts and figures supporting reform advocacy. The impetus, they suggest, was the opinion of the *Rodriguez* court that the plaintiffs failed to evidence discrimination for a definable category of students. Over a period of two decades, this sort of purposive and sustained activity contributed to significant changes as a highly equitable, redistributive finance system to the place of the one characterized by "savage inequalities" (Kozol, 1991) a decade prior.

In a similar vein, sustained, purposive activity contributed to significant changes in state control over educational delivery beginning in earnest with the Select Committee on Public Education (SCOPE), a blue ribbon commission created by Governor Mark White and spearheaded by appointed chairman H. Ross Perot.[20] White commissioned SCOPE to examine the issue of teacher pay, in part a political payback to teachers associations whose support was crucial in his gubernatorial bid. As chairperson, Perot expanded the committee's charge, taking issue with school standards, teacher competence, and student performance. Enacted in the omnibus HB 72 in 1984, the Select Committee recommendations began the twenty-year restructuring of Texas public education yielding what is termed "Texas-style accountability" (Valenzuela, 2005). Increasing teacher pay and introducing a new career ladder, HB 72 also introduced new forms of external accountability, including new performance standards for students, competency tests for teachers, and annual performance reports for school districts.

As with the sustained challenge to the school finance system, the press for greater external accountability appears to have extended well beyond the Select Committee effort. Tom Luce, Perot's protégé and the Select Committee Chief of Staff, has mounted a sustained effort to shape Texas education policy (see Luce, 1995). Luce formed the Just for the Kids (J4TK) foundation, a nonprofit watchdog group, to press his reform agenda by monitoring school progress, engage in direct-mail and media campaigns, and form coalitions with groups such as the Industrial Areas Foundation who assist in grassroots organizing and the Texas Business and Education Coalition (TBEC), a powerful corporate sector lobby (pp. 115–117). One aspect of the J4TK effort includes the use of state performance data to bring additional pressure to bear on local schools and districts through comparisons published in the popular press (see Gwynne, 2001). In 2001, this group was brought under the state umbrella, incorporated as the National Center for Educational Accountability (NCEA) at the University of Texas-Austin.

Formed in 1989, TBEC was an influential organization in Texas education reform in the 1990s. Headed by John Stevens, the group lobbied for a business community interested in workforce education and frustrated with the pace and coordination of reform (see http://www.tbec.org/history.php). Grissmer and Flanagan attest to TBEC's claim to be one of the state's most important and consistent and important forces in state educational reform (see http://www.tbec.org/index.php).

> A key aspect of business involvement in Texas is the presence of a few business leaders who became heavily involved with learning the issues in education and sustained their involvement for over a decade. These leaders became acquainted and understood all sides of educational issues, became acquainted with the decision makers at all levels and could articulate the issues to other, less involved business leaders. An illustration of this is the appointment of businesspersons to key policymaking positions like the chair of the State Board of Education. (Grissmer & Flanagan, 1998, p. 28)

Typically, this influence was directed at strategic and legislative levels, Luce's NCEA increasingly pursues more tactical and local level influence by conducting and disseminating "best-practice" research mirroring effective schools research of the 1970s and 1980s (e.g., Edmonds, 1979; Purkey & Smith, 1983).

Substantive Consequences from Subtle Choices: Path-Dependent Development

If a purposive organization induces incremental institutional change, we also note evidence of increasing returns and path dependence in the reforms whereby subtle and seemingly arbitrary choices yield significant consequences long-term. Here, we explore a number of decisions that set the state finance and accountability systems on particular courses.

DECISIONS LEADING TO CHANGE. It is generally held that the school finance landscape in Texas and across the nation would look vastly different had the *Rodriguez* case been decided differently (Bollinger, 2003; Ladd & Hansen, 1999). Despite a one-vote margin, the finding on strict scrutiny and the tradition of local control presented substantial cause for the Court to reconsider taking up the case.[21] In contrast, the *Edgewood I* decision by the State Supreme Court to overturn the appeals court reversal and the state finance system must be understood in terms of a decision that might well have gone the other way, but which has had enormous consequences.

To be certain, the attorneys for the plaintiffs and plaintiff-interveners presented an effective case and acted strategically in selecting both an effective argument and a friendly opening venue (Cardenas, 1997; Farr & Trachtenberg, 1999). Still, path dependence is a manifestation of the status quo bias of political institutions, given the ambiguity and opacity of political processes (Pierson, 2000). As in *Rodriguez*, the state court might well have found no cause to overturn the system because of the ambiguity of the state's education clause discussed above. In discussions of attempts to ascertain the framer's intent—never a clear-cut proposition—it appears that the justices found cause to dispose of the lower court's contention that the "efficiency" of the finance system was a "political" decision (i.e., to be determined by the legislature) and therefore not subject to judicial scrutiny. This case might well have been decided differently. While the decision was unanimous, a reading of the case and deliberations suggests it may have been otherwise (Farr & Trachtenberg, 1999).[22] As discussed, the consequences with regard to state control of establishing this legal precedent have been enormous, leading ultimately to a finance system that both constrains the ability of local districts to raise revenues and demands that "excess" revenues be redistributed to property poor districts.

DECISIONS ENHANCING CONTINUITY. Two elements of the state's performance accountability system also might be read as subtle choices rooted in the complexity and opacity of political processes heavily dependent on public opinion, which enabled the system to take its particular form and inhibited a course reversal. The first was a judicious choice to ratchet up the rating system over time, using then current performance measures to dictate starting a starting point. This decision obviated the declaration of large numbers of schools low-performing in the near term (as has occurred in some states under NCLB) or establishment of laudable but difficult to attain long-term targets (as occurred in states such as Virginia in the late 1990s).[23] As a result, while large numbers of students failed to perform at acceptable levels and were denied diplomas, few schools were deemed "low performing," which might have undermined public support.

A second choice concerns state-reported statistics of rapid gains for students eligible for free or reduced lunch and students of color. There has been a good deal of debate about the substantive improvement underlying the impressive statistical gains reported around the 2000 elections (Fuller & Johnson, 2001; Grissmer & Flanagan, 1998; Haney, 2000; Jerald, 2001; Judson, 1997; Klein et al., 2000). A number of indicators suggest large and persistent gaps remained in advanced course enrollment,[24] college readiness,[25] and postsecondary participation.[26] For instance, Parker (2001) notes lack of parallel improvement in passing rates and college readiness as measured by the state exit exam. The difference between the TAAS passing rates and the higher TAAS/TASP equivalence score appears to be an artifact of the placement of the cut score,[27] which might explain both the modest gains in TASP equivalence noted above and the modest gains on the National Educational Assessment of Progress (NAEP) noted by other researchers (Grissmer & Flanagan, 1998; Klein et al., 2000). This also explains the "reemergence" of twenty-point achievement gaps in many schools and districts under the new assessment system (Texas Education Agency, 2004a).

Texas has been noted for the continuity of reform agenda, avoiding the "reform du jour" pattern undermining efforts in many states (Grissmer & Flanagan,

1998). Arguably, subtle choices regarding school ratings and student cut scores contributed to public perceptions of a system that was acceptable in the main and improving, while at the same time students—particularly poor and minority students—failed at relatively high rates. It is difficult to determine, but not unlikely that the system might not have enjoyed sustained support if large numbers of schools were rated unacceptable or high failure rates were visited on more affluent students from the majority group.

Connecting Ruling Ideas to Practical Thinking: The Importance of Ideology

To avoid attributing the rise of state to an elite-imposed order, we need to make sense of the production of consent for the changing practices of government. Legitimation of late-capitalist states hinges on maintenance of an "achievement ideology" (Habermas, 1975) whereby social rewards should be distributed on the basis of individual achievement, preconditioned on equal opportunity to participate in a fair competition. We might understand the investment in institutional change noted above, the pursuit of performance accountability and finance equity, to coalesce around alternate poles of this ideological commitment. We consider now the contest of visions at play in the finance litigation of the *Rodriguez* and *Edgewood* cases and the resolution of these in the Cornyn opinion that lead to the shifting power of the state over education.

ENSURING EQUAL OPPORTUNITY. The modern period coincides with the point when authority became legitimated from below (reflected in new reliance of fair exchange in the market and demands for popular rule) and replaced legitimation from above (rooted in tradition, divine right, military might, etc.) (Foucault, 1991; Habermas, 1970). According to Habermas, the main concern of modern civilizations centers on how to *inequitably* but *legitimately* distribute the excess social product generated through increasingly efficient and effective means of production. Given the competitive advantages accruing to accumulated wealth in the market and a general antipathy toward direct redistribution of wealth among dominant groups, formal education emerged as a legitimate alternative to allocate opportunities according to demonstrated achievement (Habermas, 1975). This ideal figures prominently in the *Brown v. Board* decision:

> [Education] is the very foundation of good citizenship. Today, it is a principal instrument in awakening the child to cultural values, in preparing him for later professional training, and in helping him to adjust normally to his environment. (*Brown v. Board of Education*, 1954, p. 493)

The majority opinion in *Brown* emphasized the state's role in ensuring equity, finding education a primary function of state and local governments, and asserting that "where the state has undertaken to provide it, is a right which must be made available to all on equal terms" (*Brown v. Board of Education*, 1954, p. 493). "Indeed the underlying value in Brown is perhaps as much equity as it is desegregation. The Court concluded that it was impossible for racially segregated education to be equal—and so public education had to be racially integrated" (Bollinger, 2003, p. 2). This expression of value notwithstanding, governments often find equitable provision of educational opportunity difficult to realize, as reflected in—and, some argue, due to—the later decision regarding Texas school finance in *Rodriguez*.

While social programs including formal schooling stabilize society in part by reducing material inequality and leveling opportunity, these efforts submerge rather than eliminate class antagonism and depend on ideological maintenance to placate the public (Habermas, 1970). Schools play a central but paradoxical role in the maintenance of an *achievement ideology*, functioning as an instrument of social mobility and as an end of status attainment. This tension, at the center of the school finance litigation in Texas, is captured by Justice Powell in 1973:

> The history of education since the industrial revolution shows a continual struggle between two forces: the desire by members of society to have educational opportunity for all children and the desire of each family to provide the best education it can afford for its own children. (*Rodriguez v. San Antonio ISD*, 1973)

In finding the Texas system of school finance an inappropriate candidate for strict judicial scrutiny, the majority deemed it a matter for the people of the state and their representatives. Justice Marshall argued that the decision was "a retreat from our historic commitment to equality of educational opportunity," offering in dissent,

> I, for one, am unsatisfied with the hope of an ultimate 'political' solution sometime in the indefinite future while; in the meantime, countless children unjustifiably receive inferior educations that may affect their hearts and minds in a way unlikely ever to be undone. (pp. 71–72)

The unwillingness or inability of the Texas legislature to initiate reforms to remedy the inequities no doubt contributed to his worry.[28]

The Court's decision in *Rodriguez*, deeply unsatisfactory for those pressing for equity, reveals the difficulty reconciling demands for equitable opportunity with the traditional administration of schooling. Burch (2001) echoed Marshall's parallels between *Brown* and *Rodriguez*, but went further by drawing similarities between the *Rodriguez* decision and *Plessey v. Ferguson*. "*Rodriguez* legalizes a form of inequality that is identical in its civic consequences to the 'equal but separate' doctrine that defined *Plessey*" (p. 267). Bollinger argues that the majority was concerned about (over) stepping onto a slippery slope in declaring education a fundamental right, and thus acting as a superlegislature in disregard of principles of federalism and local control[29] (Bollinger, 2003). When the school finance system was challenged again, the State Supreme Court's reading of the constitutional obligation led to a reconciliation of the tension and an appeal to an alternate ideology of state provision of services.

THROTTLING REDISTRIBUTION AND CHANNELING ACTION. As discussed above, Texas courts ruled that the state's finance system violated of the education clause of the state constitution in *Edgewood I*, and charged the legislature with bringing the system into alignment. The opinion offered for the majority by Justice John Cornyn in *Edgewood IV* was a pivotal event in the scale-up of state power and as such assumes a prominent place in the account offered above. However, while the opinion tying the state's finance and accountability systems together altered the course of the development of institutional capacity, it differs from the path-dependence discussed above.

If continuity derives from an inability or unwillingness to reconcile deeply set ideological positions in *Rodriguez*, the *Edgewood IV* decision illustrates the role of ideas and ideology North notes in institutional development and change. The Cornyn effort to "correct" an erroneous definition of efficiency—entrepreneurial in some sense—seized on an opportunity presented in a shifting institutional framework induced by years of organizational activity on the finance and accountability systems discussed above. However, the opportunity appears to have been subtracted by a pervasive neomanagerialist public-sector reform discourse (see Maxcy, 2006b).

With the separate concurring opinion offered in *Edgewood III*, it was clear that Justice Cornyn "interpreted the word 'efficiency' much differently than either previous courts or the current majority, despite his protestations to the contrary" (Farr & Trachtenberg, 1999, p. 669). Writing for the majority in *Edgewood IV*, he literally redefined the term on which the Texas school finance decisions hinged—the operative meaning of the term "efficiency" directing legislative action through constitution's education clause. As discussed, the *Edgewood I* court delved deeply into the historical record to discern the framers' intent, ultimately determining that the term "efficiency" referred to the allocation of revenues—similar access should derive from similar tax effort. Apparently discounting the earlier court's efforts to clarify the constitutional ambiguity, Cornyn substituted a new definition of administrative efficiency—similar inputs should yield similar outcomes.

This sharp divergence may be further evidence of the ambiguity and opacity in political processes mentioned earlier. In considering this, we must ask what political cover is provided Cornyn's opinion in light of its ability to hold despite a clear break with its precedent. Is such a decision legitimated by appeals to charisma, tradition, or a rational-legal order (Weber, Gerth, & Mills, 1946)? Within American jurisprudence, such a decision cannot be founded on the author's charisma. Nor does the divergent opinion appear legitimated by a legal order that accords great respect to the principle of *stare decisis*, "to stand by that which is decided," a central tenet in the maintenance of continuity in the law.

From a Weberian perspective, lacking charismatic or rational-legal authority, the opinion must find legitimation in tradition. Arguably, the opinion does so by appealing to a traditional aversion to state power, hegemonic in a Gramscian sense, held by the people of Texas. That is, rather than recognizing the state as an instrument of the people's will—the embodiment of a public servant—the public perceives the state as a potentially pernicious interloper in local affairs, an interloper with expansionist aspirations in its pursuit of power. The law provides protection from an interventionist state that, left unrestrained, would dictate social relations unremittingly and redistribute wealth unjustly.

To many, it seemed the court was pushing the legislature into a redistribution of wealth, and for many—particularly those in high wealth districts—this was akin to state-sponsored theft (Farr & Trachtenberg, 1999). Ambivalence toward social programs used to attenuate market extremes can emerge as "utopian energies" wane in late capitalism (Habermas, 1986).

> In such a situation the social welfare state comes into danger of having its societal base slip away. The upwardly mobile voter groups, who have directly reaped the greatest benefits of the formation of the social welfare state, are capable in times of crisis of developing a mentality concerned with protecting their standard of living. They may also join with those classes oriented towards productivity, into a defensive block against underprivileged or excluded groups. Such a regrouping of the electoral base threatens, first of all, the political parties that for decades have been able to rely on a steady clientele in the welfare state. (Habermas, 1986, p. 8)

What Cornyn offers, in fusing the finance and accountability systems, is an apparent mechanism to both restrain and direct the state. In part, by employing an adequacy argument as a "shield rather than a sword" (Farr & Trachtenberg, 1999), the ruling ensures that the expansion of local enrichment in some districts does not automatically trigger similar increases across all districts.

Perhaps the more significant effect of the ruling is that it conforms to and reinforces a discursive shift relating to the roles and duties of state and local-level actors in providing public services, the former to set policy and the latter relegated to delivery. This reform discourse recasts the public agent as a narrow, self-serving individual who, lacking a disciplinary structure, is a poor steward of the public trust (Bottery, 2003; Terry, 1995). Depending on one's vantage point, the emergent disciplinary system offers a "lever for social justice"

(Skrla, Scheurich, Johnson et al., 2001), a "design for mediocrity" (Patterson, 1997), or a formula for "subtractive schooling" (Sloan, 2005; Valencia & Villareal, 2005; Valenzuela, 2002) or something altogether different not yet explored.

According to Cook (1998), this bright line between policymaking and delivery roles in provision of public services is the central tenet of the New Public Management (NPM) reform discourse. NPM has come to denote a conceptually related slate of reform principles applied to public-sector organizations such as prisons, hospitals, social service agencies, and school system in the United States, United Kingdom, Europe, and the Pacific Rim in the 1980s and 1990s (Kaboolian, 1998). Hood coined the term in 1991 in an article raising questions about the substance, ideological underpinnings, and potential organizational and societal consequences of the neomanagerialist approach. In principle, NPM reconfigures the operating environment to spur public sector reform by devolving authority over operational decisions, reconfiguring accountability relations, promoting private sector management techniques, specifying and clarifying incentives for attaining performance targets, and invoking competition among providers through market-like pressures (Pollitt, 2003). Pollitt described NPM as a "paradoxical" set of reform principles that has demonstrated some level of success, but "has achieved a level of rhetorical dominance that far outruns its impact on practice" (p. 26).

Read through NPM, the Cornyn opinion reflects and reinforces a pervasive ideology that in many ways coincides with an historical aversion to central state power in Texas, but paradoxically shifts the state–school balance of power toward the former. To be certain, he articulates a new court opinion regarding the link between revenues distributed to and outcomes expected of local providers. In doing so, the opinion empowers state actors to tighten the grip on local providers. So empowered—and arguably emboldened—state-level actors clearly do so as discussed above, by intensifying expectations and drawing down the share of revenues while maintaining a cap on local revenue generation.

However, if the court opinion offers cover for the scale-up of state-level managerialism, the opinion is likewise given cover by a reform discourse decrying an overly powerful state that is unresponsive to its clients. This is a discourse that may "ring true" in a state where dominant groups hold a long-standing antipathy toward central state power that may be intensified by fear of redistribution of wealth and power implied by the earlier *Edgewood* decisions. That is, Cornyn's divergent legal opinion—capitalizing on an opportunity to alter the course of the state school finance saga—stands because it is voiced within a potent reform discourse, an ideology, in North's terms, promulgated among a receptive public whose "utopian energies" (Habermas, 1986) are waning. Acknowledging that he voices this broader discourse, we must not underplay the power and ramifications of an official opinion voiced for and from the state's Supreme Court.

Point of Departure and Lines of Future Inquiry

In sum, making sense of the growth in institutional capacity demands close examination of the interplay between opportunities pursued and missed, paths taken and not taken, and ideological substructures more and less influential. We have attempted here to suggest needed inquiry and point to dimensions of the story we feel demand additional scrutiny. In particular, while our discussion indicates the influence of ideology, the examination of ideology might go a variety of directions. In closing the discussion, we would like to point to areas of further inquiry in accounting for the shift in the balance of power in Texas and in other states. The list is not exhaustive, but suggestive of avenues we feel are promising and have begun to explore.

First, the story suggests that inquiry into policy diffusion may offer a retrospective glimpse into adoption of particular policies in this state during a particular period of time. These theories might provide insights into how policy entrepreneurs (Kingdon, 1984; Mintrom, 1997), capitalizing on high levels of dissatisfaction in public education (Lutz, 1986), thrust Texas educational policy into the public eye. These lenses might also reveal the machinations contributing to the diffusion of the state's influence on districts and schools (Rorrer, 2001; Teece, 1980).

Explorations of ideologies among elites and non-elites might offer an account for the development of support for a system that seemed to advance state control in contradiction to conventional wisdom within the state. These might include a critical theoretical study of the Texas reforms as a legitimation project rooted in ideologies of improvement, settlement, and achievement to stave of a legitimation crisis (Maxcy, 2004, 2006a). Drawing on Habermas (1989; 1996), this line of inquiry is hinted at above, but thorough exploration is beyond the scope of the chapter.

Critical race theorists (Crenshaw, Gotanda, Peller, & Thomas, 1995; Ladson-Billings & Tate, 1997; Parker, Deyhle, & Villenas, 1999) have begun to interrogate the role of race and ethnicity in the state's school finance debate (see Alemán, 2006). Study from this perspective might examine the popular acceptance of the majority opinion that confined revenue redistribution to ends largely defined by state-level elites and business interests. Of interest is the coupling of school finance to an administrative system that seems to leverage system adjustment on the backs of students of color who are doubly failed by the educational system: failing to adequately prepare disproportionate numbers of them for high-stakes exams, then denying them diplomas. Such studies might yield insight into how depoliticized administrative systems depend on historically determined structuring of racial and ethnic privilege in American society and function by fomenting race–class divisions to undermine potential interest convergence as a managerial tool of the larger system (López, 2003; López & Parker, 2003).

Finally, inquiry drawing on postcolonial theories might interrogate the degree to which the Texas reforms reflect the application of what Said (1978) termed an "orientalist" discourse, whereby the development and administration of disciplining institutions to "serve" poor and nonwhite communities are taken up as the burden of a progressive elite. As with other forms of "governmentality" (Barthes, 1957; Foucault, 1991), such discourses inform and impose understandings of the subaltern "other" to be governed by those positioned and empowered to know and decide on that individual's behalf. A postcolonial interrogation might raise questions about the rapid diffusion of these apparently imperialist administrative discourses within a globalized context (Bhabha, 2004) and of their asymmetrical application across metropolitan areas (Lipman, 2004) and diffusion across borders (Luke, 2002; Whitty & Power, 2003). It might probe the appeal of these systems—typically promulgated within "developing" nations—in a purported "renewal" of the public sector of the "developed" world. Of interest is the apparent appeal to those concerned with the management of linguistic, religious, racial, ethnic, class, and cultural difference within school populations. Alternately, a postcolonial approach might inquire into the strategic uses of the stereotypes central to these discursive systems by subaltern groups to contest and complicate hegemonic control (Bhabha, 1994; Gandhi, 1998) as explored by Nguyen and Maxcy (Maxcy & Nguyen, 2006; Nguyen, 2006).

Conclusion

A general concern running through this volume is the growing role of states in spurring and directing school reform efforts, particularly with regard to improving the education delivered to historically underserved communities. Our discussion of Texas suggests a dramatic and rapid shift of power toward the state with the reconfiguration of the school finance and accountability systems. It seems reasonable to ask if the net result of the reconfiguration enhances system effectiveness and equity of opportunity. Without doubt, the court-mandated changes to the finance system reduced inequities in operating revenues, as did finance-related legislation between 1989 and 1993 (Alemán & Brownson, 2001). Achievement gains in schools serving students from historically underserved communities—schools that benefited disproportionately from more equitable distribution of revenues—outpaced those in schools serving more advantaged communities (Grissmer & Flanagan, 1998).

With regard to student achievement, Carnoy and colleagues found mixed effects with substantial gains on some tests but much more modest gains in other areas such as completion rates (Carnoy, Loeb, & Smith, 2000). The finding of mixed effects is reflective of a series of studies published around the 2000 campaign, as well as after the election, presenting very different pictures of the Texas system. Some praised Texas-style accountability, citing overall gains and more rapid reduction of performance gaps than other states (Grissmer & Flanagan, 1998; Jerald, 2001). Deeming it an "historic moment," some were particularly laudatory, crediting the state's performance reporting with focusing public attention on performance disparities and forcing district leaders to hold schools and districts to account for the performance of all students (Skrla & Scheurich, 2001). Others expressed skepticism about state-reported results of quick gains that did not bear out across assessments (Klein et al., 2000). Some were highly critical, arguing that the high failure rates visited on poor and minority students were discriminatory (Bernal & Valencia, 2000; Haney, 2000; Natriello & Pallas, 1998), and that, by obscuring historical inequities, the system would ultimately harm the students and schools it purports to aid (McNeil, 2000; McNeil & Valenzuela, 2000; Valencia, 2000; Valenzuela, 2005).

Perhaps this variety of assessments is to be expected since "accountability systems and their equity effects . . . are dynamic (over time), highly complex, [and] varied" (Skrla, Scheurich, & Johnson, 2001, p. 227). Parallel reforms of the state's accountability and finance systems complicate any attributions to the state's redistribution of funds or its press for performance. While some attribute gains to the increased visibility of the gaps, a case can certainly be made that many traditionally underfunded schools made good use of the resources made available by finance reform. That is, gains were registered rather than induced by the external accountability system. We note compelling accounts provided by close-in studies of beneficent practices instituted in equity-focused districts and schools (e.g., Reyes, Scribner, & Scribner, 1999; Rorrer & Skrla, 2004; Skrla et al., 2000), as well as studies revealing troubling practices visited on marginalized students induced by performance pressures (Black & Valenzuela, 2004; Sloan, 2005; Valencia & Villareal, 2005; Valenzuela, 2000). On balance, these suggest that the growing role of the state has been neither uniformly positive nor negative, nor has it been neutral.

From a less functionalist perspective, the complicating effects of the parallel (and convergent) reforms hold other meanings. As previously discussed, performance pressures engendered by the accountability regime and fiscal pressures brought about by a drawdown of the state share in school funding system combine to dramatically increase the power of the state vis-à-vis local actors. A retrospective examination of the expansion of institutional capacity must account for the interplay of these reforms. It must probe the highly path-dependent nature of the reconfiguration, given the fluid opportunity structure within which reformers and others were operating and the ideological formations influencing their analyses. Thus, we encourage further explorations of the Texas case, not as a model of efficacious reform, but as an illustration of the complex dynamics and political utility of the reconfiguration belied by the potted histories—flattering and otherwise—that are often proffered.

Notes

1. The authors note the following: "First, Texans take the notion of local control seriously. Second, all issues of property-based funding eventually encounter the uneven distribution of oil and gas across the state. Third, the Texas Constitution significantly constrains the Legislature's ability to tax. Fourth, education may be the most political issue in a state with colorful political traditions" (p. 616).

2. The vast majority of school districts are incorporated as "independent" taxing authorities, separate from municipalities.

3. The laws are named for Representative Claude Gilmer and Senator A. M. Aiken who initiated a 1947 educational reform study.

4. Green cites Hugh Roy Cullen, H. L. Hunt, Sid Richardson, and Clint Murchison among a group of "throwbacks to an era of robber barons" who took a strong interest in state politics at mid-century and gave rise to a new corporate influence that continues today.

5. In 1989 the state high court found in the initial *Edgewood* ruling that "the 300,000 students in the wealthiest districts have more than eight times the property value to support their education as the 300,000 students in the poorest districts. The average property wealth in the 100 wealthiest districts is more than twenty times greater than the average property wealth in the 100 poorest districts" (*Edgewood I*, 1989, p. 2).

6. Activity included an historic May 16, 1968, student walkout and efforts to secure influence through positions on local school boards in South Texas (Acuna, 1988; Gutierrez, 1998; San Miguel, 1987).

7. Among other things, the bill: (1) increased the basic allotment provided through the foundation program; (2) shifted the funding basis from personnel units to average daily attendance; (3) mandated class-size reductions; and (4) created a new prekindergarten program for low-income students (Hobby & Walker, 1991; Walker & Casey, 1996). The bill also increased state aid for compensatory education programs from $50 to $350 million dollars (Texas Education Agency, 2001). The 19 percent increase in educational spending, which disproportionately benefited low-income students and high-poverty schools, was funded by a $4.9 billion tax increase spread over the next three years (Walker & Casey, 1996).

8. Under the wealth-recapture plan, 90 percent of Texas students would be in a wealth neutral system and a spending gap not greater than $600 per student would exist between districts making similar tax efforts.

9. The figure increased incrementally over the next few years, to $295,000 with House Bill 4 in 1999, $300,000 for 2001–2002 and $305,000 for 2002–2003 under HB 3343 in 2001. A provision enacted in 1997 meant the recapture calcu-

lation would hold districts harmless from any lost tax revenues endured as a result of loss in taxable value due to the increased $10,000 homestead exemption.

10. The student figure is determined according to a state-weighted average daily attendance (WADA) figure adjusted for factors such as compensatory and bilingual education, transportation costs, district size, and so on.

11. By disaggregating the performance data and attaching consequences for schools that failed to attain minimum performance levels for each racial, ethnic, and socioeconomic student subgroups, the new system focused additional attention on campus and district responsibility for the performance of historically underserved students (Texas Education Agency, 2000).

12. Since 2005, a rating of Exemplary for schools and districts requires: (1) passing rate of 90 percent or more on the TAKS for both all students and each student group; (2) passing rate of 90 percent or more on the Texas State-Developed Alternative Assessment II for all eligible students; (3) completion rates at the high school are at or above 95 percent; (4) annual dropout rate for students in grades 7–8 of 0.2 percent or less for both all students and each student group. A *Recognized* rating requires: (1) passing rate of 70 percent or more on the TAKS for both all students and each student group or 65 percent floor and Required Improvement; (2) passing rate of 70 percent or more on the Texas State-Developed Alternative Assessment II for all eligible students; (3) completion rates at the high school are at or above 85 percent or 80 percent floor and Required Improvement (4) annual dropout rate for students in grades 7–8 of 0.7 percent or less for both all students and each student group or .9 percent floor and Required Improvement. A rating of *Academically Acceptable* requires: (1) passing rate of 50 percent or more on the TAKS for all students and each student group in reading/ELA, writing, and social studies, 35 percent in mathematics, 25 percent in science or meets Required Improvement; (2) passing rate of 50 percent or more on the Texas State-Developed Alternative Assessment II for all eligible students; (3) completion rates at the high school are at or above 75 percent or meets Required Improvement (4) annual dropout rate for students in grades 7–8 of 1 percent or less for both all students and each student group or meets Required Improvement.

13. In spring 2002, administration of the TAAS exit exam, 87.4 percent of low-income and 95.0 percent of non-low-income tenth grade students passed the mathematics subtest (AEIS, 2002). Passing rates for African American, Hispanic, and white students were 85.6 percent, 88.0 percent, and 96.5 percent, respectively.

14. Moving from the tenth to the eleventh-grade year, the new exit-examinations substantially increased the breadth and rigor of the exit tests and required additional tests in social studies and science.

15. Based on the passing standard recommended by a 350-member advisory committee of citizens and educators, the estimated passing rates for the

exit examination are 25 percent for low-income and 46 percent for non-low-income students. The estimated passing rates for African American, Hispanic, and white students are 20 percent, 27 percent, and 47 percent, respectively (Texas Education Agency, 2002b).

16. According to the Texas Education Agency, the scores in the initial "live" administration of the TAAS test in 1990 were ten points above the field test projections (TEA, 2002a).

17. For students slated to graduate in 2005, the estimated passing rates are 46 percent for low-income and 65 percent for non-low-income students. The estimated passing rates for African American, Hispanic, and white students are 40 percent, 48 percent, and 58 percent, respectively.

18. The state's attorneys point to large fund balances of some districts as evidence of discretion; superintendents note that the discretion is illusory as lowered fund balance can lead to lowered bond ratings, ultimately increasing borrowing costs for their local taxpayers (*WOC v. Neeley*, 2005).

19. Mintrom (1997) notes the significant role of policy entrepreneurs: "Policy entrepreneurs play an important role in articulating innovative ideas onto government agendas. They work hard at developing close ties with people through whom they can realize their policy goals and they seek to develop convincing arguments for selling their policy ideas. Naturally, policy entrepreneurs, like other actors in the policy-making process, must be aware of the constraints imposed by election cycles and interest group opposition to their proposals" (Mintrom, 1997, p. 765).

20. Perot, who Lutz (1986) called the "father of HB 72" (p. 80), reportedly used his own resources and staff. Lutz noted that the State Board of Education, Texas Association of School Administrators, principals' associations, State School Board Association, advocacy groups for vocational education and athletics, and the House and Senate Education Committees initially opposed HB 72. "Perot, his money, his staff, and his lobbyists were in Austin. One lobbyist working against the bill reported that Perot's staff had offered him a job (at higher pay) *to go home* and lobby for the bill. He turned them down. In another instance, the chairman of one of the legislature's education committees removed his arm from his right coat sleeve and, dangling the empty sleeve, said he had never been subjected to such arm-twisting in his life" (p. 72).

21. The Court expressed concern about infringing on local authority. Deeming it "one the most persistent and difficult questions of educational policy," the Court found that the inherent tension between equalization of funding and local control provided another compelling reason to reverse the district court decision. Local control "permits and encourages a large measure of participation in and control of each district's schools at the local level. . . . In part, local control means . . . the freedom to devote more money to the education of one's children. Equally im-

portant, however, is the opportunity it offers for participation in the decision making process that determines how those local tax dollars will be spent. Each locality is free to tailor local programs to local needs" (*Rodriguez v. San Antonio ISD*, 1973, pp. 49–50).

22. According to Fair and Trachtenburg (1999), "To a large degree, the true motivations of the justices remain unknown, particularly in relationship to the ever-present dual concerns of equity and adequacy in education. By basing their decision on 'efficiency,' the justices of the Texas Supreme Court held their cards close to their vests. Both the inequitable and the inadequate aspects of the Texas school finance system seemed to concern the court. Just which failures of the system most inspired each justice is a subplot that develops throughout the remainder of the Edgewood drama" (fn 171).

23. School and district ratings instituted in the early 1990s were tied to performance of disaggregated student groups (African American, Asian-Pacific Islander, Hispanic, Native American, white, and economically disadvantaged) in three categories: TAAS pass rates, dropout rates, and attendance. Schools received ratings of Exemplary (> 90 percent pass rate, < 1 percent dropout), Recognized (> 80 percent pass rate, < 3 percent dropout), or Acceptable (> 25 percent pass rate, < 8 percent dropout). The standards for acceptable schools were increased each year to a 50 percent pass rate and a 5.5 percent dropout rate.

24. From 1994 to 2000, enrollment in advanced coursework increased for both low-income and non-low-income students, but the gap between groups increased from approximately six to nine percentage points.

25. TAAS/TASP equivalence measure indicates the percentage of graduates receiving a score on the exit-level TAAS to have a 75 percent likelihood of passing the Texas Academic Skills Program (TASP) test. Unlike the TAAS passing rates, there was effectively no closure between 1994 and 2000 of the twenty-five-point performance gap between low-income students and their peers in terms of TAAS/TASP equivalency scores. Similar gaps occur between white and nonwhite student groups.

26. A national study of postsecondary education, *Measuring Up 2000*, scored states higher education systems with regard to preparation, affordability, participation, completion, and benefits. Texas received an overall score of 72 (average = 78) and ranked forty-one among the fifty states (National Center for Public Policy and Higher Education, 2001). Although figures regarding nonwhite students are not included, Texas lags top states in measures related to preparation and strategies for financial support of low-income students.

27. Because the majority of low-income students fell below the 1994 cut score (passing rate = 37.3 percent) and the majority of non-low-income students fell above the cutoff (passing rate = 60.0 percent), a marginal score improvement results in a much larger proportion of low-income students moving into the

passing range than that of their peers. In addition, as more students in the non-low-income group begin to reach the performance ceiling imposed by the TAAS, the gap appears to close even more rapidly as the test fails to reflect "real" performance gains. An identical argument can be made for the gains for African American and Hispanic students as well. Haney (2000) discusses the arbitrary process of establishing the cut score and its disparate impact on different student groups.

28. The District Court "postponed decision for some two years in the hope that the Texas Legislature would remedy the gross disparities in treatment inherent in the Texas financing scheme. It was only after the legislature failed to act in its 1971 Regular Session that the District Court, apparently recognizing the lack of hope for self-initiated legislative reform, rendered its decision" (from Justice White's dissent, cited in Bollinger, 2003).

29. A year later, the principle of local control was again emphasized by the High Court in the Detroit desegregation case, *Milliken v. Bradley* (1974, pp. 740–741): "No single tradition in public education is more deeply rooted than local control over the operation of the schools; local autonomy has long been thought essential both to the maintenance of community concern and support for public schools and to quality of the educational process" (*Milliken v. Bradley*, 1974, pp. 740–741).

References

Academic Excellence Indicator System. (2002). *2001–2002 State performance report*. Austin: Texas Education Agency.

Acuna, R. (1988). *Occupied America: A history of Chicanos* (3rd ed.). New York: HarperCollins.

Adams, J. E., Jr., & Kirst, M. W. (1999). New demands and concepts for educational accountability: Striving for results in an era of excellence. In J. Murphy & K. S. Louis (Eds.), *Handbook of research on educational administration: A project of the American Educational Research Association* (2nd ed.) (pp. 463–489). San Francisco: Jossey-Bass.

Alemán, E. (2006). Is Robin Hood the "Prince of Thieves" or a pathway to equity? Applying Critical Race Theory to school finance political discourse. *Educational Policy, 20*(1), 113–142.

Alemán, E., & Brownson, A. (2001, November 2). *Implications of Texas school finance policy on district spending behaviours.* Paper presented at the Annual meeting of the University Council of Educational Administration, Cincinnati.

Ball, S. J. (1994). *Education reform: A critical and post-structural approach.* Philadelphia: Open University Press.

Barthes, R. (1957). *Mythologies.* Paris: Éditions du Seuil.

Bernal, E. M., & Valencia, R. R. (2000). The TAAS case: A recapitulation and beyond. *Hispanic Journal of Behavioral Sciences, 22*(4), 540–556.

Bhabha, H. K. (1994). *The location of culture*. New York: Routledge.

Bhabha, H. K. (2004). Introduction (R. Philcox, Trans.). In F. Fanon (Ed.), *The wretched of the earth* (1st ed.) (pp. i–lxii). New York: Grove Press.

Black, W., & Valenzuela, A. (2004). Educational accountability for English language learners in Texas: A retreat from equity. In L. Skrla & J. J. Scheurich (Eds.), *Educational equity and accountability: Paradigms, policies and politics* (pp. 215–234). New York: Routledge Flamer.

Bollinger, L. (2003, November 1–4). *Educational Equity and Quality: Brown and Rodriguez and Their Aftermath*. Paper presented at the College Board Forum, New York.

Bottery, M. (2003). The leadership of learning communities in a culture of unhappiness. *School Leadership and Management, 23*(2), 187–207.

Bourdieu, P., & Wacquant, L. J. D. (1992). *An invitation to reflexive sociology*. Chicago: University of Chicago Press.

Brown v. Board of Education (347 U.S. 483 1954).

Burch, K. (2001). A tale of two citizens: Asking the Rodriquez question in the twenty-first century. *Educational Studies, 32*(3), 264–278.

Bush, G. W. (2001). *No child left behind*. Washington, DC: U.S. Department of Education.

Cardenas, J. A. (1997). *Texas school finance reform: An IDRA perspective*. San Antonio: Intercultural Development Research Association.

Carnoy, M., Loeb, S., & Smith, T. L. (2000, April 24–28). *Do higher state test scores in Texas make for better high school outcomes?* Paper presented at the Annual meeting of the American Educational Research Association, New Orleans.

Carollton-Farmers Branch v. Edgewood, 826 S.W.2d 489 (Supreme Court of Texas 1992).

Cibulka, J. (1996). The reform and survival of American public schools: An institutional perspective. In R. L. Crowson, W. L. Boyd, & H. B. Mawhinney (Eds.), *The politics of education, and the new institutionalism: Reinventing the American school* (Vol. 1995 yearbook of the Politics of Education Association) (pp. 7–22). Washington, DC: Falmer.

Cibulka, J., & Derlin, R. (1998). Accountability policy adoption to policy sustainability: Reforms and systemic initiatives in Colorado and Maryland. *Education and Urban Society, 30*(4), 502–515.

Coase, R. (1937). The nature of the firm. *Economica, 4*, 386–405.

Cook, B. J. (1998). Politics, political leadership, and public management. *Public Administration Review, 58*(3), 225–230.

Crenshaw, K., Gotanda, N., Peller, G., & Thomas, K. (Eds.). (1995). *Critical race theory: The key writings that formed the movement.* New York: New Press.

Davidson, C. (1990). *Race and class in Texas politics.* Princeton, NJ: Princeton University Press.

Eby, F. (2004). The first century of public education in Texas. In *Sesquicentennial Handbook* (pp. 35–59). Austin: Texas Education Agency.

Edgewood v. Kirby, 777 S.W.2d 391 (Supreme Court of Texas 1989).

Edgewood v. Kirby, 804 S.W.2d 491, (Supreme Court of Texas 1991).

Edgewood v. Meno, 917 S.W.2d 717, 737 (Supreme Court of Texas 1995).

Edmonds, R. (1979). Effective schools for the urban poor. *Educational Leadership, 37*(1), 15–24.

Elazar, D. J. (1994). *The American mosaic: The impact of space, time, and culture on American politics.* Boulder, CO: Westview Press.

Elmore, R. F., Abelman, C., & Fuhrman, S. (1996). The new accountability in state education reform: From process to performance. In H. Ladd (Ed.), *Holding schools accountable: Performance based reform in education* (pp. 65–98). Washington, DC: Brookings.

Farr, J. S., & Trachtenberg, M. (1999). The Edgewood drama: An epic quest for education equity. *Yale Law and Policy Review, 17*, 607–727.

Foucault, M. (1980). *Power/knowledge: Selected interviews and other writings, 1972–1977.* New York: Pantheon.

Foucault, M. (1991). Governmentality. In G. Burchell, C. Gordon, & P. Miller (Eds.), *The Foucault effect: Studies in governmentality, with two lectures by and an interview with Michel Foucault* (pp. 87–104). Chicago: University of Chicago Press.

Friedman, M. (1962). *Capitalism and freedom.* Chicago: University of Chicago Press.

Friedman, M. (1977). *From Galbraith to economic freedom* (Vol. 49). London: Institute of Economic Affairs.

Friedman, M., & Friedman, R. D. (1980). *Free to choose: A personal statement.* New York: Harcourt Brace Jovanovich.

Fuhrman, S. H. (1999). *The new accountability* (CPRE Policy Brief). Philadelphia: Consortium for Policy Research in Education.

Fuller, E. J., & Johnson, J. F. (2001). Can state accountability systems drive improvements in school performance for children of color and children from low-income homes? *Education and Urban Society, 33*(3), 260–283.

Fusarelli, L. D. (2002). Tightly coupled policy in loosely coupled systems: Institutional capacity and organizational change. *Journal of Educational Administration, 40*(6), 561–575.

Galbraith, J. K. (1956). *American capitalism: The concept of countervailing power.* Boston: Houghton Mifflin.

Galbraith, J. K. (1958). *The affluent society*. Boston: Houghton Mifflin.

Gandhi, L. (1998). *Postcolonial theory: A critical introduction*. New York: Columbia University Press.

Giddens, A. (1979). *Central problems in social theory: Action, structure, and contradiction in social analysis*. Berkeley: University of California Press.

Gordon, C. (1991). Government rationality: An introduction. In G. Burchell, C. Gordon, & P. Miller (Eds.), *The Foucault effect: Studies in governmentality, with two lectures by and an interview with Michel Foucault* (pp. 1–52). Chicago: University of Chicago Press.

Green, G. N. (1979). *The establishment in Texas politics: The primitive years, 1938–1957*. Westport, CT: Greenwood Press.

Grissmer, D. W., & Flanagan, A. (1998). *Exploring rapid achievement gains in North Carolina and Texas*. Washington, DC: National Education Goals Panel.

Gunn, S. (2006). From hegemony to governmentality: Changing conceptions of power in social history. *Journal of Social History, 39*(3).

Gutierrez, J. A. (1998). *The making of a Chicano militant: Lessons from Cristal.* Madison: University of Wisconsin Press.

Gwynne, S. C. (2001). How good is your kid's school? *Texas Monthly Magazine*.

Habermas, J. (1970). *Toward a rational society: Student protest, science, and politics.* Boston: Beacon Press.

Habermas, J. (1975). *Legitimation crisis*. Boston: Beacon Press.

Habermas, J. (1979). *Communication and the evolution of society* (T. McCarthy, Trans.). Boston: Beacon Press.

Habermas, J. (1986). The new obscurity: The crisis of the welfare state and the exhaustion of utopian energies. *Philosophy and Social Criticism, 11*(2), 1–18.

Habermas, J. (1989). *The structural transformation of the public sphere: An inquiry into a category of Bourgeois society*. Cambridge, MA: MIT Press.

Habermas, J. (1996). *Between facts and norms: Contributions to a discourse theory of law and democracy*. Cambridge, MA: MIT Press.

Hall, S. (1996). The problem of ideology: Marxism without guarantees. In D. Morley & K.-H. Chen (Eds.), *Stuart Hall: Critical dialogues in cultural studies* (pp. 25–46). New York: Routledge.

Haney, W. (2000). The myth of the Texas miracle in education. *Educational Policy Analysis Archives, 8*(41).

Hayek, F. A. (1988/2000). The fatal conceit: The errors of socialism. In R. Blaug & J. Schwartzmantel (Eds.), *Democracy: A reader* (pp. 362–366). New York: Columbia University Press.

Hayek, F. A. (1994). *The road to serfdom* (50th anniversary ed.). Chicago: University of Chicago Press.

Hobby, W., & Walker, B. (1991). Legislative reform of the Texas public school finance system. *Harvard Journal on Legislation, 23*(379), 379–394.

Jerald, C. (2001). *Real results, remaining challenges: The story of Texas education reform*: Business Roundtable.

Judson, J. (1997). *The true state of Texas education*. Austin: Texas Public Policy Foundation.

Kaboolian, L. (1998). The new public management: Challenging the boundaries of the management vs. administration debate. *Public Administration Review, 58*(3), 189–193.

Key, V. O. (1949). *Southern politics in state and nation*. New York: Vintage Books.

Kingdon, J. 1984. *Agendas, alternatives, and public policies*. New York: HarperCollins.

Klein, S., Hamilton, L., McCaffrey, D., & Stecher, B. (2000). *What do test scores in Texas tell us?* Santa Monica, CA: Rand.

Kozol, J. (1991). *Savage inequalities: Children in America's schools*. New York: Crown.

Ladd, H. F., & Hansen, J. S. (1999). *Making money matter: Financing America's schools*. Washington, DC: National Academy Press.

Ladson-Billings, G., & Tate, W. (1997). Toward a critical race theory of education. *Teachers College Record, 97*(1), 47.

Lipman, P. (2004). *High stakes education: Inequality, globalization, and urban school reform*. New York: Routledge Falmer.

López, G. R. (2003). The (racially neutral) politics of education: A critical race theory perspective. *Educational Administration Quarterly, 39*(1), 68–94.

López, G. R., & Parker, L. (2003). *Interrogating racism in qualitative research methodology*. New York: Peter Lang.

Luce, T. (1995). *Now or never: How we can save our public schools*. Dallas: Taylor.

Luke, A. (2002). *Curriculum, ethics, metanarrative: Teaching and learning beyond the nation*. Retrieved March 31, 2005, from http://www.education.tas.gov.au/english/luke.htm.

Lutz, F. (1986). Education politics in Texas. *Peabody Journal of Education, 63*(4), 70–89.

Malen, B. (2003). Tightening the grip? The impact of state activism on local school systems. *Education Policy, 17*(2), 195–216.

Maxcy, B. D. (2004). *Emerging democracy in an urban elementary school: A Habermasian framework for examining school governance reculturing in response to systemic reform.* Unpublished doctoral dissertation, the University of Texas at Austin.

Maxcy, B. D. (2006a). *Managing leadership: Asymmetrical impacts of new public management logics on democratic leadership of public schools.* Paper presented at the Annual meeting of the American Educational Research Association, San Francisco.

Maxcy, B. D. (2006b). Policy commentary and book review: Leaving children behind, A. Valenzuela (ed.). *Educational Administration Quarterly, 42*, (256–284).

Maxcy, B. D., & Nguyen, T. S. T. (2006). The politics of distributing leadership: Reconsidering leadership distribution in two Texas elementary schools. *Educational Policy, 20*(1), 169–196.

McNeil, L. M. (2000). *Contradictions of school reform: Educational costs of standardized testing*. New York: Routledge.

McNeil, L. M., & Valenzuela, A. (1998, December 4). *The harmful impact of the TAAS system of testing in Texas: Beneath the accountability rhetoric.* Paper presented at the Harvard Civil Rights Project Conference: High-stakes testing in K–12: Reconciling standards-based reforms with civil rights and equity, New York.

McNeil, L. M., & Valenzuela, A. (2000). The harmful impact of the TAAS system of testing in Texas: Beneath the accountability rhetoric. In M. Kornhaber & G. Orfield (Eds.), *Raising standards or raising barriers? Inequality and high stakes testing in public education* (pp. 127–150). New York: Century Foundation.

Milliken v. Bradley 740–741 (418 U.S. 717 1974).

Mintrom, M. (1997). Policy entrepreneurs and the diffusion of innovation. *American Journal of Political Science, 41*(3), 738–770.

National Center for Public Policy and Higher Education. (2001). *Measuring up 2000: The state-by-state report card for higher education*. Washington, DC: Author.

Natriello, G., & Pallas, A. (1998, December 4). *The development and impact of high stakes testing.* Paper presented at the Harvard Civil Rights Project Conference: High-stakes testing in K–12: Reconciling standards-based reforms with civil rights and equity, New York.

Neeley v. West Orange Cove Consolidated (Supreme Court of Texas 2005).

Neeley v. West Orange Cove Consolidated Independent School District, 176 S.W.3d 746 (2005).

Nguyen, T. S. T. (2006). *Politics of place: Managing linguistic difference through a population specific (Vietnamese) program within and against one public elementary school.* Unpublished doctoral dissertation, the University of Texas at Austin.

North, D. C. (1990). *Institutions, institutional change, and economic performance.* New York: Cambridge University Press.

Parker, L. (2001). Statewide assessment triggers in urban school reform: But how high the stakes for urban minorities? *Education and Urban Society, 33*(3), 313–319.

Parker, L., Deyhle, D., & Villenas, S. A. (1999). *Race is—race isn't: Critical race theory and qualitative studies in education.* Boulder, CO: Westview Press.

Patterson, C. (1997). *Design for mediocrity: A report on current reforms in Texas public schools.* Austin: Texas Public Policy Foundation.

Pierson, P. (2000). Increasing returns, path dependency, and the study of politics. *American Political Science Review, 94*(2), 251–267.

Pierson, P. (2004). *Politics in time: History, institutions, and social analysis.* Princeton, NJ: Princeton University Press.

Pollitt, C. (2003). *The essential public manager.* Philadelphia: Open University Press.

Purkey, S. C., & Smith, M. S. (1983). Effective schools: A review. *Elementary School Journal, 83*(4), 426–452.

Reyes, P., Scribner, J. D., & Scribner, A. P. (1999). *Lessons from high-performing Hispanic schools: Creating learning communities.* New York: Teachers College Press.

Rodriguez v. San Antonio ISD (411 U.S. 1 1973).

Rorrer, A. (2001). *Leadership and equity: From reproduction to reconstruction: An institutional analysis.* (Doctoral dissertation, the University of Texas at Austin). (UMI No. 3049260).

Rorrer, A. (2003). Intersections in accountability reform: Complexity, local actors, legitimacy, and agendas. In L. Skrla & J. Scheurich (Eds.), *Educational equity and accountability: Paradigms, policies, and politics* (pp. 251–266). London: Routledge-Falmer.

Rorrer, A. K., & Skrla, L. (2004). Leaders as policy mediators: The reconceptualization of accountability. *Theory Into Practice, 44*(1).

Said, E. W. (1978). *Orientalism.* New York: Pantheon.

San Miguel, G. (1987). *"Let all of them take heed": Mexican Americans and the campaign for educational equality in Texas, 1910–1981.* Austin: University of Texas Press.

Scheurich, J. J., Skrla, L., & Johnson, J. F. (2000, April). Thinking carefully about equity and accountability. *Phi Delta Kappan, 81*(8), 293–299.

Serrano v. Priest (5 Cal. 3d 584, 487 P.2d 1241 (CA) 1971).

Shirley, D. (1997). *Community organizing for urban school reform*. Austin: University of Texas Press.

Sipple, J., Kileen, K., & Monk, D. (2004). Adoption and adaptation: School district responses to state imposed learning and graduation requirements. *Educational Evaluation and Policy Analysis, 26*(2), 143–168.

Skrla, L., & Scheurich, J. (2001). Displacing deficit thinking in school district leadership. *Education and Urban Society, 33*(3), 235–259.

Skrla, L., Scheurich, J., & Johnson, J. (2001). Introduction: Toward a new consensus on high academic achievement for all children. *Education and Urban Society, 33*(3), 227–234.

Skrla, L., Scheurich, J., Johnson, J., Hogan, D., Koschoreck, J., & Smith, P. (2000). *Equity driven achievement focused school districts: A report on systemic school success in four Texas school districts serving diverse student populations*. Austin: Charles A. Dana Center.

Skrla, L., Scheurich, J. J., Johnson, J. F. J., & Koschoreck, J. W. (2001). Accountability for equity: Can state policy leverage social justice? *International Journal of Leadership in Education, 4*(3), 237–260.

Sloan, K. (2005). Playing to the logic of the Texas accountability system: How focusing on "ratings"—not children—undermines quality and equity. In A. Valenzuela (Ed.), *Leaving children behind: How Texas-style accountability fails Latino youth* (pp. 153–178). Albany: State University of New York Press.

Staff. (2005, November 27). Focusing on taxes, not schools. *The Austin American Statesman*, p. H2.

Teece, D. (1980). The diffusion of an administrative innovation. *Management Science, 26*(5), 464–470.

Terry, L. D. (1995). *Leadership of public bureaucracies: The administrator as conservator*. Thousand Oaks, CA: Sage.

Texas Business and Education Coalition. (2001, November 14). *TBEC: A history of commitment*. Retrieved 11/17, 2001, from http://www.tbec.org/history.htm.

Texas Education Agency. (1996). *The development of accountability systems nationwide and in Texas* (Statewide Texas Educational Progress Study (STEPS) No. 1). Austin: Author.

Texas Education Agency. (2000). *Glossary for the academic excellence indicator system*. Retrieved November, 2002, from http://www.tea.state.tx.us/perfreport/aeis/2000/glossary.html.

Texas Education Agency. (2001). Compensatory education guidelines, financial accountability treatments, and an auditing and reporting System. In *Texas Education Agency Financial Accountability System Resource Guide* (Vol. 7, pp. 10). Austin: Author.

Texas Education Agency. (2002a). Press release: TAKS phase-in approved by State Board of Education. Austin: Author.

Texas Education Agency. (2002b). *Texas Assessment of Knowledge and Skills (TAKS) standard setting: Summary of projected impact of possible standards.* Austin: Author.

Texas Education Agency. (2004a). *Academic Excellence Indicator System: 2003–2004 state performance report.* Austin: Author.

Texas Education Agency. (2004b). *Texas public schools: Sesquicentiennial handbook, 1854–2004.* Austin: Author.

Timar, T. B. (1997). The institutional role of state education departments: A historical perspective. *American Journal of Education, 105*(3), 231–261.

Timar, T. B., & Kirp, D. L. (1987). Educational reform and institutional competence. *Harvard Educational Review, 57*(3), 309–330.

Valencia, R. R. (2000). Inequalities and the schooling of minority students in Texas: Historical and contemporary conditions. *Hispanic Journal of Behavioral Sciences, 22*(4), 445–459.

Valencia, R. R., & Villareal, B. J. (2005). Texas' second wave of high-stakes testing: Anti-social promotion legislation, grade retention, and adverse impact on minorities. In A. Valenzuela (Ed.), *Leaving children behind: How Texas-style accountability fails Latino youth* (pp. 113–152). Albany: State University of New York Press.

Valenzuela, A. (2000). The significance of the TAAS test for Mexican immigrant and Mexican American adolescents: A case study. *Hispanic Journal of the Behavioral Sciences, 22*(4), 524–539.

Valenzuela, A. (2002). High-stakes testing and U.S.-Mexican youth in Texas: The case for multiple compensatory criteria in assessment. *Harvard Journal of Hispanic Policy, 14*, 97–116.

Valenzuela, A. (Ed.). (2005). *Leaving Children Behind: How Texas-style accountability fails Latino youth.* Albany: State University of New York Press.

Walker, B., & Casey, D. T. (1996). *The basics of Texas public school finance* (6th ed.). Austin: Texas Association of School Boards.

Weber, M., Gerth, H. H., & Mills, C. W. (1946). *From Max Weber: Essays in sociology* (H. H. Gerth & C. W. Mills, Trans.). New York: Oxford University Press.

West Orange Cove Consolidated v. Neeley (250th Judicial District (TX) 2005).

Whitty, G., & Power, S. (2003). Making sense of education reform: Global and national influences. In C. A. Torres & A. Antikainen (Eds.), *The international handbook on the sociology of education: An international assessment of new research and theory* (pp. 305–324). Lanham, MD: Rowan & Littlefield.

Chapter 7

Kansas

Bruce D. Baker and Preston C. Green

Kansas—Separate and Unequal by Design: What's the Matter with the Rising State Role in Kansas Education?

Does increased state involvement in public schooling necessarily increase equality of educational opportunity? Do state legislatures pursue greater control over public school finance only when forced to by state courts? It is commonly perceived that state school finance litigation in particular has helped to fuel the emerging role of state control of financing and accountability in public education. It is also believed that state control of school finance may result in equality of educational opportunity.

Critics of school finance litigation argue that Kansas provides an alternative to school finance reform through litigation. Several scholars have suggested that, in the early 1990s, district court judge Terry Bullock, Governor Joan Finney, and legislative leaders overcame their differences through a contentious political process, rather than a judicial one, and came together to implement a truly revolutionary system of funding for the state, adopting a much stronger state role as well as a more rational system of financing schools for the good of all Kansas children (Berger, 1998; Johnston & Duncombe, 1998).

However, a closer look at the constitutional and statutory history of the state of Kansas in relation to public schooling reveals a far more nuanced and incremental story in which the Kansas legislature may have used centralized state control of school funding to maintain racially separate but equal educational systems. Moreover, the state legislature has consistently responded to judicial intervention by maintaining funding inequities through centralized state control.

Race, Education, and the Kansas Constitution

A review of Kansas's constitutional history reveals the importance of public schooling even before statehood. The Organic Act of 1854 set aside certain sections of land to be used for education and designed a Territorial Superintendent of Common Schools, who certified teachers and organized school districts (*Montoy v. State*, 2005). Article 6 of the 1859 constitution provided funding for public education through taxation and the sale of public lands (*Montoy v. State*, 2005). Article 6 also specified that the "legislature *shall encourage the promotion of* intellectual, moral, scientific and agricultural improvement, by establishing a uniform system of common schools, and schools of a higher grade, embracing normal, preparatory, collegiate and university departments" (p. 316, emphasis added).

Of particular importance was that the adopted language specified that the legislature was compelled (shall) to encourage promotion of intellectual, moral, scientific, and agricultural improvement by establishing a uniform system of common schools, and schools of a higher grade. It was not optional. Further, that system was to be *uniform*, suggesting not only a preference for the minimum adequacy of schooling—sufficient to *encourage the promotion of*—but also a preference that all Kansas children would have access to equitable common schools and higher schools, regardless of their location in the state or, arguably, even the color of their skin.

Racial segregation of schooling in Kansas had not been a central policy issue in the immediate aftermath of statehood and the drafting of the 1859 constitution, largely because Kansas was not home to many blacks until the decade following the Civil War as blacks fled nearby southern states. The push to permit racial segregation of schools in state legislation began with an 1879 statute permitting *cities of the first class* (those of approximately 15,000 or more residents) to operate separate elementary (common) schools for black children. Under the same legislation, cities of the first class were delineated as separate, autonomous school districts, while cities of the second class were governed partially by county superintendents (*Reynolds v. Board of Education of the City of Topeka*, 1903). Without specific exemption for cities of the first class, racially segregated elementary schools might have violated the state's *uniform systems* clause that applied to common schooling. At the time, few Kansas blacks attended high school. However, as black high school attendance increased, in 1905, the legislature adopted a special statute allowing Kansas City, Kansas, to operate segregated high schools.

A string of legal challenges to Kansas's "separate but equal" educational policies in state court preceded *Brown v. Board of Education of Topeka*. Most of the state court challenges affirmed the state's authority to permit segregation in specific locations, but denied segregation in those areas where not permitted under state statute. In the final case before *Brown*, *Webb v. School District #90, Johnson*

County (1949), the Kansas Supreme Court denied the establishment of impermissible segregated schools in Johnson County. District #90 in then-rural Johnson County had attempted to establish its own racially segregated elementary schools. Regarding the segregation plan, the court noted that the district had the authority to establish two schools and to designate areas of attendance for each. However, the designation of the areas had to be made on a reasonable basis, and the two schools were required to have comparable facilities and standards.

Concurrently, the few (fifteen) black high school students residing in Johnson County, in the Shawnee Mission High School District were exported to segregated schools in Kansas City, a few miles to the north (*Kansas City Star*, June 11, 1949). No blacks attended the Shawnee Mission High School. To some extent, it is surprising that any black families lived within the attendance boundaries of the Shawnee Mission High School District or in District #90. Since the turn of the century, legislators and local government officials had been complicit to a regional real estate industry that gained national notoriety for designing and constructing vast expanses of racially restricted housing development. Gotham (2000) shows that between 1900 and 1947, 97 percent of the developed acreage in Johnson County was racially restricted as were 96 percent of Johnson County subdivisions.

Eventually, *Brown* invalidated the special exception provisions for cities of the first class and for Kansas City that permitted establishment of segregated schooling. Baker and Green (2005) show that by that time, however, the state's black population had, through racially restricted real estate development, been boxed in tightly to only a handful of zip codes in a handful of cities, primarily the pre-*Brown* cities of the first class. Those patterns of racial residential segregation remain largely in place to this day. As in many southern states, the *Brown* decision did not eliminate the role of race in Kansas public schooling, but instead ushered in a new era of public policy development in Kansas requiring, in the eyes of some, a stronger state role.

Progressive Legislative Reforms of the 1960s

The first major wave of education reform that occurred in the post-*Brown* era in Kansas involved the reorganization of Kansas public schools. These attempts included the School Unification Act of 1963 (revised in 1965). Previous attempts at consolidation had been overturned on the partial basis that the legislature lacked the authority to delegate control to county level committees to oversee and manage consolidation (*Donaldson v. Hines*, 1947; *School District, Joint No. 71, Rooks County v. Throckmorton*, 1962). In the 1963 act, the legislature adopted an alternative strategy of delegating oversight to the State Superintendent of Public Instruction. Every significant procedure in the process, including ratification of local elections, required the state superintendent's decision or approval (State Department of Public Instruction, 1967).

Perhaps questioning whether they were again walking on tenuous ground in allocating so much authority to the State Superintendent of Public Instruction, legislators sought to redraft the state's constitution to specifically grant themselves the authority to do what they had already done. An eleven-member citizen task force was formed to make recommendations to legislators regarding guiding principles for revision of Article 6 of the constitution. The proposed language for a new Article 6 included, among other things, the following:

> Section 1: The legislature *shall* provide for intellectual, educational, vocational, and scientific improvement by establishing and maintaining public schools, educational institutions, and related activities which may be organized and changed in such manner as may be provided by law.
>
> Section 2: (a) The legislature *shall* provide for a state board of education which shall have general supervision of public schools, educational institutions and all the educational interests of the state, except educational functions delegated by law to the state board of regents. The state board of education shall perform such other duties as may be provided by law.
>
> Section 5: Local public schools under the general supervision of the state board of education shall be maintained, developed, and operated by locally elected boards. When authorized by law, such boards may make and carry out agreements for cooperative operation and administration of educational programs under the general supervision of the state board of education, but such agreements shall be subject to limitation, change, or termination by the legislature.
>
> Section 6: The legislature *shall* make suitable provision for finance of the educational interests of the state. No tuition shall be charged for attendance at any public school to pupils required by law to attend such school, except such fees or supplemental charges as may be authorized by law. The legislature may authorize the state board of regents to establish tuition, fees, and charges at institutions under its supervision.

A notable omission in the new Article 6 was any mention of a preference for uniformity or equality of educational opportunity. The uniform systems clause had played a major role in pre-*Brown* segregation litigation under the "separate but equal" standard. The uniformity clause defined a high standard of equality, but uniformity had now been replaced with suitability, a more subjective standard granting the legislature the opportunity to treat individuals differently, at least under Article 6.

The new Article 6 was ratified in 1966 just as the Unification Act of 1963 reached completion of phase-in. Eventually, under the School Unification Law of 1963, the total number of school districts in the state was reduced from approximately 1,600 to 306. Concurrently, in 1965 the legislature enacted the first organized state level system for allocating aid to local public schools: the School Foundation Act. Major provisions of the act included a basic allotment of $760 per pupil and included two major adjustments to that allotment: (1) an adjustment based on teacher education and experience levels; and (2) a multiplier based on each district's pupil-to-teacher ratio relative to the state average. In addition, the legislature implemented strict limits to budget growth (limits to local taxing authority) under the act. With the School Foundation Act, the state share of school funding rose from about 23.7 percent in 1960–1961 to about 35.3 percent in 1965–1966. At this point in time, state funding was at nearly the same level as local school district funding (35.6 percent), with county level funding making up 20 percent (State Department of Public Instruction, 1967). This balance of revenues placed Kansas at slightly lower state control than the national average at that time (Institute of Education Sciences, National Center for Education Statistics, 2005).

Reflecting on the 1960s Reforms

On the one hand, Kansas education governance reforms of the 1960s are consistent with the view of the *old* Kansas as a progressive, populist state. However, while the reforms of the 1960s might be seen as purely progressive in the *old* Kansas tradition, they may also be evaluated in an alternative light. For example, the Unification Act of 1963 served to solidify the boundaries between black and white school districts in the state during a period when those school districts had been forced to eliminate racially segregated schooling within. As such, within those districts, whites could no longer escape blacks, leading to white flight into neighboring districts where residential housing remained racially restricted at least through 1962, despite U.S. Supreme Court precedents rendering such restrictions unenforceable (Gotham, 2000). The Unification Act strengthened the operational viability of rural and small town districts adjacent to cities and towns serving nearly 100 percent of the state's black population. In some cases, predominantly white unified school districts were formed within the municipal boundaries of cities of the first class. School districts were retained as separate and segregated even where the land on which the districts sat had been annexed into cities of the first class (History of the KCKs Public Schools Beginning July 1, 1844, n.d.). Population had already begun declining in rural outlying districts and pressure was already being felt to consolidate rural and small town districts with larger towns and nearby cities (State Department of Public Instruction, 1967). By reorganizing rural and small town districts amongst themselves, those districts would not be forced to consolidate and integrate with larger towns or cities.

One might also perceive implementation of an organized system of finance to be a step that could lead only to greater equity and adequacy of school funding over time. Yet, the Kansas legislature managed to use state control over school funding to create and perpetuate school funding disparities that, for the next forty years, would systematically disadvantage those few districts in cities and towns of over 15,000 residents serving nearly all of the state's black population (Baker & Green, 2005). Baker and Green (2005) as well as the Education Trust (2005) identify Kansas as having among the largest, systematic gaps in funding across school districts serving high and low minority concentrations.

What is so unique about Kansas is that these black–white disparities in question came about as a direct function of highly centralized reorganization of public schooling in Kansas and highly centralized control over the financing of schools. Without such a high degree of state control, it is unlikely that Kansas legislators would have been able to perpetuate this combination of racial segregation and financial disparity. In short, taking full state control of the Kansas system of public schooling in the 1960s allowed the Kansas legislature to codify, through district boundaries, highly racially segregated schooling and then through school finance policy to systematically disadvantage predominantly black schools for decades to follow.

The Role of School Finance Litigation

By the time the first legal challenge to state financing of public schools came about in Kansas, the legislature, under its newly drafted constitutional authority, had already taken full control over the organization and governance of public schools in Kansas and was already allocating over 35 percent of public school funding, with an additional 20 percent coming from county sources. That is, local unified school district control over finances had already been reduced to well less than a majority share. As such, it would be a stretch, at best, to attribute centralization of Kansas schooling to activist judicial interpretations of the legislature's role, under Article 6, Section 6 in financing schools. Article 6, Section 6 had just been adopted and no litigation invoking Article 6 had yet been filed. Further, the legislature had already adopted policies regulating school district budget growth and increases to local taxation for public schools.

Early Litigation over Legislative Actions in School Finance

Specific provisions of the 1965 School Foundation Act brought about the first round of school finance litigation in the state in 1973. In particular, the court was asked to address three major deficiencies with the school finance formula. First, districts with well-trained and experienced teachers received more state funding than districts with less experienced teachers. That is, they got more simply because they had more. Second, the pupil-to-teacher ratio multiplier put large, urban districts at a disadvantage by placing significantly more state funding into the coffers of small, rural districts with fewer pupils per teacher (Green & Baker, 2005). Third, the index used for determining local tax effort harmed poor school districts in rich counties because the expected contribution of a poor district was computed as equal to that of more affluent districts in the same county (Berger, 1998).

Another provision of the act restricted the budgetary authority of school districts. School districts were prohibited from increasing their budgets annually by more than 4 percent. This provision had the effect of codifying existing inequalities between rich and poor school districts because the provision was put into place on top of (a) provisions of the 1965 Act that granted more funding to already advantaged districts and (b) disparities in local revenue raising that had existed prior to the 1965 act.

In 1972, the Johnson County District Court ruled in *Caldwell v. State* that the school finance system violated the Equal Protection Clause to the extent that it "[made] the educational system of the child essentially the function of, and dependent on, the wealth of the district in which the child resides" (quoted in *Unified School District No. 229 v. State*, 1994, p. 1177). Note again that funding was highly related to local wealth NOT because of local discretion over school district taxes, but because the legislature had defined a system whereby lower wealth and especially larger districts would receive a smaller defined allotment and were then not allowed to increase their budgets at a higher rate to catch up. The court did not deny the legislature's authority to implement strict limits on school district budget growth.

Following legal challenges to the School Foundation Act, the legislature adopted the first iteration of the School District Equalization Act (SDEA). SDEA replaced the pupil-to-teacher ratio adjustment with different-sized base budgets for districts of different size. SDEA provided districts with fewer than 400 students a base budget of $936 per pupil and districts with more than 1,300 students a base budget of $728 per pupil. That is, the previous mechanism was replaced with state-defined allotments not directly associated with staffing parameters, but ultimately replicating the distributional effect of the previous mechanism.

In addition, the state established new limits on annual budget growth and tied those limits to district size groups. Districts above the median spending of districts in their size group could increase their budget by 5 percent per year. Districts below the median spending of districts in their size group could increase their budget to the lower of (a) 5 percent above the median or (b) a 15 percent increase over the previous year. This policy would lead to a ratcheting effect over the next eighteen years, whereby higher-funded enrollment categories (small districts) could significantly outpace revenue growth of lower-funded enrollment categories (large districts). That is, the same patterns of disparity would not only continue to exist, but the state-defined disparities would widen in dollars over time since state-controlled growth rates were established on a percentage basis and districts could adjust their budgets relative to others in their same size group. In effect, the legislature was micromanaging the system toward increased disparity, with the biggest losers being larger cities and towns that were home to the state's minority population.

The second round of challenges to state school finance policy came in 1976, in *Knowles v. State Board of Education* (1976). Plaintiffs challenged the constitutionality of the SDEA on the ground that it violated the Bill of Rights of the state constitution and the Equal Protection Clause of the U.S. Constitution. The Chautaqua County District Court struck down the SDEA because "the distribution of state funds under the formula provided in the Act resulted in unequal benefits to certain school districts and an unequal burden of ad valorem school taxes on taxpayers in various districts with no rational classification or basis" (p. 700). The district court also held that the SDEA's provision for school funding "was not sufficient to enable the plaintiffs to provide a fundamental education for the students within the respective districts on a rationally equally basis with students of other school districts within the state as required in the state constitution" (p. 700).

However, the district court took judicial notice that the state legislature was in session when it entered judgment and gave the legislature time to correct the inequalities. The legislature then amended the SDEA to address the deficiencies identified by the district court. For instance, the limitation on school budget increases was raised from 5 percent to 10 percent, and in some instances 15 percent. That is, under pressure from the court, legislators relaxed the restrictions on budget growth they themselves had pro-actively implemented. "District wealth" was also redefined to be an average of the previous three years to "soften any sharp increase or decrease in either the adjusted valuation or the taxable income within a district" (p. 700). The district court then dismissed the case as moot because the amendments to the SDEA were substantial enough to constitute an entirely new law.

The Kansas Supreme Court vacated the lower court's dismissal because "[t]he ultimate effect of the formula depends upon the use of similar factors contained in the prior law such as district wealth, local effort, budget per pupil and sales ratio to local assessed valuations" (p. 705). Thus, the constitutional questions raised by the plaintiffs' claims still remained unsolved. The case was remanded to the Shawnee County District Court because the record was insufficient to decide on these constitutional issues. The district court upheld the SDEA in 1981—seven years after *Knowles* had been originally filed. Again, no pressure was provided by the courts to substantially alter the legislature's approach to financing schools.

Mock & USD 229

SDEA came under fire in the late 1980s through 1991, with forty-two districts across the state taking four separate legal challenges to Shawnee County District Court. District Court Judge Terrence Bullock consolidated these cases into a single case and issued a pre-ruling indicating that if the case went to trial, he would likely declare SDEA in violation of both equal protection and Article 6, Section 6 of the state constitution that mandates that the legislature "make suitable provision for finance of the educational interests of the state." Judge Bullock as an individual and through his actions during this time period is often credited with orchestrating the shift from a system of locally controlled schools to the new highly centralized system of Kansas schooling. Yet, we have already shown that the assumption that Kansas schooling was locally controlled in the pre-*Mock* era is largely incorrect.

Judge Bullock's pre-ruling was issued October 14, 1991, after which Governor Joan Finney immediately convened a task force that produced its recommendations for reforming the school finance formula in November. The eleven-member task force (déjà vu) recommended a financing method that would set an equal tax rate across Kansas school districts and provide each district with a flat amount of basic operating aid. The task force also recommended that it would be appropriate to include some adjustment to that general fund budget to help sustain small, rural districts, and other adjustments to help districts cope with increased numbers of at-risk and limited English-speaking children.

During the legislative session of the spring of 1992, it appeared as if no solution would be reached on a new school finance plan. In April 1992, after the regular session of the legislature adjourned failing to pass two separate plans, Judge Bullock warned the legislature that if they failed to comply with his preliminary ruling by June 1, he would order the schools closed in the fall. During the "veto session" that convened on April 29, the School District Finance (SDF) Act, coupled with accountability legislation, the Quality Performance Accreditation Act (QPA), was passed into law (together, SDFQPA).

In general, the legislature followed the task force recommendations. Notable features of the new state school finance formula included a very large adjustment to compensate small school districts, based solely on what they had been spending in 1991, a sizeable adjustment (25 percent) for the number of children attending new school facilities, received initially by only a handful of suburban districts and relatively small adjustments for children qualifying for free lunch (6 percent) and children participating in bilingual education programs.[1] In addition, the legislature carried on its tradition of tax and expenditure limits by setting a strict revenue cap of 25 percent above districts basic per pupil allotment.

In short, like previous funding formulas dating back to 1965, the School District Finance Act froze into place prior disparities, leaving specifically large cities and towns at the bottom of the spending distribution. Under SDF in the 1990s, more than 90 percent of the variations in school funding across Kansas school districts were a function of state control, not local control (Baker, 2003). Arguably, the Kansas legislature could have achieved a much fairer system with a much lower degree of state control. Instead, the Kansas legislature chose to adopt an unfair system—built almost entirely on past funding disparities—almost entirely under state control.

State Control and Inequality: Contrasting Kansas and Missouri Reforms

Contrasting Kansas and Missouri school finance reforms of the 1990s illustrates this point. Interestingly, Missouri, like Kansas, faced a state district court decision over their school finance formula in 1993. District court judge Byron Kinder declared the system of finance unconstitutional in *Committee for Educational Equality v. State*. Missouri's system of school funding was, in fact, more highly locally controlled than the Kansas system of the day, with no limits to local taxation and no specific floor of local tax effort or state support. The Missouri legislature responded to the CEE decision with the Outstanding Schools Act. In contrast to the highly state controlled School District Finance Act in Kansas, the Missouri legislature increased the local share requirement and also increased matching aid that could be received by districts choosing to levy higher local tax rates, with additional weighting for children in poverty and an adjustment to district matching aid rates based on district income levels. No other "cost" adjustments or major factors differentiating funding levels were introduced in Missouri.

Figure 7.1 tracks the events in Kansas and Missouri, alongside national trends in the percent of schooling revenue from state sources from 1990 to 2000. Nationally, state share of school funding climbed toward 50 percent during this

FIGURE 7.1 Litigation and Reforms in Kansas and Missouri and the State Share of Education Funding

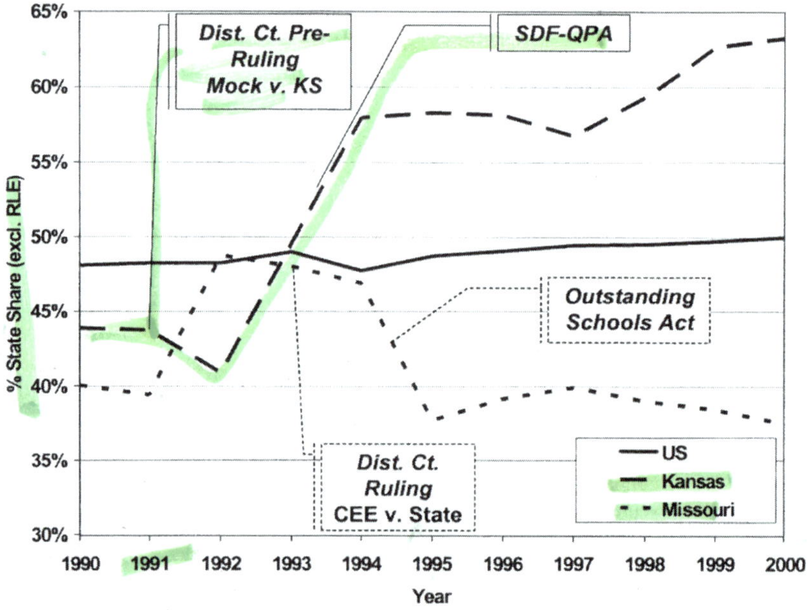

FIGURE 7.2 Cost Adjusted Coefficients of Variation of Current Expenditures per Pupil for Kansas and Missouri Districts from 1990 to 2000

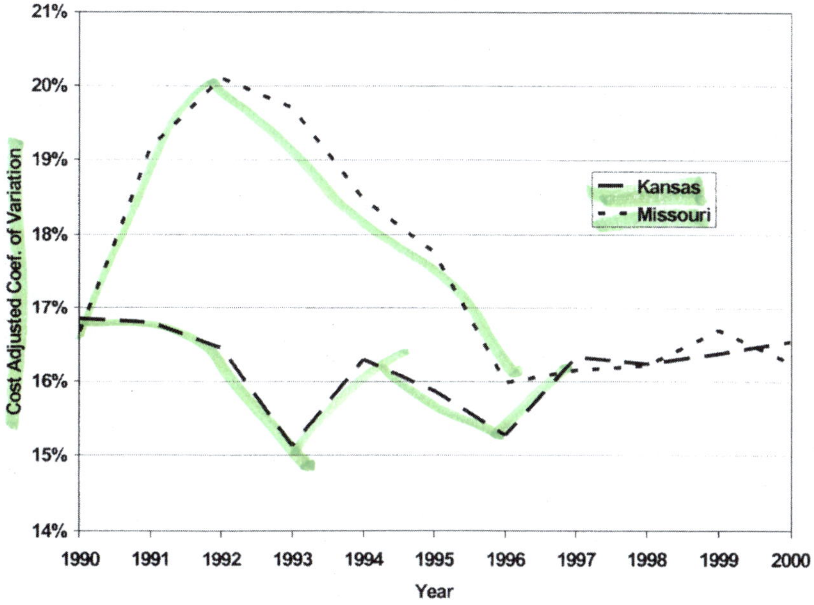

period. In 1990, both Kansas and Missouri fell between 40 and 45 percent state funded. Following Judge Bullock's *Mock* ruling, the Kansas share of state source funding climbed toward 60 percent. The Kansas share jumped above 60 percent in 1998 when the Kansas legislature chose to cut dramatically local property taxes. By contrast, following the CEE ruling, under the Outstanding Schools Act the state share in Missouri actually decreased to below 40 percent, as local districts raised additional local taxes to gain access to additional state aid.

The common assumption would be that equity must have improved far more in Kansas than in Missouri because the Kansas legislature had adopted much greater state level control. Not only that, but Kansas had adopted numerous major adjustments in aid allocation, on the argued basis of different costs of education. Missouri had introduced only one weight for children in poverty, and allowed their system to be driven primarily by local taxing decisions. Figure 7.2, however, shows the cost adjusted coefficients of variation for Current Expenditures per Pupil in Kansas and Missouri districts from 1990 to 2000. In each state, district current expenditures per pupil are adjusted for differences in the costs of achieving state-mandated outcome levels on state assessments, given districts student population characteristics, economies of scale, and regional labor costs. An education cost function methodology was used to estimate cost indices for each district. For Kansas, cost function estimates prepared by Duncombe and

Yinger (2006) for the Division of Post Audit for the Kansas legislature were used. In Missouri, cost function estimates were generated by the authors, and appear in Baker (2006). Duncombe and Johnston (2004) and Reschovsky and Imazeki (2004) use similar approaches to evaluating cost adjusted equity.

Figure 7.2 shows that equity in Kansas improved slightly between 1992 and 1993, but from 1996 through 2000, the coefficient of variation remained between 16 and 17 percent. Duncombe and Johnston (2004) also find that "disparities in cost-adjusted spending have not generally been reduced since the reform." (p. 147) By contrast, Missouri, which reduced rather than increasing its state share of funding, managed to dramatically reduce the coefficient of variation for cost-adjusted current expenditures between 1993 and 1996. From 1996 to 2000, the two state systems were similarly equitable, or similarly disparate.

The major difference in resource distribution between the two states is that, in Missouri, poor urban, predominantly black school districts were able to raise their own tax rates to disproportionately high levels to achieve more adequate funding. Notably, the Kansas City School District had its high local property tax rate forced on it by federal court in the case of *Missouri v. Jenkins*. In contrast to Kansas, Missouri is among those states where districts with higher concentrations of black children have systematically higher nominal (though lower adjusted) spending per pupil, albeit by inequitable taxation, highly statistically associated with district black concentration (Baker, 2006). In Kansas, under greater state control, districts with higher concentrations of black children were first provided less need-adjusted general funding, and then prohibited from raising additional funding locally in order to meet their actual rather than state-defined needs. Imazeki (2001) describes a similar effect of Wisconsin tax and expenditure limits on Milwaukee schools, and Baker (2005) shows that Nebraska's school finance formula, which applies budget growth limits by district groupings (similar to SDEA in Kansas in the 1970s), prohibits the city of Omaha from achieving its necessary funding. In short, by exercising a high degree of state control, the Kansas legislature was not attempting to promote greater equity, but rather actively micromanaging inequity, deciding from Topeka who should be advantaged and who disadvantaged across the state.

Nonetheless, the appearance of a more rational system was sufficient for Judge Bullock to dismiss some of the consolidated cases and transfer jurisdiction of the remaining cases, based on the new law, to Judge Marla Luckert (Shavers, 2005). After a trial, Judge Luckert ruled in 1993 that the SDF did not violate Article 6, Section 6 of the state constitution. Luckert did find that the act's small school district adjustment provision violated the state equal protection provision. Luckert was the first state court judge since *Caldwell* and *Knowles* to raise concerns over the way the Kansas legislature was exercising state control over school funding.

The Kansas Supreme Court agreed with the lower court's assessment that the act did not violate the state's "suitable provision for finance" clause because the school districts were presently meeting the accountability standards developed by the legislature. However, the Kansas Supreme Court reversed the lower court's finding that the SDF's low enrollment weighting policy violated state equal protection provision, noting that "[p]lain common sense advises there is a rational basis for the allowance of extra funding for low enrollment situations" (*Unified School District No. 229 v. State*, 1994, p. 1192).

In short, the state courts had again merely affirmed the legislature's authority to (1) adopt a highly centralized system of financing schools, (2) provide vastly different amounts of funding to schools and districts across the state, and (3) apply strict limits to supplemental local property taxation for schools. The Supreme Court's decision went to the extreme of granting the legislature wide latitude to create whatever disparities in funding they might so choose, so long as the legislature could articulate a reason that met the *common sense* test. The Supreme Court at that time was unwilling to suggest that the legislature had used its substantial control over school funding inappropriately.

The decision to implement SDF, while under pressure of county district court, was under no formal judicial ruling and largely followed guidelines laid out in a citizen task force convened under the governor. The Kansas legislature, while significantly divided, had taken another incremental step toward increased state control. That said, the legislature had merely re-codified in school finance policy, twenty-five years of legislatively managed funding disparities resulting in roughly the same winners and losers that existed in the immediate post-*Brown* era.

Recent School Finance Litigation Challenging Legislative Actions

The most recent round of challenges placed renewed scrutiny on the ways in which the legislature had exerted its control over school funding toward creating inequities. The issue of misapplication of state control over school funding, raised by Judge Luckert in 1994, was again raised in district court by Judge Terry Bullock in 2003. Until this point, the judicial branch and most onlookers, except for Judge Luckert, had simply assumed that a more highly state-controlled system of school finance must be fairer and more rational and therefore allowed the legislature to go on their way, micromanaging a system of carefully disguised policies to perpetuate educational inequality.

In fact, in pre-*Brown* cases heard (1) under the *Plessy v. Ferguson* separate but equal standard for black and white accommodations and (2) under the previous 1859 constitutional language mandating a *uniform system* of schooling, the Kansas courts often imposed an even stricter standard of teacher credential and school facilities quality for black and white children. It is possible that modern comparison of facilities quality and teacher qualifications across predominantly black and predominantly white schools in Kansas would fail to meet the "equal" or "uniform" standard applied in pre-*Brown* cases. In retrospect, the removal of the *uniform systems* clause in 1966 may have been an intentional act to increase legislative authority to apply differential treatment across Kansas schoolchildren.

In *Montoy v. Kansas*, Bullock first reflected on the 1992 decision and subsequent reforms: "At the time of the adoption of this new financing scheme, this Court believed that funds under the new plan would be equally distributed for the benefit of all Kansas children." Judge Luckert, however, was concerned about whether the low enrollment weighting (extra funds for "small districts") would eventually skew the equity of funding distribution. Nevertheless, the Supreme Court, impressed that the scheme contained objective criteria for fairness and quality and a high-powered committee, consisting primarily of legislative leaders, to oversee future fairness in implementation, approved it conceptually. Sadly, for the children of Kansas, Judge (now Justice) Luckert's concerns were prophetic (*Montoy v. State*, 2003, p. 31).

Regarding the small district weighting, Judge Bullock noted:

> [T]his weighting factor was also based solely on the spending history from the prior, unconstitutional SDEA and not from any actual or even estimated costs to operate such schools. Once again, *the inequities of the old law were frozen into the new*. (p. 30, emphasis added)

The Kansas Supreme Court adopted a peculiar *split-the-difference* perspective, agreeing with Judge Bullock that the current system of finance violated Article 6, Section 6 of the constitution but determining that the system did not violate the equal protection clause, applying the *common sense* test used in 1994 to evaluate the differences in funding created by the legislature. However, the Supreme Court did determine that the various differences in funding created by the Kansas Legislature were *politically distorted* and therefore in violation of Article 6 (not suitable). That is, the state-controlled system of inequity was on the one hand *common sense*, but on the other hand *politically distorted*.

While the Supreme Court recognized that the legislature had created a politically distorted system, the court applied little or no pressure on the legislature to actually correct the distortions across Kansas children by race, ethnicity, and socioeconomic status. Instead, the court gave the legislature total spending targets to reach, granting the legislature wide latitude as to who would receive more and who would receive less funding. While under court oversight between 2005 and 2006, the Kansas legislature did correct, to some extent, the political distortions that had emerged over the past forty years. In addition, the legislature raised but did not eliminate caps on revenue raising, likely leading to a reduction in state share, but possibly compromising equity.

However, the legislature also introduced new, legislatively controlled inequities, including a new cost adjustment for districts with housing unit values in excess of 25 percent above state average. This adjustment, it was argued, would allow districts with high-priced houses to recruit and retain teachers. While the high court noted that "the evidence at trial demonstrated that it is the districts with high-poverty, high at-risk student populations that need additional help in attracting and retaining good teachers," the court eventually let this new distortion pass, just as previous Kansas courts had let other substantial distortions pass or be replicated under new disguise. In the summer of 2006, the court dismissed *Montoy* on the basis that the legislature had allocated a large portion of the total amount the court mandated; they allowed this new distortion and others to be implemented. However, the court deferred on whether current law was constitutional.

Conclusions and Implications

In short, the Kansas saga paints a very different view from common perception about judicial and legislative roles in state school finance and governance and the relationship between state control and equity. Kansas legislators themselves, through no prompting by the courts, made a bold power grab in the 1960s, first through statutes governing organization of schools then through revising the constitution to grant them more power and responsibility. Further, the legislature removed language requiring uniform treatment of the state's children. From that point forward, Kansas legislators actively used greater state control to create inequity in school funding, across school districts that they had actively organized to be racially segregated—even in the face of judicial opposition.

Amazingly, after implementation of supposed bold, progressive 1990s reforms, Kansas school finance remained as inequitable as Missouri school finance, a state often credited with one of the least equitable school funding systems in the nation (see *Education Week*, 2005). While we lack direct measures, one might suspect that previous reforms in 1965, 1973, and 1976 were comparably ineffective. All along, while the legislature has incrementally stepped up control over state financing of schools, the role of the courts has merely been to affirm that the legislature did indeed have the authority exert significant control over school funding. Only in a handful of circumstances have the courts questioned the use of that authority and even more rarely have the courts actually demanded that the legislature use their control over financing to improve rather than erode equity.

Kansas policymakers past and present have favored strong state control over public elementary and secondary education for a variety of reasons. Consistent threads over time include the legislature's desire to maintain a high level of control over who goes to school where and who wins and who loses, especially in terms of finance. Further, greater state control has allowed the legislature to forestall scrutiny on their actions because, in school finance, inaction is perceived to be the most significant source of inequity. Not so in Kansas.

Note

1. The weight was set at 20 percent, but only attainable for Full Time FTE Bilingual Education Program students, where Full Time meant six full contact hours per day. On average children received only two to three contact hours, effectively halving this weight, making well less than half the weight used for children in new facilities.

References

Baker, B. D. (2006). Missouri's state school finance formula fails to guarantee equal or minimally adequate educational opportunity to Missouri schoolchildren. Prepared for plaintiff districts in *Committee for Educational Equality v. State.*

Baker, B. D. (2005). Nebraska's state school finance policy fails to provide equal opportunity for Nebraska school children. Prepared for plaintiff districts in *Douglas County School District v. Heineman.*

Baker, B. D. (2003) *Wide of any reasonable mark: Evaluating the suitability of the Kansas School District Finance Act.* Expert Testimony in the case of *Montoy v. Kansas.* Report commissioned by Schools for Fair Funding, Inc., Newton, KS.

Baker, B. D., & Green, P. C. (2005). Tricks of the trade: Legislative actions in school finance that disadvantage minorities in the post-*Brown* era. *American Journal of Education 111* (May), 372–413.

Berger, C. (1998). Equity without adjudication: Kansas school finance reform and the 1992 School District Finance and Quality Performance Act. *Journal of Law and Education 27* (January), 1–46.

Committee for Educ. Equal. v. State, No. CV190-1371CC (Cir. Ct. Cole County Jan. 15, 1993)

Donaldson v. Hines, 182 P.2d 865 (Kan. 1947).

Duncombe, W. D., & Johnston, J. (2004). The impacts of school finance reform in Kansas: Equity is in the eye of the beholder. In J. Yinger (Ed.), *Helping children left behind: State aid and the pursuit of educational equity* (pp. 147–194). Cambridge, MA: MIT Press.

Duncombe, W. D., & Yinger, J. (2006) *Estimating the costs of meeting student performance outcomes mandated by the Kansas State Board of Education.* Topeka: Kansas Legislative Division of Post Audit, 2006—January. Retrieved March 1, 2006, from http://www.kslegislature.org/postaudit/audits_perform/05pa19a.pdf.

Education Trust. (2005). The Funding Gap Report 2005: Low-income and minority students shortchanged by most states. Washington, DC: Author (www.edtrust.org).

Education Week. (2005). No small change: Targeting money toward student performance. Quality Counts 2005.

Gotham, K. F. (2000). Urban space, restricted covenants, and the origins of racial residential segregation in a U.S. city. *International Journal of Urban and Regional Research 24*(3), 616–632.

Green, P., & Baker, B. (2005). *Montoy v. State* and state racial finance disparities: Did the Kansas courts get it right this time? *West's Education Law Reporter, 195*, 681–696.

History of the KCKs Public Schools. (n.d.). Available at http://www.kckps.org/disthistory/pdf%20files/school_history_1-short.pdf.

Imazeki, J. (2001, November 8–10). School revenue limits: Evidence from Wisconsin. National Tax Association 94th Annual Conference, Baltimore, MD.

Institute of Education Sciences, National Center for Education Statistics. (2005). Digests of education statistics, tables, and figures: 2005. Available at http://nces.ed.gov/programs/digest/d05/tables/dt05_152.asp.

Johnston, J., &Duncombe, W. D. (1998). Balancing conflicting policy objectives: the case of school finance reform. *Public Administration Review 58*(2), 145–158.

Knowles v. State Bd. of Educ., 547 P.2d 699 (Kan. 1976).

Montoy v. State, 2003 WL 22902963 (Kan. Dist. Ct. Dec. 2, 2003).

Reschovsky, A., & Imazeki, J. (2004). School finance reform in Texas: A never-ending story? In J. Yinger (Ed.), *Helping children left behind: State aid and the pursuit of educational equity* (pp. 251–282). Cambridge: MIT Press.

Reynolds v. Board of Educ. of City of Topeka, 72 P.2d 274 (Kan. 1903).

School Dist., Joint No. 71, Rooks County v. Throckmorton, 370 P.2d 89 (Kan. 1962).

Shavers, A. (2005). Closing the school doors in the pursuit of equal education opportunity: A comment on *Montoy v. State*, 2003 WL 22902963. *Nebraska Law Review, 81*, 901–914.

State Department of Public Instruction. (1967). The state department of public instruction 1945–1967: Part III—division of administrative services. Available at http://www.kckps.org/disthistory/state_school_history/throckmorton/throckmorton_1945-1967_pt3.htm.

Unified Sch. Dist. No. 229 v. State, 885 P.2d 1170 (Kan. 1994).

Webb v. School Dist. No. 90, Johnson County, 206 P.2d 1066 (Kan. 1949).

Part II

Comparative and National Trends

Chapter 8

The Roots of Difference in State Educational Policy

Karen Seashore, Molly Gordon,
Judy Meath, and Emanda Thomas

In the United States, "ownership" of educational policy is hotly contested. Historically, there has been a tension over who sets educational policy. Over time, there have been periods in which the state has taken the initiative to control education, while at other times, local interests have prevailed (Timar, 1997). The Web site of the federal Department of Education proclaims that in "the U.S., the federal role in education is limited. Because of the Tenth Amendment, most education policy is decided at the state and local levels" (http://www.ed.gov/policy/landing.jhtml). However, following the enactment of the federal No Child Left Behind legislation, some observers have suggested that the traditionally decentralized state and local approach to educational policy was under serious challenge (Bracey, 2004). In addition, there has been a strong thrust in the last twenty-five years toward private and/or parent-controlled education, which has increased since the introduction of charter schools and the authorization of home schooling in most states, along with efforts to introduce school vouchers. One of the consequences of the patchwork of individual, local, state, and federal decisions is that the landscape of educational policy in the United States is unusually fragmented and even chaotic compared to most other developed countries.

In this chapter, we focus on understanding only one piece of this broader landscape. Our emphasis is on the way in which *state policy culture* both enables and constrains the development of state initiatives in education. Of course we cannot ignore the broader debates about national–state trends, but, based on an analysis of three states, we concentrate on the distinctive nature of policy histories and cultures and the way in which these have led to differences in legislation around standards, accountability, and other initiatives designed to improve educational quality. We focus on three states that are not discussed in the other chapters of this volume, and that receive relatively limited attention in the more popular press and policy analyses.

A Framework for Analyzing Policy Cultures

The concept of policy cultures has shallow roots in the social sciences. The first empirical research using the concept began appearing in the 1960s, inspired by cross-national investigations of civic culture (Almond & Verba, 1963). By the early 1970s, political scientists began to borrow the idea of political culture, and to look at the way in which collective values and norms affected political decision-making (Elazar, 1970; Lehman, 1972; Putnam, 1971), and only a few years later the concept was sufficiently embedded that there were calls to reexamine and redefine it (Elkins & Simeon, 1979). By the late 1980s, the empirical evidence was sufficient that authors claimed, with certainty, that "measures of political culture can help explain both differences between states and variations within a state in political mobilization processes" (Conway, 1989), and shortly thereafter critical theorists had come to see the concept as a constraint to more in-depth empirical analysis of political systems (Somers, 1995). Here we will briefly describe how the concept has been used, and its empirical application to state policymaking. We then present our working definition that will be used in this chapter.

What Is Policy Culture?

Chilton (1988) notes that there is some consensus among both political scientists and sociologists that the concept of political culture is an important one, but he argues that there is little agreement over the meaning of the term, and he advocates a continued effort to determine how best to "redeem its promise" through empirical verification (Chilton, 1988). The traditional definition of political culture is the set of enduring political attitudes, values, and behaviors associated with groups that live in a defined geographical context (Elazar, 1970). Simple geographic proximity is, however, not enough: Evidence is also needed that there is a sense of shared membership, that the values are influenced and affirmed by group members and are publicly common, that they are associated with behavior regularities that have meaning for members, and that the dimensions that define the culture can be compared (between cultures) and are observable and testable.[1] Others follow a more traditional definition that associates political culture primarily with predominant attitudes that underlie the assumptions and rules governing political behavior (Wirt, Mitchell, & Marshall, 1985). Sociologists have also been involved in refining the conceptual underpinnings, drawing on European as well as U.S. theorists. Berezin (1997), for example, emphasizes the importance of boundaries, the intersection between political culture and concepts of "the civil society," democracy, social meaning, and collective action. Nevertheless, the concept is still relatively vague, and more often defined by the author's selection of indicators than by a simple, straightforward consensus about what it means. In this chapter, we focus exclusively on states, which, based on the literature, we assume have cultures that can be distinguished from the national political culture that is distinctively American.

Empirical Research on State Policy Culture

It is beyond the scope of this chapter to provide a comprehensive review of the empirical research on political culture, but it is important to illustrate that the concept has enduring value explaining political outcomes. Most studies of political culture have, until recently, looked at comparisons among national cultures (Almond, 1956; Merelman & Foster, 1978). Applications within the United States to states have been, however, increasing, and there is considerable evidence that state political cultures are associated with a wide variety of policy outcomes. Elazar's initial formulation and classification of three types of state political cultures—traditional, moralistic, and individualistic—was largely impressionistic, but political scientists quickly began to look for its ability to predict differences among states (Sharkansky, 1969). One early study (Johnson, 1976) achieved modest success in replicating Elazar's classification, and found associations between the state political culture types and dependent variables such as innovative government activity, encouragement of popular participation, and the level of party competition. Others have supported this finding. Wirt (1991) reported that there was extensive empirical evidence to link state policy initiatives and Elazar's simple classification, noting at the same time that embedded state policy cultures were sometimes temporarily overridden by "national tides of reform" (Wirt, 1991). A more recent review reported relatively consistent support across studies for the explanatory power of political culture on the state budgeting process and outcomes (Koven & Mausolff, 2002). Recent studies have continued to find effects of political culture, as distinct from political party affiliation, on outcomes as varied as state budget allocations, the election of women, and legislative activity around abortion (Arceneaux, 2001; Cook, Jelen, & Wilcox, 1993; Norrander, 2000). Others suggest that political culture is a more powerful explanatory variable in determining state actions than other contextual characteristics, such as affluence or industrialization (Morgan & Watson, 1991). In education, the use of political culture as a variable has been more limited, but a number of studies support both its descriptive utility and its ability to explain differences in some aspects of state policy initiatives (Merelman & Foster, 1978; Rice & Sumberg, 1997; Wirt, Mitchell, & Marshall, 1988; Wirt et al., 1985; Wong, 1989).

It is important to distinguish the concept of political culture from the increasingly popular notion of civic culture, although the two were linked in Almond and Verba's (1965) research. Civic culture includes at least four dimensions—civic engagement, political equality, tolerance, and trust, and social structures of cooperation—that are not, typically, a component of empirical research on political culture. While state political and civic cultures are, empirically, strongly related at the state level, at least one study suggests that they are not the same (Rice & Sumberg, 1997), and confounding them contributes, in our view, to some of the null findings in empirical research (Jackman & Miller, 1996).

Working Definition and Indicators of State Political Culture

We do not attempt to resolve the continuing muddiness in discussions of political culture, but use a definition that emphasizes its observable roots: Political culture is the repeated patterns of behavior that can be observed in the policymaking process within a permanent political entity, and the espoused values and beliefs that help to explain these regularities.[2] Under this definition, any permanent entity, ranging from an organization to a nation, may have a political culture.

As noted above, in the absence of a tight definition, political scientists have tended to identify specific social relations as key indicators that distinguish among states' political cultures (Herzik, 1985). Each of those elements has a corresponding pattern of political behavior. For example, in more open political cultures, the general public has substantial influence in determining the nature of government structures and political processes, while the more closed political cultures have stringent requirements for participation that may lessen the public's influence. The long-term effects of culture may not be visible in every legislative session because no government is entirely consistent. However, they become apparent over longer periods of time.

In pursuing our research, we have developed a definition of political culture that draws heavily on Elazar's formulation, which, along with later applications, reinforces the significance of four distinct dimensions of political culture (Herzik, 1985):

1. *Openness:* broad availability of political participation as contrasted with constrained or elite dominance.
2. *Decentralism:* distributed power sources; no one center versus concentration of power in the legislature or governor's office.
3. *Rationalism:* policies based on comprehensive and coherent solutions to social problems as contrasted with either multiple, unrelated initiatives or limited government activity.
4. *Egalitarianism:* persistent policies to redistribute resources to minimize disparities versus limited efforts in redistribution.

In addition, we rely on the empirical research that has applied the concept of political culture to educational settings (Marshall, Mitchell, & Wirt, 1986; Wirt et al., 1988), and incorporate the following additional dimensions:

5. *Efficiency:* an emphasis on economic cost-benefits and optimization of policy performance versus limited attention to input-output considerations (Wood & Theobald, 2003).
6. *Quality:* an elaborated and comprehensive state system of social/educational indicators and monitoring, versus a less systematic, laissez-faire approach to determining quality[3] (Bryk & Hermanson, 1993).
7. *Choice:* an emphasis on increasing options available to individual citizens (and, in the case of education, families) (Mazzoni, 1993; Whitty & Power, 2000).

Methods

This chapter draws on research conducted as part of a larger study of educational leadership. We used a qualitative methodology to compare education-related policymaking in nine states, which were randomly sampled to ensure regional representation. We utilized two sources of data in this study: state-level interviews states and reviews of easily accessible documents from journals, newspapers, and the Web.

The structured state-level interviews, our primary data source, were conducted via telephone with approximately ten education policy experts in each state between October 2004 and February 2005. We designed the state interview instrument to elicit respondents' assessments of the major education policy initiatives and issues of the past ten or so years, how those policies were developed, and by whom. Probes were used to ensure that respondents remarked on any policy activity in the areas of administrator licensure, evaluation and accountability standards, and capacity development.[4] State interview subjects were selected based on their professional positions. We identified positions that would yield, cumulatively, a comprehensive set of perspectives on state-level education policy and policymaking. Therefore, people interviewed included elected representatives, commissioners of education, chairs of state boards of education, teacher and administrative union leaders, university deans and faculty, heads of local/state foundations, and business leaders engaged in state education initiatives. We sent potential respondents letters of invitation, followed up with phone calls to schedule telephone interviews. State-level interviews lasted one hour. Trained interviewers tape-recorded each interview, with the respondent's consent, and all interviews were then transcribed for analysis. The literature and Web scans were conducted to obtain demographic information, and to verify findings that were discussed in the interviews.

In this chapter, we compare education policymaking in three of the nine states: Oregon, New Mexico, and Missouri. These states were selected because they are all of moderate size (thus eliminating the inherent complexity of policymaking in states like New York and Texas), but illustrate variations in their history of involvement with setting state policy in the areas under investigation.

Three State Policy Cultures

We have organized the presentation of our data using three narrative cases that provide background information about the state, a summary of recent legislative activity (focusing on standards and accountability), and a description of the role various actors have played in developing policy. In these narrative accounts we have embedded information that is reflective of the dimensions of political culture outlined above. In the subsequent section we will pull the culture dimensions out of the narrative in order to compare them.

Oregon

Historically, Oregon has created and enacted education policies that favor locally controlled progressive reforms. Oregon's political culture encourages large numbers of participants to come to the table to discuss issues and create policy. Specific groups, however, have higher levels of influence over issue development and policymaking in the state than others. These inner circle and near inner circle political groups usually get together to talk over issues and reach consensus prior to lobbying the legislature. This tendency to informally consult and create short-term but strong alliances may be due, in part, to a long-standing fear of any one group gaining too much power. Broad-reaching grassroots participation encourages organizations and political groups to collaborate with each other in order to be viewed as legitimate, but appears to discourage permanent alliances. Politically, the state is governed by voter initiatives and while many issues make it onto the ballot, most fail or are not enacted by the legislature.[5] This initiatives-based system, according to some state-level players, makes the process of getting special interest issues onto the ballot an open and easy process, but also time consuming and cumbersome since most initiatives fail.

Oregon has maintained this sense of local control even while plagued by fiscal concerns that placed primary control for education funding in the hands of the state, and a 1.5 percent property tax limit with the passage of Measure Five in 1991. Even though Oregon is moving in the direction of increasing state mandates, the culture and mentality of Oregonians have remained consistent. By 1993, several educational groups in Oregon cooperated to produce a comprehensive and rationalized system of standards and accountability called "Bringing Oregon Schools into the 21st Century." Although the state played a large role in helping to create standards, school districts were left to design their own assessment methods, a decision that is still contested today.

EDUCATIONAL ATTAINMENT. The creation of state standards and local assessments in Oregon has a long history, predating NCLB by a decade. Despite Oregon's early start, the standards and accountability reform movement in Oregon has garnered mixed results. According to the Quality Counts at 10 Report (*Education Week*, 2006), Oregon received a C+ on its standards and accountability system, slightly lower than the B− average of all states. Although the report indicated that Oregon has clear, specific, and content-grounded standards in four core subjects, state assessments are not well aligned with the standards. The Fordham Foundation Report, developed by a more conservative think tank, gave Oregon standards and accountability reforms an even lower evaluation. Overall, the state received a D in education reform and was ranked thirty-third out of the fifty states (Fordham Foundation, 2006). In addition, the Fordham Foundation reported that Oregon is making only minimal progress on achievement trends.

Even though the state received less than stellar marks from national policy analysts, it scores close to the U.S. average on NAEP assessments. Nevertheless, NCLB has revealed new challenges. Although the achievement gap for blacks and whites mirrors the U.S. gap, the gap between Hispanic students and white students is larger in Oregon. The state has made greater gains, however, in reducing the gap between school lunch eligible and non-eligible students compared with overall U.S. scores. Furthermore, in 2002, Oregon had a slightly higher rate of high school graduation than the overall United States, but, when broken down into subgroups, American Indian, Asian, Hispanic, and white students had below-average graduation rates. All of Oregon's largest high schools have failed to meet Adequate Yearly Progress. Only a fourth of Oregonian high school students graduate ready for college, yet the college bound students are among the highest scoring on the ACT/SAT tests.

In many ways, the standards and accountability movement, which had considerable momentum a decade ago, has been overshadowed by the concerns over finance equalization. Several key players argue that funding inequities have stalled the progress of revamping the current standards and the alignment process; this is the key reason cited for the downsizing of standards from all subjects to only the four core subjects. Because K–12 funding is determined by the state's economic performance, resource allocation is unstable and burdensome to districts, but efforts to overturn Measure Five have been unsuccessful.

LEGISLATIVE HISTORY. In 1993, "Bringing Oregon Schools into the 21st Century" launched the creation of standards-based curriculum across grade levels. In the beginning, the standards reform was seen as both a driver for education policy and a divider: On one side, this legislation sparked broad school reform conversations, but on the other, its most immediate effect was an increasing emphasis on testing students. Following the recommendation of national experts, the state tweaked that act in 1995 and added two levels of certification for students to reach during high school called the Certificate of Initial Mastery (CIM) and the Certificate of Advanced Mastery (CAM). By 1999, Oregon established school report cards; the calculation of the report uses both current levels of tested performance and a measure of continuous improvement over time. In addition, the report now also provide a snapshot of the percentage of student meeting standards every year, a by-product of adapting to federal No Child Left Behind legislation. Another policy adaptation in response to NCLB has been to change the state tests, which had originally been covering several subject matter areas, including the arts, to align them with required tenth grade testing.[6] The tweaked reform (HB 2744) reduced CIM/CAM to mathematics, science, and English standards and assessments, subjects with existing and implemented statewide assessments already aligned with NCLB. This move in 2003 was seen by many as chipping away at the original plan, a compromise that was reached reluctantly due to competing fiscal priorities. HB 2744 also postponed mandatory implementation of CAM until 2008, again due to budgetary concerns, and a call for streamlining of existing CAM assessments. Whether the implementation of the CIM/CAM initiative will be successful is yet to be determined; participation is not mandated, and few students pursue the CAM.

Despite the narrowing of curricular standards, Oregon has remained committed to multiple, locally created assessment methods. Although the state was the dominant player in creating the original standards, it was reluctant to determine the specifics of the district-level assessment methods because of the state's commitment to local participation. Thus, most school district assessment methods include a combination of state-developed paper-and-pencil tests that meet NCLB requirements, student work samples or portfolios, as well as grades. In addition, state assessments go beyond multiple-choice and include extended response and short-answer sections, a feature that was lauded by the 2006 *Education Week* report (*Education Week*, 2006).

Because of concerns over large high schools not meeting AYP and preliminary results from national comparisons, Oregon amended its high school graduation requirements in 2005 to include a greater number of credit hours and increased requirements in mathematics and English. According to the 2006 Fordham Foundation Report, the department of education in Oregon is reviewing all of its standards and accountability reforms over the next year (Fordham Foundation, 2006). A push to increase achievement in Oregon is not new; during the mid-1990s, the speaker of the house was authorized to develop a measure of education outcomes based on ideal schools that became known as the "Quality Education Act." The language of the act linked full state funding to student achievement, but this component of the act has not been implemented.

The issue of school choice is fairly new in Oregon and resulted in a 1999 law authorizing charter schools. By the mid-2000s, the number of charter schools in Oregon grew to fifty-seven, but, compared to other states, the total enrollment of students in charter schools is quite small, totaling only 5,076 students (Heritage Foundation, nd). Other recent efforts to increase parental choice in education include a voluntary interdistrict transfer policy.

WHO IS INVOLVED IN POLICYMAKING AND HOW THEY WORK TOGETHER. Because of the strength of localized control, local policy players appear to have as much or more power than the state over interpretation and implementation of new policies (with the exception of finance). Local leaders, therefore, do not see their job as part of any statewide effort to improve education. However, coalitions and groups band together to lobby at the state level—Oregon operates in a collaborative tradition in which groups, rather than individuals, are recognized as state policymakers. Consistent with Oregon's openness and preference for bringing several players to the table, large groups and coalitions talk about and decide the direction of educational policy. One informant described the State Department of Education as a "convener" because it invites all educational groups and organizations for open dialogue and discussion around educational issues in the state.

This intense push for building coalitions and collaboration in the education circles is fairly recent. Some influential players argue that the standards and accountability push, along with the funding shortages, has intensified the movement to collaborate at the state level, a trend one senator has said has grown in his twelve years in office. Yet, Oregonian political culture has consistently been known for its lack of "turf" and the ability to get every major and minor player in a room together to discuss and make policy. The Oregonian political party culture is strong, but reliably "purple," with Oregonians electing both Republicans and Democrats and expecting them to cooperate. In this way, communities and state education organizations often do come together and lobby for educational policies changes.

The main groups that regularly collaborate and convene at the state level are the Oregon School Boards Association (OSBA), the Confederation of Oregon School Administrators (COSA), the Oregon Business Council (OBC), and the Oregon Education Association (OEA). In recent years, Oregon governors have not prioritized K–12 education, focusing more on higher education. The Oregon Education Association (OEA) has a long history of working with professional educators and the state in lobbying for the interests of teachers and administrators. The OEA has been influential in all of the major funding initiatives in the state and was active in helping create the CIM/CAM and school report cards that are linked to the state standards. OEA works in collaboration with the Confederation of Oregon School Administrators (COSA) to lobby the legislature to increase school funding.

Businesses also have a strong voice on educational issues in Oregon. For example, the Oregon Business Council (OBC) is highly active and visible in education. The group had a role in the development of the 1993 as well as the CIM/CAM laws. Businesses in Oregon are well represented on education committees at the state level, lobbying for the enactment of various policies. Another group involved in education is the Oregon Business Association (OBA) although not to the extent of the OBC. Recently, the OBC, in collaboration with the OSBA, helped create the Employers for Educational Excellence (E-3) group. E-3 brings together various education stakeholders in an effort to build community support and will for change in the schools. The group plans to help communicate and develop plans that will push for a more aggressive timeline to make necessary changes so that all Oregon students meet standards.

Political participation is also encouraged at the local level where there are many grassroots organizations lobbying alone or more often with the state-level organizations mentioned earlier for particular policy issues. One initiative, "The Chalkboard Project," is a coalition of five foundations that have developed a civic engagement process with an action research component in public education. The project takes the pulse of education around the state and shares insights with state organizations in an effort to work with them to influence the direction of state policy. Out of that information gathering, the group plans to make recommendations to the legislature. Grassroots organizations have also popped up recently to try and combat the issue of funding in Oregon. One group called "Coalition for School Funding Now" consists of schools, parents, locally elected officials and business leaders who advocate for school funding in the legislature.

SUMMARY DISCUSSION OF STATE POLICY CULTURE. Oregon has remained consistent in its political culture throughout the years, even with changes in parties (currently Republicans control the house, but Democrats control the senate) and shifts in funding responsibilities. The commitment to localism remains despite a push toward more statewide uniformity that began before NCLB. Because of the tradition of decentralized policymaking, local players appear to have a dominant influence over interpretation and implementation of new educational policies. Local leaders do not see their job as part of a statewide program to improve education, but as policymakers at the local level. Community is also highly influential in education initiatives as well. Nevertheless, the state's emphasis on high standards determines the performance expectations of districts and their students. How districts achieve those goals, however is determined at the local level.

New Mexico

New Mexico is the poorest of the three states that we are examining, and its poverty rates, combined with the large numbers of immigrant and minority children, are an important backdrop to its political culture. In contrast to Oregon and Missouri, for example, New Mexico is a "majority minority" education state, with fewer than 35 percent of its K–12 enrollment classified as white, and nearly 60 percent of the children are eligible for free and reduced price meals—nearly 20 percent more than in the other two states. The state's weak economic climate may have contributed to a historically laissez-faire approach to education, which has largely relied on bootstrapping at the local level.

As a consequence of high poverty and recent immigration, New Mexico has one of the country's most serious gaps in educational attainment for adults: over 30 percent of adult Hispanic Americans and nearly as many Native Americans have less than a high school education (Kelley, 2005). However, analyses that connect the projected declines in the level of educational attainment in the state and the state's economic future have reinforced a sense of pressure about educational reform, and, in the past few years, the state has become one of the most active in pushing a state-wide educational agenda.

EDUCATIONAL ATTAINMENT. As assessed by NAEP scores, New Mexico's educational attainment has consistently been below the national average. There has been improvement in test scores over time, but performance for fourth and eighth graders in math and reading is still low and the gap between New Mexico averages and the national average in eighth grade mathematics is widening.[7] The achievement trends for low-income and minority students show little progress in "closing the gap."

Although student achievement is relatively low, two recent reports have given New Mexico high marks for its recent education reform efforts. The Fordham report ranks New Mexico among the top ten to fifteen states in the country for most of its policies relating to education reform, including the rigor of state standards and its insistence on including most of its minority and poor students in the national and state testing programs (Fordham Foundation, 2006). According to the recent *Education Week* analysis, the state also rated among the best in its standards and accountability, and its efforts to improve teacher quality—and it received an overall "grade" of B, one of only eight states to do so (*Education Week*, 2006). This dichotomy elicits many questions about how state policies and policy culture are intertwined with student achievement initiatives in the short and long run. One question that arises is what policy initiatives impress the outside reviewers with a national perspective. The one that we address, however, is how these policies have emerged in a state that appeared to have limited interest in active educational policymaking until recently.

LEGISLATIVE HISTORY. Prior to 2003, the New Mexico state legislature played the primary role in initiating educational policymaking in education. State policies around education were not uncommon, but were ad hoc and frequently focused on policies that affected specific districts, schools, or clusters of schools. These policies exemplify the limited state efforts to create a comprehensive solution to the challenges in education and the state's long history of weak academic achievement. Even adjustments to state law to accommodate the federal No Child Left Behind Act were limited in nature during the first two years after its passage.

This characteristic of New Mexico's legislative history and political culture changed markedly with the election of Governor Bill Richardson in 2003. He quickly made the issues of state standards and accountability systems a hallmark of his agenda, with an eye not simply to comply with NCLB but to improve test scores and graduation rates. However, his primary focus was on putting a quality teacher in every classroom, an issue that was a state concern prior to his inauguration. Although New Mexico has an extensive legislative history of involvement in local educational matters, New Mexico respondents identified no policies related to statewide accountability prior to Richardson's tenure. Earlier state initiatives, in addition to those targeted at specific schools, emphasized fiscal appropriations. However, even in that arena, the state was judged among the least adequate in providing funding to students with limited English proficiency (a large group in the state) (Baker, 2001). In the 1990s, the state began conversations about the problem of teacher shortages and salaries, as well as initiating a roundtable on K–16 initiatives, but few significant specific policies were initiated during this time.[8] The only policy initiative prior to 2003 that was highlighted by respondents was the Public Schools Finance Act of 1974, which addressed finance equalization.

Respondents described the 2003 New Mexico House Omnibus Bill 212, the School Reform Act, as a landmark. The bill included accountability provisions and measures to improve educational leadership, and outlined a plan for increasing teacher salaries, a top priority for Governor Richardson. The bill illustrates a three-tiered teacher licensure system, which compensates teachers for their quality and continuous professional development. The latter was also included in the bill as a requirement for licensure advancement. Improving the quality of school administrators was another focus of the bill. It outlined stringent expectations of principals to have increased competencies, be instructional leaders, and enforce accountability in their buildings. A task force has been formed to create a policy framework for professional development, as required by current state law.[9]

Another important aspect of the legislative process is the inclusion of greater stakeholder involvement and centralized decision-making authority. For example, a provision to House Bill 212 resulted in the creation of the Office of Education Accountability in the Department of Finance and Administration. This office provides independent assessments and support around educational reform, leadership, and accountability. Included in the bill was a shift in hiring personnel from the local school boards to district superintendents. This policy was contested in smaller districts where hiring became no longer a community process.

Moreover, Constitutional Amendment 1 (2003), called for a change in educational governance at the state level. The amendment shifted power from the Superintendent of Public Education and the State Board of Education to the State Secretary of Education and the New Mexico Public Education Dept (NM PED). As a cabinet position, the State Secretary of Education plays a primary role in working closely with the governor and shaping education policy.

Although comprehensive state leadership for school improvement is recent, New Mexico has a longer history of finance equalization. For example, in 1974, New Mexico's State Board of Education and legislature passed the Public Schools Finance Act that included a School Equalization Guarantee. Consequently, the funding formula is perceived as highly equitable, in that there are not wide differences in how schools are funded across the state. Constitutional Amendment 2, also introduced in 2003 and passed by voters, increased the distribution from the Land Grant Permanent Fund for Education to pay for increased teacher salaries instituted by Governor Richardson. By 2004, New Mexico finished its legislative session with a 6 percent budget increase for public education. Governor Richardson also proposed an increase in spending for K–12 education for 2005, which included putting $35 million in a lockbox for future improvements, increasing spending on charter schools, and reallocating 1 percent of local spending to classroom instruction.

The state has also passed legislations regarding educational attainment aimed at early childhood education. In 2005, the state passed HB 337, the Pre-Kindergarten Act that apportioned $2.5 million from the Public Education Department and $2.5 million from the Children, Youth, and Family Department to pilot a voluntary full-day kindergarten program. This is part of an Early Childhood Education Initiative and includes a voluntary pre-K program component. During this year, the state also continued to direct funding toward the full-day kindergarten program, which was an adopted legislation in 2000.

Other important New Mexico reforms illuminate the recent flurry of activity in educational policy in the state legislature. In 2003, New Mexico enacted the Indian Education Act (SB115) to create an Indian Education Division within the Public Education Department. An assistant secretary was appointed to spearhead an Indian Education Advisory Council, whose focus was on assisting in the evaluation, coordination, and consolidation of all activities related to educating New Mexico's Native American students. Furthermore, in 2005, the legislature passed SB215, the American Indian Advanced School Curriculum Act. This bill directed the State Department of Education (Indian Education Division and Rural Education Division) to develop a challenging and culturally relevant curriculum as well as support to school districts and tribes for capacity building to meet the needs of American Indian students. Finally, school choice is also available for families in the state. New Mexico passed its Charter School Act in 1999, and added recent amendments in 2005 and 2006. The Fordham Foundation gives high ratings to New Mexico's support for charters; as of 2005, there were forty-two charter schools enrolling about 2 percent of the students in the state (http://www.heritage.org/Research/Education/SchoolChoice/New Mexico.cfm).

WHO IS INVOLVED IN POLICYMAKING AND HOW THEY WORK TOGETHER. Prior to 2003, policymaking in New Mexico appears to have been closed and centralized at the executive branch, the legislature, and the State Board of Education. Since 2003, other stakeholders have become involved in policymaking conversations. However, initiation of new legislation is concentrated in the governor's office, and in the house education committee, and is a direct result of the governor's agenda for education.

The 2003 School Reform Act involved a broad range of top and mid-level policy and political leaders, including New Mexico State Board of Education members, the Secretary of Education, and the staff of the New Mexico Public Education Department. Support for the initiative also came from the New Mexico Business Roundtable for Educational Excellence, the Governor's Council of Teachers, the Greater Albuquerque Chamber of Commerce, and the elected New Mexico Public Education Commission. Constitutional Amendments 1 and 2 were introduced by the governor, and the Legislative Education Study Committee (LESC), and passed in the legislature.

Stakeholder groups are able to participate in other education policy initiatives as well. For example, the Legislative Education Study Committee (LESC) holds meetings throughout the state and businesses host roundtable discussions on key educational issues. The governor also works closely with the State Secretary of Education, who has further opened the policymaking process to include school and district administrators to inform the governor about educational issues they face. Thus, although much of the political power in New Mexico is concentrated, it is also evident that many players are able to come to the table to voice their opinions on educational policies.

Moreover, there is a newer presence of policies affecting the quality of education and accountability for American Indian students, as evident through SB115 (2003) and SB215 (2005). Policies such as these are examples of the increased importance on providing greater quality and more equitable education for marginalized groups in the state.

SUMMARY DISCUSSION OF STATE POLICY CULTURE. There is a virtual consensus among respondents that the level of activity that can be observed in New Mexico is a break from the previously low-key environment for educational policy. Most of this consensus is due to the leadership of Governor Bill Richardson, who, with the chair of the House Education Committee (Rick Miera), was cited by most respondents as the chief architect. Governor Richardson and Rick Miera have both made active efforts to open the education policy arena to both new actors, while simultaneously increasing state control over education. New initiatives are quite comprehensive and focus on system change, capacity building with the intention of developing an infrastructure that can more efficiently provide needed inputs that will yield a desired improvement in quality of schools and increased student achievement. Finally, choice is an increasingly important issue as well.

It is clearly too soon to determine whether the tide of activity represents a shift in political culture away from incremental legislative initiatives that have little impact on most schools toward a more comprehensive and directed approach from Santa Fe. While the governor's actions bespeak his intent to change not only policy, but who is involved and the way in which policy is made, we do not know whether this new reality will remain after he is no longer in office.

Missouri

Missouri's education reform efforts of the past decade were ranked overall as average when compared with other states by the 2006 *Quality Counts* report (*Education Week*, 2006). However, Missouri received a D+ on their standards and accountability system, considerably lower than the B− average of all states (and lower than both Oregon and New Mexico). According to the report, Missouri "lacks standards that are clear, specific, and grounded in content" (p. 2). The Fordham Foundation Report also assigned Missouri a D− in quality of state standards, ranking thirty-seven out of forty-nine states.[10]

Student achievement in Missouri hovers around the national average for both fourth and eighth graders: Student achievement in mathematics in Missouri as measured on the NAEP is slightly lower than the national average, while scores for reading are just above the national average. Missouri scores higher than the rest of the country in high school graduation rates. In 2002, 77 percent of Missouri seniors graduated compared to 69 percent for the country. The achievement gaps between white and black students put Missouri in the middle of the states, as do gaps between white and Hispanic students, and students ineligible for free and reduced lunch and those eligible. Like Oregon, Missouri received an average score (C) for resource equity, although other analyses suggest that Missouri's inequitable distribution of funding has been extreme among the group of proximate states that serve as its comparison group (Podgarsky & Springer, 2006). It was ranked above average in its efforts to improve teacher quality and school climate.

RECENT LEGISLATIVE HISTORY. The largest, most far-reaching piece of legislation directed at improving education in Missouri of the past fifteen years was Senate Bill 380, the "Outstanding Schools Initiative" of 1993. The bill made broad changes in education funding, state standards, and professional development for both teachers and administrators. The Outstanding Schools Initiative established statewide, performance-based assessment standards well in advance of No Child Left Behind. State education policy leaders viewed the

"Show Me Standards" as more rigorous than those eventually handed down from the federal Department of Education. Senate Bill 380 specified outcomes for districts to accomplish, but gave them considerable latitude in how those outcomes would be reached.

The Outstanding Schools Initiative revised the school funding formula in an attempt to address inequities in school funding. The new funding scheme was met with opposition, resulting in lawsuits that continue to this day. Finally, in 2005, the legislature shifted the basis from the highly inequitable local property taxes to student need, and tied this controversial decision to NCLB requirements for "reducing the gaps."

Another important feature of Senate Bill 380 was the stipulation that 1 percent of the budget of the Department of Elementary and Secondary Education (DESE) was to be spent on professional development. This expenditure was a substantial investment in teacher quality. SB 380 further required that members of district school boards obtain annual professional development, and represents an area of state investment that is tied to its continuing interest in fostering teacher quality.

Senate Bill 380 had broad aims and effects, but it was light on accountability mechanisms. Although it required districts to have comprehensive improvement plans, there was little oversight to see that those plans were implemented. The bill required schools to meet at least ten standards to remain certified, but again lacked enforcement mechanisms. An important move toward accountability came in 2001 when the Missouri General Assembly enacted (HB 865) requiring districts to report assessment results. In 2005, HB 297 transferred the responsibility for report cards from the districts to the Department of Elementary and Secondary Education. With these exceptions, most legislation relating to accountability provides minimal adjustments to meet the reporting requirements of No Child Left Behind.[11]

State standards and student testing were introduced in 1998, and were not revised until early 2006, when the Missouri Assessment Program was revised and renormed so that more students would score at the "proficient" and "advanced" levels (http://dese.mo.gov/news/2006/revisedMAP.htm).

Teacher quality has been addressed several times since the Senate Bill 380 was passed in 1993. In 2002, the Missouri legislature signed into law HB 1711, which accelerated the process through which experienced teachers from other states could achieve certification in Missouri. An out-of-state teacher with five years' teaching experience could obtain provisional certification, which would be permanent after five years of teaching in Missouri. The following year, Senate Bill 296 was passed that required new teachers to participate in a two-year mentoring program, obtain thirty hours of professional development, and participate in a beginning teacher assistance program. As with Senate Bill 380, the particulars of these programs were left to the districts, in keeping with Missouri's decentralized policy culture.

WHO IS INVOLVED AND HOW THEY WORK TOGETHER. The primary actors in crafting state education legislation in Missouri are the governor, the legislature, the State Board of Education, and the Department of Elementary and Secondary Education (DESE). Missouri's commissioner of education and members of the State Board of Education are appointed by the governor, and therefore the direction and flavor of education policy are clearly controlled at the executive level, and can be partisan. This partisan bias is tempered, however, by the fact that the governor's nominations to the Board of Education must be approved by the senate. Moreover, once appointed, Board of Education members tend to serve multiple terms that overlap governorships. Missouri governorships flip-flop reliably between Republican and Democrat (since 1900, Missouri has had nineteen Democratic governors and nine Republican governors). The Board of Education works closely with DESE (where the commissioner is usually appointed from among the ranks of sitting Superintendents) and depends on the state agency to funnel information about the state's education-related needs up from the schools and districts. When the legislature is considering a given bill, ad hoc committees are formed to study the issue and craft bill language. In sum, participation in education policymaking in Missouri is less a function of the party in power than membership in the groups and agencies that have a role in influencing education legislation and subsequent regulations.

A number of additional groups—outside of the permanent government actors noted earlier—exert influence over legislation through lobbying and by forging relationships with legislators. Probably the most influential are business interests, represented by several groups including the state Chamber of Commerce and the National Alliance of Business. While, these groups have historically focused on fiscal matters (i.e., taxes and funding) of education initiatives, they have more recently expressed interest in curricula and professional development. The business groups are cited as having more influence over the content of legislation than other groups.

Educational professional groups have a more limited role, although the teacher and administrator associations employ full-time lobbyists. The School Administrators Coalition comprises several administrators' associations, but is viewed as more effective at stopping legislation than initiating it. There are three teacher organizations, but they often differ over legislative goals and operate in a nonunion environment. Other education groups that try to influence state legislation include the Missouri School Boards Association, the Missouri Association of School Librarians, and the Missouri State PTA, but they are not regarded as key players. Higher education representatives do not appear to be very involved in crafting education-related legislation, but they do contribute to the implementation of education policy once it is outlined by the legislature, particularly in the areas of preparation and evaluation of teachers and administrators.

Citizen participation in educational discussions is also limited. The Board of Education invites groups or individuals who are affected by a given proposed policy to speak before it, and uses this information to advocate for legislation. There is an Education Roundtable composed of many education groups, but it has no institutional support and has not coalesced into a legislative force. Thus, participation of groups outside the traditional legislation making bodies occurs largely at the discretion of those bodies.

SUMMARY OF MISSOURI'S POLICY CULTURE. Missouri's state political machinery lacks clear mechanisms for participation by new groups. Outside of the legislature, however, Missouri's tradition of decentralization has ensured that local districts have considerable influence in how a given piece of law in enacted. The comprehensive Senate Bill 380 in 1993, for example, made stipulations concerning curriculum and professional development, but left particulars largely to districts. The most centralized educational policies in Missouri relate to funding and accountability.

Educational equity has long been contested in Missouri. The funding formula implemented by Senate Bill 380 in 1993 was an attempt to rationalize the distribution of public education in the state, but it resulted in litigation that continues to the present. School choice is not a high priority with the Missouri state legislature. The state's two urban centers do have high numbers of children, especially middle- and upper-middle-class children, attending parochial or private school.

In summary, Missouri's political culture tends to favor a small number of participants in making education policy, little direct public involvement, and a fractious approach to achieving equity in educational access and attainment.

Comparing the Three States

Historically, Oregon has created and enacted education policies that favor locally controlled progressive reforms, and has been classified as having a "moralistic" political culture in every study that has been conducted using Elazar's classification. According to most scholars, a moralistic political culture is one that emphasizes the values underlying political action, and regards government as a vehicle for securing the common good. What does this mean in the current context of educational reform? Oregon's political culture encourages large numbers of political participants to come to the table to discuss issues and create policy. Specific groups, however, have higher levels of influence over issue development and policymaking in the state than others. These inner circle and near inner circle political groups usually get together to talk over issues and reach consensus prior to lobbying the legislature. This tendency to informally consult and create short-term but strong alliances may be due, in part, to a long-standing fear of any one group gaining too much power. Broad-reaching grassroots participation encourages organizations and political groups to collaborate with each other in order to be viewed as legitimate, but appears to discourage permanent alliances. Politically, the state is governed by voter initiatives and, while many issues make it onto the ballot, most fail or are not enacted by the legislature and, as noted earlier, its initiative law is considered one of the most populist. This initiatives-based system, according to some state-level players, makes the process of getting special interest issues onto the ballot an open and easy process, but also time consuming and cumbersome since most initiatives fail.

Even though Oregon is moving in the direction of increasing state mandates, the culture and mentality of Oregonians have remained consistent. By 1993, several educational groups in Oregon cooperated to produce a comprehensive and rationalized system of standards and accountability called "Bringing Oregon Schools into the 21st Century." Although the state played a large role in helping to create standards, school districts were left to design their own assessment methods—a decision that is still contested today.

Missouri's political culture stands in contrast to Oregon's, although in terms of demographics and size, they are relatively similar. Missouri's political culture is classified as highly "individualistic." In many ways, Missouri's recent history of educational policymaking is a classic case of individualism in practice. Its policymaking process is not impermeable, but is deeply affected by electoral politics and the competition for good ideas and practices. In this context, key players in policymaking in the state are well known to all parties, and are concentrated in and around the governor and the Board of Education, while the marketplace, through lobbying and interest group competition, stimulates public discussion of different alternatives. Direct citizen involvement is reported to be significantly lower, and is concentrated through competing interest groups who rarely collaborate. Although it is not a closed system of elites, it is, reportedly, hard to influence policy except through activist players. There is a high tolerance for differences—among schools as well as between individuals—which means that state educational policies do not have a comprehensive character.

Throughout the two decades of increasing state activism in educational policy, Missouri has remained committed to a philosophy of decentralism and a preference for local control. A modest-sized state with only two significant urban areas, the state gives considerable autonomy to its over five hundred school districts. This commitment to localism must be viewed against the backdrop of the continuing controversies (and court cases) around desegregation and state finance reform. There are, for example, state standards, but curriculum decisions are clearly in the hands of local districts. While, on the surface, this is also the case for Oregon, Missouri lacks the "buzz" of broad conversations about what constitutes desirable standards and higher levels of learning, and what citizens around the state want from education.

According to a number of respondents, Missouri's competitive political environment permeates election rhetoric and the legislative process, privileging party line rhetoric over substantive discussion of serious educational issues. Policymaking is logical but piecemeal, not guided by a comprehensive vision. There is agreement that the decades-long struggle over how to deal with educational inequity, particularly in urban centers, has not been satisfactorily addressed with accountability legislation.

New Mexico stands in distinct contrast to Missouri and Oregon, where political culture (and the policy issues that emerge over and over in policymaking) have a durable and familiar quality. There is a virtual consensus among respondents that the political culture of New Mexico is a break from the previously low-key environment that emphasized the importance of both individual and local autonomy, and in which the state played a minimal role. Most of this change is due the leadership of Governor Bill Richardson, whose efforts have opened the education policy arena to both new and old actors. This activism has been accompanied by increased centralization of government decision-making, in contrast with the history of localized citizen control except in matters of funding. New policy initiatives are quite comprehensive and focused on addressing social problems by dealing with issues of equity, efficiency, and quality of education. Finally, choice is an increasingly important issue as well.

But to what degree does the current political initiative signal a fundamental change in political culture? Sharkansky (1969) and all subsequent empirical studies have classified New Mexico's political culture as "traditional," which means that it has been generally predisposed to turn decisions over to elites (usually landowners), and to give preference to stability over dramatic change. The average citizen and citizen groups are not expected to have a high level of active participation in setting educational policy directions. This has certainly been the case in educational policy in New Mexico, which accounts for the relatively low level of state initiative during the last several decades of pressure for reform.

When reform arrived in New Mexico, it was primarily a result of changing priorities among the elite.[12] While the level of policy activity has gone from routine to jet-fueled, it has proceeded with an emphasis on additional centralization (especially in the governor's office) rather than popularizing educational policy. Our respondents point to the effort that has gone into opening up state policy discussions, but most of this effort has focused on fleshing out and getting reactions to initiatives rather than generating new and different alternative policies. However, given that citizen participation in politics in New Mexico has been highly class biased compared to Missouri or Oregon (Hill & Leighley, 1992), it will take more that a few initiatives to make the system more open for most people. Given the state's long tradition, not only in education but in other areas, collective preferences that are being challenged by a popular elected official may simply be an example of the temporary effects of popular waves of reform.

Discussion

This chapter focused on a description of state accountability and standards initiatives over the past few years in order to explore whether the concept of political culture could explain how legislatures and elected officials have responded to calls for reform. Our analysis suggests that, despite the contention that federal initiatives are undermining the state's role in education, there is still a great deal of variation among states. This distinctiveness is apparent not only in the nature of specific reform policies, but the way in which they get on to the policy agenda and into legislation. We find, furthermore, that in spite of the belief that we are in a long wave of national conversations about educational reform, a system of political culture indicators that emerged in the 1950s and 60s has continuing power in discriminating among the states. When we viewed differences among the three states in this study holistically, their policy paths and practices conform quite clearly to Elazar's initial impressionistic classification of differences in state culture that are rooted in deep history. Whether this stability in political culture and its apparent impact on educational policy is good or bad for children's development and learning should be explored in more depth, paying attention to the permanent features of our state policy landscape as well as the immediacy of annual agendas.

Notes

1. Chilton also argues that political cultures must have a basis in moral reasoning.

2. This definition follows the early calls for using the concept as an explanatory variable rather than as a focus of study in itself (Lehman, 1972).

3. State tests, if used as a single indicator, would not constitute a quality focus.

4. A copy of the interview protocol may be found in Learning from Leadership Project: *Year 1 Report to the Wallace Foundation* at http://education.umn.edu/CAREI/Leadership/Reports.html.

5. To get an initiative on the ballot requires signatures from 4 percent of the population. Oregon's initiative law is considered one of the most populist in the country.

6. A number of respondents commented that NCLB introduced a more punitive and sanctions-based policy into the Oregon system, which made it contentious precisely because this kind of policy lever has not been used historically in the state.

7. See http://nces.ed.gov/nationsreportcard/states/profile.asp

8. We confirmed this assessment of the respondents by examining the list of educational policy initiatives, outlined by ECS, between 2000 and 2006. We agree with our respondents that most of the legislation and rule making in the

first few years of 2000 were not earthshaking, and many of the quality initiatives passed by the legislature were vetoed by Governor Gary Johnson. Beginning in 2000, a review of state legislative initiatives indicates that there were a series of efforts to develop policies to improve teacher quality and accountability, but these were not part of a comprehensive reform agenda.

9. More details of this large and complex bill may be found on the Education Commission of the States Web site: http://www.ecs.org/ecs/ecscat.nsf/Web StateView?OpenView&count=500&RestrictToCategory=New+Mexico.

10. The only significant point of difference between these two recent reports concerns school choice; the Fordham Foundation report graded Missouri a D, while the Quality Counts report praises Missouri's "relatively strong charter school law" an gives it a B.

11. See http://www.ecs.org/html/Doucment_noID.asp?ChouseID=2184.

12. New Mexico does not pay its legislators, which means, to an even greater extent than in other states, that only citizens from wealthier backgrounds can afford to participate.

References

Almond, G. (1956). Comparative political systems. *The Journal of Politics, 18*(3), 391–409.

Almond, G., & Verba, S. (1963). *The civic culture: Political attitudes and democracy in five nations*. Princeton: Princeton University Press.

Arceneaux, K. (2001). The "gender gap" in state legislative representation: New data to tackle an old question. *Political Research Quarterly, 54*(1), 143–160.

Baker, B. (2001). Living on the edges of state school-funding policies: The plight of at-risk, limited-english-proficient, and gifted children. *Educational Policy, 15*(5), 699–723.

Berezin, M. (1997). Politics and culture: A less fissured terrain. *Annual Review of Sociology, 23*, 361–383.

Bracey, G. (2004). *Responses to misconceptions about public education in the U.S.* (2nd ed.). Portsmouth, NH: Heineman.

Bryk, A. S., & Hermanson, K. L. (1993). Educational indicator systems: Observations on their structure, interpretation, and use. *Review of Research in Education, 19*, 451–484.

Chilton, S. (1988). Defining political culture. *The Western Political Quarterly, 41*(3), 419–445.

Conway, M. M. (1989). The political context of political behavior. *The Journal of Politics, 51*(1), 3–10.

Cook, E. A., Jelen, T. G., & Wilcox, C. (1993). State political cultures and public opinion about abortion. *Political Research Quarterly, 46*(4), 771–781.

Education Week. (2006). *Quality counts at 10: A decade of standards-based reform*. Retrieved August 1, 2006, from http://www.org/ew/toc/2edweek006/01/05/index.html.

Elazar, D. J. (1970). *Cities of the prairie*. New York: Basic.

Elkins, D. J., & Simeon, R. E. B. (1979). A cause in search of its effect, or what does political culture explain? *Comparative Politics, 11*(2), 127–145.

Fordham Foundation. (2006). *The Fordham Report 2006: How well are states educating our neediest children?* Retrieved December 15, 2006, from http://www.edexcellence.net/foundation/publication/publication.cfm?id=363.

Heritage Foundation. (n.d.). *Issues, education, choice*. Retrieved December 14, 2006, from http://www.heritage.org/Research/education/schoolchoice/Oregon.cfm#SchoolChoiceStatus.

Herzik, E. B. (1985). The legal-formal structuring of state politics: A cultural explanation. *The Western Political Quarterly, 38*(3), 413–423.

Hill, K. Q., & Leighley, J. E. (1992). The policy consequences of class bias in state electorates. *American Journal of Political Science, 36*(2), 351–365.

Jackman, R. W., & Miller, R. A. (1996). A renaissance of political culture? *American Journal of Political Science, 40*(3), 632–659.

Johnson, C. A. (1976). Political culture in American states: Elazar's formulation examined. *American Journal of Political Science, 20*(3), 491–509.

Kelley, P. (2005). *As America becomes more diverse: The impact of state higher education inequality*. Retrieved December 12, 2006, from www.highered.org.

Koven, S., & Mausolff, C. (2002). The influence of political culture on state budgets. *American Review of Public Administration, 32*(1), 66–77.

Lehman, E. W. (1972). On the concept of political culture: A theoretical reassessment. *Social Forces, 50*(3), 361–370.

Marshall, C., Mitchell, D., & Wirt, F. (1986). The context of state-level policy formation. *Educational Evaluation and Policy Analysis, 8*(4), 347–378.

Mazzoni, T. L. (1993). The changing politics of state education policy making: A 20-year Minnesota perspective. *Educational Evaluation and Policy Analysis, 15*(4), 357–379.

Merelman, R. M., & Foster, C. R. (1978). Political culture and education in advanced industrial societies: West Germany and the United States. *International Review of Education / Internationale Zeitschrift fur Erziehungswissenschaft / Revue Internationale de l'Education, 24*(4), 443–465.

Morgan, D. R., & Watson, S. S. (1991). Political culture, political system characteristics, and public policies among the American states. *Publius, 21*(2, State Political Subcultures: Further Research), 31–48.

Norrander, B. (2000). The multi-layered impact of public opinion on capital punishment implementation in the American states. *Political Research Quarterly, 53*(4), 771–793.

Podgarsky, M., & Springer, M. G. (2006). *K–12 public school finance in Missouri: An overview.* Retrieved December 20, 2006, from http://research.stlouisfed.org/publications/red/2006/01/PodgurskySpringer.pdf.

Putnam, R. (1971). Studying elite political culture: The case of "ideology." *American Political Science Review, LXV*, 651–682.

Rice, T. W., & Sumberg, A. F. (1997). Civic culture and government performance in the American states. *Publius, 27*(1), 99–114.

Sharkansky, I. (1969). The utility of Elazar's political culture: A research note. *Polity, 2*(1), 66–83.

Somers, M. R. (1995). What's political or cultural about political culture and the public sphere? Toward an historical sociology of concept formation. *Sociological Theory, 13*(2), 113–144.

Timar, T. B. (1997). The institutional role of state education departments: A historical perspective. *American Journal of Education, 105*(3), 231–260.

Whitty, G., & Power, S. (2000). Marketization and privatization in mass education systems. *International Journal of Educational Development, 20*(2), 93–107.

Wirt, F. (1991). "Soft" concepts and "hard" data: A research review of Elazar's political culture. *Publius, 21*(2), 1–13.

Wirt, F., Mitchell, D., & Marshall, C. (1988). Culture and education policy: Analyzing values in state policy systems. *Educational Evaluation and Policy Analysis, 10*(4), 271–284.

Wirt, F., Mitchell, D. E., & Marshall, C. (1985). Perceptions of state political culture by education policy elites. *Peabody Journal of Education, 62*(4, State Politics of Education), 48–60.

Wong, K. K. (1989). Fiscal support for education in American states: The "parity-to-dominance" view examined. *American Journal of Education, 97*(4), 329–357.

Wood, B. D., & Theobald, N. A. (2003). Political responsiveness and equity in public education finance. *Journal of Politics, 65*(3), 718–738.

Chapter 9

State Power and Equity

Kevin P. Brady

In this chapter, the rapid and significant expansion of state power will be examined in relation to issues of educational equity. One of the primary questions this chapter will explore is, given the status of state control and power over the organization and governance of public schools, how can states more effectively and efficiently manage educational policy goals, such as equity with competing demands from local school districts for increased autonomy and control (Conley, 2003). Beginning in the 1980s, the major school reform strategy adopted by many states has been toward more centralized legislative and administrative controls (Timar, 1997).

As educational reformers increasingly expect states to carry the burden of school improvement, there is a concern that states vary widely in the level of equity provided to local schools through the implementation of state-led educational policy initiatives. This chapter will examine two major equity issues that have coincided with the national trend of raising state power: (1) the passage of the No Child Left Behind Act (NCLB) and its state-level implementation through adequate yearly performance (AYP) measures and (2) school finance litigation reform throughout the states.

The passage of NCLB in 2002 created assessment and accountability systems in nearly every state and requires states to provide data on student test performance as well as comparing that data to other schools (Goertz & Duffy, 2001). Evidence suggests that each of the fifty state legislatures in the United States has taken increasingly more control over selected educational policies, such as educational accountability and school funding issues (Hirth, 1996). The influence of states can be seen in such major educational policy areas as school finance, educational accountability, administration of large-scale grants, implementation of educational programs for students with special needs, and policy efforts to increase student academic standards. While substantial evidence that drastically increasing state influence in public educational policy is significantly influencing the school curriculum (Cohen & Hill, 2001; Firestone,

Mayrowetz, & Fairman, 1998; Fuhrman, 2001), there is little written regarding the direct relationship between rising state power and its impact on equity considerations in education.

Over the past two decades, public education has increasingly become a major political topic in many states, most notably because public education-related expenses are usually the most expensive service in state budgets (Conley, 2003). Since the historic meeting between former President George H. W. Bush and the fifty governors in Charlottesville, Virginia, in 1989, the United States has witnessed a massive expansion in state leadership involving educational policymaking as evidenced by the political actions by state governors and legislators within the educational policy arena (Welburn, 2002). For example, state governors now play an appreciably more important role in educational policy. In a 1995–1997 study of nine states, Gittell and McKenna (1999) observed that state governors were significant political players in major educational reforms, including school vouchers, standards, and the formation of important coalitions with the business and religious communities. Since 1989, state legislatures across the United States have passed thousands of education-related bills, numerous state commissions on education were created, and state gubernatorial education plans were promulgated.

Indeed, the evolution and dramatic increase of the state role in public educational policy has been remarkable in the past few decades (Wirt & Kirst, 2005). A 2001 Institute of Educational Leadership (IEL) report titled "Leadership for Student Learning: Recognizing the State's Role in Public Education" found that states are presently in a historically unprecedented position to address contemporary educational policy challenges, including the improvement of teaching and learning in schools, the implementation of systemic educational reform, the narrowing of achievement gaps, and the enhancement of equity through policies of school finance equalization.

Despite being the nation's primary units of educational governance and policy, states are extremely varied with their 50 individual governors, 7,400-plus state legislators, and approximately 508 state education board members. This notable variation among states has definite implications on educational equity considerations. While states historically delegated much of their policymaking power in education to local governments, during the last twenty-five years, states have increasingly reasserted their power over educational policy issues—a trend that is likely to continue throughout the twenty-first century (First, 1992; Fowler, 2000; Mazzoni, 1993; Wirt & Kirst, 2005). Fowler (2000) contends that the gradual and significant increase in state power, especially involving educational policymaking, has two implications: first, state policymakers are now considered more important compared to their federal and local level counterparts and, second, since the mass media often overemphasizes educational policymaking at the federal level, state-level policymaking is often poorly understood by the public-at-large.

Kirst (1988) contends that growing state power in public education resulted primarily from a gradual, but consistent loss of public confidence in the local public school district's ability to provide a high-quality education to its students. Beginning in the 1960s, educational policy issues, including bilingual education, students' rights, and civil rights were largely monitored under the auspices of local school district governance.

By the 1970s, however, local districts were facing declining student enrollments, public resistance to increases in local property taxes, and court decisions calling for increases in student rights. Despite this consistent decrease in the political power of local school districts, many Americans are still largely unaware that local school boards and officials, including principals and superintendents, have been losing political power in public education compared to state officials as well as state education agencies (SEAs) (Kirst, 1988; Wirt & Kirst, 2005). As educational reformers increasingly expect states to carry the burden of school improvement, there is a real concern because states vary markedly in the level of equity afforded to students.

State Policymaking in Public Education: An Overview

Historically, states varied in the level of local control they afforded school districts. In an attempt to categorize these governance approaches, McGivney (1984) offers a typology model that details the evolution of state-level educational politics. The four typologies include: Stage I: localistic decentralized, where the decision-making process involves each local unit as well as the state legislature; Stage II: statewide monolithic, where the decision-making process involves state-wide coalitions; Stage III: state-wide fragmented, where the decision-making process involves the state governor, state legislature, and the courts; and Stage IV: state-wide bureaucratization, where the decision-making process involves bureaucracy. In McGivney's study of twenty-two states, these four stages helped classify "stages of evolutionary typology" in state politics. For example, in McGivney's study, five states (Connecticut, Massachusetts, Maine, New Hampshire, and Vermont) were classified as localistic decentralized states, whereas only one of the twenty-two states studied, Hawaii, was classified under the fourth stage, state-wide bureaucratization, where the educational decision-making process involves bureaucracy.

At the state level, political influence and the individuals and groups who exert power over the educational policy discourse are crucial to the policymaking process. Based on their study of six states, Marshall, Mitchell, and Wirt (1989) ranked the influence of policy actors at the state level in educational policymaking and found that individual legislators, the legislature as a whole, chief state school officers, interest groups, and teachers' organizations exerted the most significant influence on education policy.

State Power, Centralization, and Local Control: An Uneasy Alliance?

Although the loss of local autonomy troubles some educators, others welcome more centralized state control in the educational policymaking process. According to McDermott (1999), centralization of the educational policy process can be more effectively achieved at the state and local levels through the three functions of regulation, support, and resource allocation. For instance, from 1990 to 1997, both North Carolina and Texas experienced the largest average increases in student test scores on the National Assessment of Educational Progress (NAEP) by actively adopting these three functions. Grissmer and Flanagan's (1998) study concluded that the most plausible explanation for significant test score increases in these two states was the policy environments established in each state. According to this study, both states succeeded in significantly raising NAEP student test scores by radically changing both their organizational environment and incentive structures for educators. These specific changes included: creating an aligned system of state testing standards, curriculum, and assessments; holding individual schools accountable for improvement by all students; and receiving influential support from the business community in the development and implementation of these changes over time (Grissmer & Flanagan, 1998).

Ironically, this increasing trend toward state-level centralization of educational policy seems to contradict some states' attempts to increase local school district-level autonomy through policies, such as site-based management, school-based budgeting, as well as efforts to increase teacher and parental involvement at the local decision-making level (Spring, 2005). While some states are clearly more aggressive in the implementation of education policy reforms, efforts in every state to enhance equity in public education through the improvement of student and teacher performance have considerably diminished local school district controls over school funding, testing standards, curricular reform, and accountability. Usdan (2002) contends that the politics of education at the state level is presently undergoing major change due to the standards-based reform movement and NCLB. NCLB continues to be a major catalyst in educational policymaking, particularly at the state level. This chapter will now take a closer look at the impact of state power on the equity considerations of both NCLB and state-level school funding reforms.

State Power, High-Stakes Testing, and Equity: The Equity Implications of NCLB

On January 8, 2002, President George W. Bush reauthorized and renamed the Elementary and Secondary Education Act (ESEA) as the No Child Left Behind Act of 2001 (NCLB). NCLB requires states to test specific subjects and grade levels as well as establish minimum academic performance standards for students, schools, and school districts (Goertz, 2005). In terms of equity, one of the negative legacies of a public school system that has until fairly recently been largely governed by local control has been the nonstandardized reporting of data from schools to the state (Conley, 2003). In terms of equity, one of the most important changes to arise out of increases in state power in the educational policymaking process has been the focus of the individual school, not the school district, as the unit of accountability toward assessing student performance on state-level, standardized exams. Today, states increasingly analyze and compare schools in relation to other schools with comparable socioeconomic and student populations.

In order to comply with NCLB regulations, states have made school improvement and performance data available to the larger public. Due to massive dissemination efforts by state agencies, such as state departments of education, the public has been given unprecedented access to school-level information. This public access to performance data has the potential to strengthen equity by creating public pressure for school improvement. An additional benefit is that both local school officials and the public-at-large are increasingly more aware of the data-driven environments in which schools operate. However, some critics worry that school officials and the public have been barraged with too much information to process it properly.

Fusarelli (2004) presents another concern, namely that the promise of NCLB to enhance equity by reducing the student achievement gap will likely remain unfulfilled due to insufficient funding and an overly simplistic definition of what constitutes this gap. Therefore, despite acting as a catalyst for the dissemination of standardized school level data, due to variations in school funding across the states, NCLB has not yet created greater equity for students. Still, because of NCLB, every state is now implementing some form of standards-based testing reform. This NCLB-related testing expanded responsibilities for states in terms of implementation (Jennings et al., 2002). In addition to requiring states to institute standards, NCLB also requires them to implement assessments, disaggregate student test data, and ensure that migrant students, student with disabilities, and students from different racial and socioeconomic levels achieve state-determined benchmarks of academic achievement (Jennings et al., 2002). Unfortunately, however, states are currently facing significant challenges with changing their student testing systems to conform to the requirements of NCLB. According to *Education Week*, for example, only nine states are even close to fulfilling the NCLB requirements. (Olson, 2002)

Since NCLB provides states with nearly complete autonomy to develop benchmarks as to what students must learn, how to test this knowledge, and what specific scores students need to achieve to demonstrate proficiency in a particular curriculum area, there are noticeable state-to-state variations. For example, Mississippi and Nebraska have the highest percent proficient students

(89 percent each), while Nevada (42 percent) and South Carolina (35 percent) have the lowest (Carey, 2006).

The 2013–2014 school year is the target year set by NCLB for having all students across the country be proficient or advanced in reading and math. Consequently, states have the enormous task of measuring the amount of student progress necessary to meet this goal in their particular state. The federal government will impose sanctions on schools and districts that do not meet the benchmark performance goals that they set as a precondition of receiving federal aid. Specifically, each state must set testing performance benchmark goals to determine whether the state's schools and districts are satisfying Adequate Yearly Progress (AYP) toward teaching students what they need to know. In 2004–2005, Oklahoma and Rhode Island reported the highest percentage of schools meeting AYP (97 and 95 percent, respectively), while Hawaii (34 percent) and Florida (28 percent) had the lowest (Carey, 2006).

When Congress passed NCLB legislation, lawmakers attempted to make the AYP provisions detailing state-level accountability clear. Under AYP, states have the responsibility of ensuring that schools meet "clearly defined goals" and teach "all students" to state-level standards. According to NCLB, "clearly established goals" require each state to set specific testing benchmark goals of the percentage of students in each school that are expected to demonstrate proficiency on state tests in language arts and math. It is expected that these "clearly established goals" will increase over time. Under NCLB, schools are now accountable for the testing outcomes of all students and this focus on the testing of all students has brought attention to the unique testing concerns of certain student groups, including students with special needs and students whose native language is not English.

After NCLB was passed, states were left with the overwhelming task of enforcing NCLB's mandates, but lacked the legal capacity to enact the reforms into policy as required by the federal mandates. McDermott and Jensen (2005) argue that, as a result of NCLB, there has been a "reordering of intergovernmental relationships in education policy" (p. 54). The federal government's new role under NCLB essentially mandates that not only states adopt standards-based reforms, but that they adopt these reforms under very specific federally mandated guidelines.

Many states have claimed that they do not have enough financial resources to effectively and equitably administer NCLB. Recent estimates of the financial cost associated with administering new, state-level student testing assessment systems range from \$1.9 billion to \$7 billion (McDermott & Jensen, 2005). In 2005, Connecticut became the first state in the nation to file a lawsuit against the U.S. Department of Education, claiming that the NCLB law was illegal. Connecticut charged that the federal government did not provide enough funding to pay for the implementation of testing and required programs (Cohen, 2006).

Federal funds for NCLB implementation were allocated for only one year and were not substantial enough to cover student testing and assessment mandates as well as other related costs (Thomas & Brady, 2005). Therefore, states were left with the burden of financing NCLB educational reform initiatives. Due to necessary budgetary cuts to other essential state-supported educational services, financial concerns were increased in many school districts across the country. Researchers at the Harvard University Civil Rights Project conducted an equity-based study of the implementation of NCLB and how the policies operated in different educational systems (Sunderman & Kim, 2004). The results of the Harvard study indicated that the development and implementation of new NCLB-mandated student testing and assessment systems resulted in a "disruptive and costly process" for many states (p. 5).

There are growing equity concerns regarding states' capacity to comply with NCLB's mandates and meet the policy's timetable for bringing U.S. students to academic proficiency (Cohen, 2006). In terms of equity implications, opponents and supporters alike agree that NCLB will ultimately lead to a more unified, tightly coupled educational system, especially within states and possibly across states (Fusarelli, 2004). However, given implementation problems arising from significant variations among states in student testing standards and accountability policies as well as the costs associated with fully implementing NCLB, the increased state power in implementing NCLB has some real concerns associated with enhancing equity.

State Power, Equity, and Funding the Nation's Schools

As noted by Conley (2003), the states' increasing control over public school funding has paralleled the academic standards movement. Odden (1998) argues that the impact of both a national and state policy focus of teaching toward higher standards has resulted in a shift from the traditional school funding focus on equity to an expanded concept of adequacy, which was designed to facilitate the goal of more students successfully satisfying higher academic standards. Undoubtedly, one of the primary driving forces in the states' role toward shaping educational policies has been the shift of responsibility for school funding from the local to state level (Picus & Blair, 2004).

Substantive legal challenges to inequitable state school funding systems were initiated in the 1970s by local school districts unable to generate enough local revenue, mainly property tax, compared to other school districts within a particular state. The ultimate goal of these local school districts was to achieve increased fiscal resources. One of the effects of moving school funding policy decisions to the state level has been a corresponding decrease in political authority and responsibility at the local level (Conley, 2003). Since the end of the

1970s, for example, the financial contribution of local school districts has noticeably declined from 52 percent to 43 percent, while the corresponding state's fiscal contribution has increased from 39 percent to 47 percent (Odden & Picus, 2000). The state's fiscal share of funding public schools during the 2002–2003 school year was 48.7 percent compared to the local contribution of 42.8 percent (National Center for Education Statistics, 2004).

Even as state control over school funding increased, state success toward minimizing fiscal inequities between high- and low-property-wealth local school districts has been limited. Over a thirty-year period, Odden's (1998) research reveals that although many states have undergone court-ordered school finance reform, the results of efforts to improve equity among local school districts are mixed. While state-initiated school finance reforms reduced the rising fiscal gap between wealthy and poorer school districts overall, these reforms did not address fiscal disparities in per pupil spending levels, which are linked to variations in local property wealth. Therefore, states have generally not been successful in improving disparities in local property wealth among school districts even though the state's revenue contribution to public schools has been growing in recent years.

While funding disparities between school districts within a state challenge equity, so do the disparities in school funding that occur between states. Even though the overall contribution of state revenues to public K–12 education has increased from approximately 20 to 50 percent since 1900, variations among individual states are significant (Wirt & Kirst, 2005). The majority of state funds for public schools are drawn from state sales and income taxes and, to a lesser degree, from lotteries, tobacco legal settlements, and alcohol taxes (Collen & Underwood, 2005). Each state has a different capacity to generate revenues. Further complicating the situation is that today states are expected to do more than supply a basic level of funding. Since the 1980s, school finance concerns have heightened to include not only the equitable distribution of financial resources to schools, but the provision of sufficient resources to meet the goals for student learning presented in state and local standards. If a state fails to provide an appropriate level of funding for its schools, it faces legal action. One of the first school finance lawsuits was *San Antonio Independent School District v. Rodriguez* (1973).

In 1973, the U.S. Supreme Court ruled in *San Antonio Independent School District v. Rodriguez* that public education is not a fundamental right under the U.S. Constitution. The *Rodriguez* case was an unsuccessful legal attempt to address school funding inequities in Texas under the Equal Protection Clause of the U.S. Constitution (Lefkowits, 2004). The U.S. Supreme Court in *Rodriguez* ruled that taxation for public schools and educational reforms are state matters. After the Supreme Court's *Rodriguez* decision, individuals and groups frustrated with the level of funding given public schools by state legislatures were limited largely to state-level courts and state constitutions for remedies (Collen & Underwood, 2005).

The early school finance cases focused on legal questions of equity, or whether students were being treated equally regardless of the wealth of the school district in which they lived. These particular type of school finance reform cases centered on eliminating the discriminatory impact of disparate property taxes among school districts with the goal of all districts being able to equally support educational services (Collen & Underwood, 2005).

More recently, school finance litigation has shifted from equity and fairness considerations to whether or not resources are available to provide an adequate education to all students. In contrast to equity-based school finance litigation, adequacy-based lawsuits focus on exactly how much money is necessary, or adequate, to provide all students in a particular state with a constitutionally guaranteed education (Lefkowits, 2004). More specifically, adequacy-based school finance lawsuits require school districts to determine funding on the basis of how much money is required to reach a specified result (Collen & Underwood, 2005).

Some educational reformers have come to the realization that the allocation of the same amount of resources for each public school district is not an effective strategy for more equitably funding schools. For instance, some students, such as students with disabilities, usually require more funding. Legal challenges of state school finance systems have been on the rise. According to the Campaign for Fiscal Equity, a not-for-profit corporation and coalition of parent organizations, community school boards, concerned citizens, and advocacy groups seeking reform of New York State's school finance system, only five of fifty states (Delaware, Hawaii, Mississippi, Nevada, and Utah) have not had litigation challenging the constitutionality of their state's K–12 school funding system. Still, states are in an unenviable position when it comes to school finance reform. States were left a legacy of significant inequities in local school funding along with increased responsibilities to provide viable solutions.

States, Coalition Building, and Enhancing Equity: Future Implications of State Power for the Twenty-first Century

Local school districts and schools were not originally organized to be responsive to state policy directives. Therefore, it should be no surprise that implementation issues surround the state and local control of educational policies. In terms of equity, there are clearly some benefits associated with increased state control over educational policies, namely more standardized data collection systems and fiscal accounting systems, which have lead to the dissemination of this information to the public-at-large and pressured local school officials to improve the overall quality of their schools. Wirt and Kirst (2005) indicate that the use of public resources to maximize the educational values of quality, efficiency, equity, and choice is not new. More specifically, reconciling the ideal of equity in education policymaking has long been and continues to be a dilemma in public education. While it is clear that state involvement with local school districts has increased significantly over the last several decades, the U.S. traditional value of local control in public education still provides a check on uncontrolled state activism.

McDermott (1999) argues that a more equitable public educational system can be achieved by centralizing many of the school finance decisions at the state level and delegating curriculum-based decisions to local governing bodies. If policy initiatives in education are to improve America's schools, then policy leaders at all levels of the educational system must be involved in cooperative ventures.

The major political players in state-level educational policymaking, namely governors, state legislatures, and state boards of education, each have powerful resources at their disposal to significantly alter the public education landscape. However, the organizational structure of the various state educational policymaking bodies, coupled with significant differences across states, constitute a messy system for making equitable educational policies. Among state-level educational policy influences, the greatest potential for advancing equitable educational policies comes from state boards of education, or SEAs. Additionally, state board of education members increasingly represent not only geographic, but the ethnic, racial, and gender diversity of the state and include parents, business leaders, and in some states, educators and students (Welburn, 2002). According to a report by the National Association of State Boards of Education (NASBE) titled, "State Education Governance for the 21st Century," state political leaders must provide state boards of education with greater access, independence, resources, and ongoing professional development in the educational policy process if they are going to accurately and equitably represent the voice of the citizenry of their respective states (Welburn, 2002).

Indeed, no one individual or institution can effectively control the institution of public education. Similarly, achieving complete educational policy parity among the fifty states is a pipe dream. However, individual states can effectively learn equitable elements of state governance and educational policy implementation from other states. For instance, several states have used collaborative leadership by adopting the advisory roles of "outside" coalitions, such as business leaders, local civic leaders, lawyers, parents, and students themselves as catalysts for equitable changes in educational policies. For example, South Carolina developed a joint subcommittee, named the South Carolina Business-Education Subcommittee that was responsible for promoting the 1984 Education Improvement Act (EIA) as well as reviewing evaluations and assessments encompassing the educational needs of the state and current education reforms requiring updates (Fuhrman, 1994). Another example of coalition building in state educational policymaking is seen in Kentucky's Prichard Committee for Academic Excellence, a nonprofit, volunteer group composed of private citizens, including business leaders, local civic activists, parents, professionals, as well as former governors. With funding from private corporations and foundations, Kentucky's Prichard Committee for Academic Excellence monitors and supports state-level educational reform initiatives. The Prichard Committee was pivotal in the political processes that developed the 1990 Kentucky Education Reform Act (KERA).

In their 2001 report, *Leadership for Student Learning: Recognizing the State's Role in Public Education*, the Task Force on State Leadership recognized that state education leadership needs to be more equitable because this leadership should reflect a diverse collection of values. Additionally, the task force articulated eleven guiding principles that can support more effective leadership at the state level. Inherent in these eleven principles are a focus on equity. Indeed, the evidence is clear that state power in the area of educational policymaking has markedly increased over the past few decades.

With increased state power come increased responsibilities in educational policymaking, often with limited financial resources to accomplish meaningful educational reforms. These eleven principles acknowledge the fact that states need to embrace inclusive partnerships in order to continue meaningful educational reform initiatives. From a practical perspective, the successful implementation by states of NCLB mandates via Adequate Yearly Performance (AYP) benchmarks requires additional fiscal contributions by the federal government. Otherwise, the states are being set up for failure. In this chapter's overview of school finance reform, states, on average, are overburdened with the fiscal responsibilities of funding America's public K–12 educational infrastructure. Indeed, a by-product of increasing state power has yielded a substantially greater utilization of state resources, both financial and otherwise. State leadership needs to be more mindful that equity concerns are a major source of its responsibilities. For states to lose sight of their responsibilities toward maintaining high standards of equity in our educational policies, especially in light of the state's growing political power, would be a grave error with immeasurable, negative consequences.

Conclusion

While disagreements continue to exist concerning to degree to which states can control or change public school systems, there is general consensus that many local school districts want to maintain independence from states. In fact, evidence suggests that, historically, some local school districts have been quite successful at thwarting attempts by their respective state to implement educational policies. Usdan (2001) has referred to this desire for autonomy and territoriality by local school districts as the "theology of localism."

Nevertheless, as states continue to exercise control over educational policies, especially policies regarding fiscal accountability and increased student achievement, they need to restructure their governance relationships with local school districts. The question of how states can effectively balance centralization and decentralization and state incentives versus sanctions continues to be an elusive goal for many states (Conley, 2003). The ultimate goal is for states to create greater student equity through fiscal and governance reforms that allow for the dominance of state educational policies coexisting with the sanctity of local control.

References

Augenblick, J. G., Meyers, J. L., & Anderson, A. B. (1997). Equity and adequacy in school funding. *Financing schools, 7*(3), 63–78.

Carey, K. (2006, May). *Hot air: How states inflate their educational progress under NCLB.* Retrieved June 11, 2006, from http://www.educationsector.org/analysis/analysis_show.htm?doc_id=373044#end.

Cohen, D. K., & Hill, H. C. (2001). *Learning policy.* New Haven: Yale University Press.

Cohen, K. (2006, April 26). *NCLB and the states.* Retrieved June 11, 2006, from http://www.pbs.org/newshour/bb/education/nclb/federalvsstate.html.

Collen, A., & Underwood, J. (2005, May). Taking adequacy to the courts: A look at current trends in school finance litigation. *Leadership insider: Practical perspectives on school law and policy.* Alexandria, VA: National School Boards Association.

Conley, D. T. (2003). *Who governs our schools? Changing roles and responsibilities.* New York: Teachers College Press.

Danzberger, J. P. (1992). School boards: A troubled American institution. In *Facing the Challenge: The Report of The Twentieth Century Fund Task Force on School Governance.* New York: The Twentieth Century Fund.

Doyle, D. P., & Finn, C. E. (1984). American schools and the future of local control. *Public Interest* 77, 77–95.

Erikson, R. S, Wright, G. C., & McIver, J. P. (1993). *Statehouse democracy: Public opinion and policy in the American states.* Cambridge: Cambridge University Press.

Firestone, W., Mayrowetz, D., & Fairman, J. (1998). Performance-based assessment and instructional change: The effects of testing in Maine and Maryland. *Educational Evaluation and Policy Analysis, 20*(2), 95.

First. P. F. (1992). *Educational policy for school administrators.* Boston, MA: Allyn and Bacon.

Fowler, F. C. (2000). *Policy studies for educational leaders.* Upper Saddle River, NJ: Prentice-Hall.

French, D. (1998, November). The state's role in shaping a progressive vision of public education. *Phi Delta Kappan,* 185–194.

Fuhrman, S. (1994, April). Politics and systemic education reform. CPRE Policy Briefs, RB-12. New Brunswick, NJ: Consortium for Policy Research in Education, Eagleton Institute of Politics, Rutgers University. Retrieved June 14, 2006, from http://www.gse.upenn.edu/cpre/docs/pubs/rb12.pdf.

Fuhrman, S. (Ed.). (2001). *From the capital to the classroom: Standards-based reform in the states.* Chicago: University of Chicago Press.

Fusarelli, L. D. (2004, March). The potential impact of the No Child Left Behind Act on equity and diversity in American education. *Educational Policy, 18*(1), 71–94.

Gittell, M., & McKenna, L. (1999, September). Redefining education regimes and reform: The political role of governors. *Urban Education, 34*(3), 268–291.

Goertz, M. (2005). Implementing the No Child Left Behind Act: Challenges for the States. *Peabody Journal of Education, 80*(2), 73–89.

Goertz, M. E., & Duffy, M. C. (2001). *Assessment and accountability across the 50 states.* (RB-33). Philadelphia: Consortium for Policy Research in Education.

Gray, V. (1973, December). Innovation in the states: A diffusion study. *American Political Science Review, 67*(4), 1174–1185.

Grissmer, D., & Flanagan A. (1998, November). *Exploring rapid achievement gains in North Carolina and Texas.* Washington, DC: National Eduication Goals Panel. Retrieved June 9, 2006, from http://www.negp.gov/reports.

Hirth, M. (1996). Systemic reform, equity, and school finance reform: Essential policy linkages. *Educational Policy, 10*(4), 468–479.

Iannaccone, L. (1967). *Politics in education.* West Nyack, NY: Center for Applied Research in Education.

Jennings, J., Rentner, D. S., & Kober, N. (2002, Spring). *What to expect from the No Child Left Behind Act.* Retrieved June 19, 2006, from http://www.cep-dc.org/fededprograms/newfedroleedfeb2002.pdf.

Kirst, M. W. (1988). Recent state education reform in the United States: Looking backward and forward. *Educational Administration Quarterly, 24*(3), 319–328.

Lefkowits, L. (2004, March). *School finance: From equity to adequacy.* Aurora, CO: Mid-continent Research for Education and Learning (McREL).

Marshall, C., Mitchell, D., & Wirt, F. (1989). *Culture and education policy in the American states.* New York: Falmer Press.

Mazzoni, T. L. (1994). State policy-making and school reform: Influences and influentials. In J. D. Scribner and D. H. Layton (Eds.), *The 1994 Commemorative Yearbook of the Politics of Education Association* (pp. 53–73). Washington, DC: Falmer Press.

McDermott, K. A. (1999). *Controlling public education: Localism versus equity.* Lawrence: University Press of Kansas.

McDermott, K. A. (2003). What causes variation in states' accountability policies? *Peabody Journal of Education, 78*(4), 153–176.

McDermott, K. A., & Jensen, L. S. (2005). Dubious sovereignty: Federal conditions of aid and the No Child Left Behind Act. *Peabody Journal of Education, 80*(2), 39–56.

McDonald, J., Kaplow, R., & Chapman, P. (2006). School finance reform: The role of U.S. courts from 1968–1998. *National Forum of Educational Administration and Supervision Journal, 23*(4).

McGivney, J. H. (1984). State educational governance patterns. *Educational Administration Quarterly, 20*(2), 43–63.

Odden, A. R. (1998). *Improving state school finance systems: New realities create need to re-engineer school finance structures*. Paper prepared for the Consortium for Policy Research in Education, University of Wisconsin–Madison, Wisconsin Center for Education Research.

Odden, A. R., & Picus, L. O. (2000). *School finance: A policy perspective*. New York: McGraw-Hill.

Olson, L. (2002, January 9). Testing systems in most states not ESEA-ready. *Education Week, 11*.

Picus, L. O., & Blair, L. (2004, March). *School finance adequacy: The state role.* Austin, TX: Southeast Educational Development Laboratory (SEDL).

Spring, J. (2005). *Conflict of interest: The politics of American education*. Boston: McGraw-Hill.

Sunderman, G., & Kim, J. (2004, February). Inspiring vision, disappointing results: Four studies on implementing the No Child Left Behind Act. Harvard Civil Rights Project. Retrieved June 16, 2006, from http://www.civilrightsproject.harvard.edu/research/esea/nclb.php.

Thomas, J. Y., & Brady, K. P. (2005). The Elementary and Secondary Education Act at 40: Equity, accountability, and the evolving federal role in public education. *Review of Research in Education, 29*, 51–67.

Timar, T. B. (1997). The institutional role of state education departments: A historical perspective. *American Journal of Education, 105*(3), 231–260.

Timar, T. B., & Kirp, D. L. (1988). *Managing educational excellence.* London: Falmer Press.

Usdan, M. D. (2002, Spring). The new state politics of education. *The State Education Standard.* Retrieved June 12, 2006, from http://www.nassbc.org/Standard9_Spring2002/Usdan.pdf.

Usdan, M.D., McCloud, B., Podmostko, M., & Cuban, L. (2001). *Leadership for student learning: Recognizing the state's role in public education*. Washington, DC: Institute for Educational Leadership.

Walker, J. L. (1969, September). The diffusion of innovations among the American states. *American Political Science Review, 63*(3), 880–899.

Welburn, B. L. (2002, Spring). State education governance for the 21st century. *The State Education Standard*. Retrieved June 13, 2006, from http://www.nasbc.org/Standard9_Spring2002/Exec._summary_03-02.html.

Wirt, F. M., & Kirst, M. W. (2005). *The political dynamics of American education*. Richmond, CA: McCutchan.

Chapter 10

The Incremental Revolution

Nationalizing Education Accountability Policy

Kathryn A. McDermott and Elizabeth DeBray-Pelot

The No Child Left Behind Act of 2001 (NCLB) significantly extended federal power over states' assessment and accountability policies. As a condition of receiving Title I compensatory education funds (the largest single source of federal education aid), the states must annually administer tests to every student in grades 3–8, plus one high school grade, monitor whether or not schools and districts are making adequate yearly progress in their students' test scores, and ensure that corrective action occurs when schools and districts receiving Title I funds consistently fail to improve their scores. NCLB specifies how states must define "adequate yearly progress," as well as the range of acceptable options for corrective action. Since the law's passage, several states have criticized it as an intrusion on their freedom to set educational policy. There has also been controversy over whether NCLB constitutes an unfunded mandate on states and localities (Mathis, 2003). States' resentment of NCLB is ironic, since the law is actually based on accountability models that were first developed by states and added to federal law by the reauthorization of the Elementary and Secondary Education Act (ESEA) in 1994. Beginning in President Bill Clinton's second term, Congress considered measures that would tighten the accountability requirements placed on states by the 1994 law. This process culminated in the NCLB provisions governing adequate yearly progress (AYP) and corrective action.

In this chapter, we argue that many members of Congress did not understand the extent to which NCLB increased federal control over states' accountability policy choices when they voted to pass the bill. In making the federal definitions of adequate yearly progress and corrective action more stringent, Congress followed a path that was already well trodden in the history of federal mandates and regulations; frequently, Congress takes models from a few states' laws and imposes them on all states as mandates or grant conditions. A small number of senators and representatives actively pushed for more stringent statutory language on AYP and corrective action, and their colleagues followed their lead. In the context of a massive omnibus bill, which was moved through both houses very quickly with few hearings and whose final passage occurred during the aftermath of the September 11, 2001, terrorist attacks, the adjustments seemed to many to be incremental, technical changes. However, these incremental changes produced a revolutionary extension of federal power over education policy. Congress legislated in haste, and many states are now repenting at leisure.[1]

State Influence on Federal Policymaking

Since the 1930s, public policy in the United States evolved from a system of "dual" federalism, with clearly separate state and federal spheres of authority, into one in which state and federal governments share authority for domestic policy. A stronger federal role in domestic policy did not produce a withering away of state governments. Rather, they broadened their revenue bases and increased their administrative capacities (Teaford, 2002; Walker, 2000). Laws expanding the federal role in education policy, such as the Elementary and Secondary Education Act of 1965 and the Education for All Handicapped Children Act of 1975, included provisions designed to build up state departments of education (Timar, 1997). Just as federal laws influenced state political development, the states have also influenced federal policymaking. Despite pressure to consolidate federal programs into block grants during the 1980s, the compensatory education component of ESEA (Title I, known as Chapter I between 1981 and 1994) remained separate, largely because of pressure from its constituency of state and local Title I program directors (Peterson, Rabe, & Wong 1986). During Clinton's first term, current and former "education governors" and their allies profoundly influenced federal policy (Jennings, 1998). During Clinton's second term, Congress passed a welfare reform bill based quite explicitly on a few states' experiments with work requirements and time limits (Derthick, 1999).

Ironically, the "unfunded mandates" that arouse the ire of state and local officials often have their origins in state policies. Posner (1998) argues that the growth in federal mandates in the late twentieth century was in part because "state and local leaders themselves sought the nationalization of their own policies, whether it be to protect against intergovernmental competition or to promote their own national policy ideas or political ambitions" (p. 223). State programs can stimulate interest in a policy, demonstrate its feasibility, or produce inconsistencies among states that Congress is then called upon to eliminate (Posner, 1998, pp. 63–65).

The States and the 1994 Improving America's Schools Act

The provisions of the 1994 Improving America's Schools Act that require states to enact particular assessment and accountability policies followed essentially the trajectory that Posner describes. Several states enacted their own accountability reforms. National-level organizations (and public officials who had previously worked with those organizations) pushed to have standards and accountability enacted both in the states and as federal policy. Their goal was for federal Title I policy to become consistent with existing state accountability reforms, and also to use Title I as leverage so that more states would enact accountability measures. Undersecretary Marshall Smith said of IASA, "Title I was used to help drive the notion of having every state have standards. . . . Once Congress has said there's going to be a time schedule on this thing, you're going to have standards-based reform in your states" (DeBray, 2006, p. 31).

The National Movement for Standards-Based Education Reform

Standards-based education reform grew in popularity in the United States during the 1980s and 1990s, largely through the efforts of the National Governors' Association (NGA). The core of standards-based reform is the idea that education policy should be made "coherent" and organized around clear statements of what students should know and be able to do, coupled with assessments that would determine whether or not students were attaining the standards. Standards-based reform also includes expanding the state government's power to hold local schools and educators accountable for students' test results. This expansion of state control was intended to reduce variability among schools' curricula and students' experiences in school. NGA outlined its reform agenda in *Time for Results*, a report released in 1986, and tracked progress toward reform in an annual series of reports entitled *Results in Education*. The NGA also held a summit in Charlottesville, Virginia, in 1989 at which it endorsed a set of National Education Goals, with the support of President George H. W. Bush. Members of the Business Roundtable joined with their states' governors to push the standards-based reform agenda. Other organizations, such as Achieve, Inc., the New Standards Project, and the Pew Forum on Standards-Based Reform, also produced research and advocacy for standards in education.

Although the standards-based reform movement was national in scope, the actual policies were enacted at the state level because of constitutional necessity. Although ESEA, the federal special education law, and decades of desegregation litigation had expanded the federal role in education well beyond what it had been in the days of pure dual federalism, states retained their power and authority over matters of curriculum and testing. It was also a matter of politics, since a federally determined curriculum or testing regime would have been anathema to most citizens and state policymakers.[2] By 1994, forty-two states had developed, or were developing, content standards, and thirty states had, or were developing, student performance standards based upon the content standards (Jennings, 1998).

The Improving America's Schools Act: Standards-Based Reform Goes Federal

When President Bill Clinton, himself a former "education governor" who had been president of the NGA at the time of the Charlottesville summit, took office in 1993, the direction of federal education policy changed. Gordon Ambach of the Council of Chief State School Officers, Michael Cohen of President Clinton's White House staff, and Marshall Smith, Dean of the School of Education at Stanford University, played an important role in Clinton's transition team (Jennings, 1998). Veterans of state education reform and advocates of standards-based reform moved into key positions at the U.S. Department of Education (including Secretary of Education Richard Riley). The Clinton administration's goals were to bring federal education policy, especially the programs run under Title I of the ESEA, in line with states' existing standards-based policies and to push more states in a standards-based direction. In the spring of 1994, Congress passed Clinton's "Goals 2000" bill, which established the National Education Goals, provided grants for states to use in implementing standards-based reform, and created the National Education Standards and Improvement Council (NESIC) to provide leadership for state efforts.

After passing Goals 2000 in the spring of 1994, Congress then turned its attention to reauthorization of ESEA. The reauthorization bill, entitled the Improving America's Schools Act of 1994 (IASA), clearly had its origins in the standards-based reform movement. The law's "Statement of Policy" declared that the purpose of Title I programs was "to enable schools to provide opportunities for children served to acquire the knowledge and skills contained in the challenging State content standards and to meet the challenging State performance standards developed for all children" (P.L. 103-382, Secs. 1001c and 1001d). Toward this end, IASA required that assessment of Title I students be integrated with the assessments the states were using for the mainstream student population.[3]

IASA also required states to assess whether district and school performance on the assessments was showing "adequate yearly progress," and to impose sanctions if a school or district repeatedly failed to make such progress. The law allowed the states latitude in arriving at their own definitions of adequate yearly progress as long as those definitions were linked "primarily" to students' performance on required assessments and were

> consistent with [Federal] guidelines . . . that result in continuous and substantial yearly improvement of each local educational agency and school sufficient to achieve the goal of all children served under this part meeting the State's proficient and advanced levels of performance, particularly economically disadvantaged and limited English proficient children. (Sec. 1111b)

Districts were to identify for "improvement status" any school that did not achieve adequate yearly progress for two consecutive years, and to take "corrective action" in schools that still did not make adequate yearly progress after two years in improvement status.

Corrective actions, "consistent with State and local law," ranged from implementing Opportunity to Learn standards or strategies under the state's Goals 2000 plan, or entering into "interagency collaborative agreements" to improve service delivery, to more punitive measures such as withholding funds or "decreasing decision-making authority at the school level" in favor of "alternative governance arrangements" such as conversion into a charter school (Sec. 1116c). If an entire school district failed to make adequate yearly progress, the state education agency was to place it in improvement status, which could lead to corrective actions, including withholding funds, reconstituting (i.e., replacing) district personnel, removing one or more schools from the LEA's jurisdiction, implementing opportunity to learn standards or strategies under the state Goals 2000 plan, placing the LEA in receivership, abolishing or restructuring the LEA, allowing students to transfer to other school districts, and establishing a joint state–local plan for addressing performance problems.

State-Level Results of IASA

By 2001, nearly all states had defined academic performance standards for students and were testing students to determine their mastery of those standards. However, states' goals for the percentage of students that would be rated as "proficient" and their definitions of "adequate yearly progress" (AYP) toward that goal varied greatly (Goertz, Duffy, & LeFloch, 2001). Not surprisingly, so did the proportion of schools that states identified as not making AYP, from 1 percent in Texas and 5 percent in North Carolina to 76 percent in Michigan and 80 percent in the District of Columbia (Cohen, 2002, p. 4). Accountability policies also varied. Some states had no consequences for underperforming schools and districts other than a requirement that a "report card" or rating system indicate the underperformance. Other states had the power to take over or reconstitute failing schools (McDermott, 2003), but few had actually used the power.[4]

The IASA seems to have had no effect on the rate at which states enacted policies permitting state takeover, closure, and reconstitution of schools and school districts. By 1994, nineteen states had enacted district-level sanctions. Only seven more states enacted such sanctions prior to 2001.[5] Of the twenty-eight states that enacted school-level sanctions prior to 2001, fourteen had already done so in 1994 (see Figure 10.1). These policies thus appear to have been a response to state-level issues and conditions as much if not more than to federal pressure.

Clearly, states were taking full advantage of the flexibility of IASA's accountability requirements. Many states did not even comply with the IASA requirements for state assessments based on curriculum standards. As of March 2002, twenty-seven states had received federal waivers for the testing deadlines in IASA, and four states plus the District of Columbia had entered into compliance agreements with USED (U.S. General Accounting Office, 2002, pp. 10–11).

John Jennings, the former General Counsel for the House Committee on Education and Labor, and a principal participant in passage of both Goals 2000 and IASA, said that the Clinton administration "thought that if they pressed hard on states to comply with the new law, they would be shaking the foundations of the federal role in education, and giving ammunition to the far right that wanted to eliminate any federal role" (Robelen, 2001). Given that Republican candidates for Congress in 1994 had successfully campaigned against Democrats for creating a "national school board" with Goals 2000 and IASA, this fear was probably well founded. Put more positively, during the 1990s there was still no national consensus on what types of educational accountability policies worked best, and states' policies were responding to fifty different combinations of issues, institutions, and legal environments.

FIGURE 10.1 Ultimate State-level Sanctions for Schools and Districts

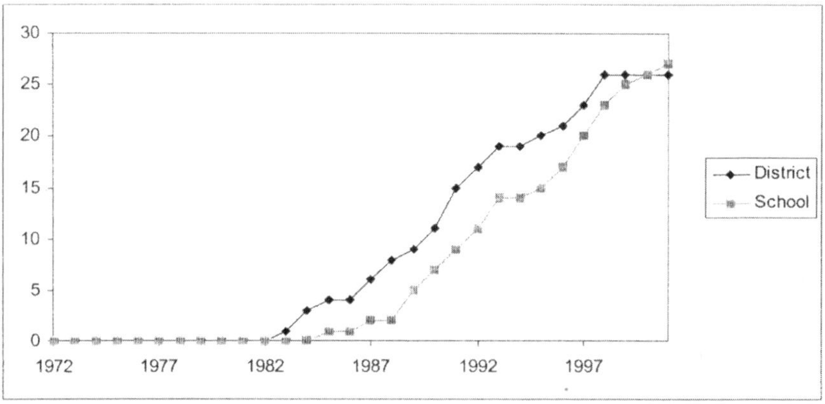

From IASA to NCLB: The Incremental Revolution

Dissatisfaction with the states' responses to IASA led officials in the Clinton administration and members of Congress to explore ways in which federal accountability policies might be tightened. When the 106th Congress (the last one during the Clinton administration) took up reauthorization of ESEA, the accountability advocates had their chance. Although more stringent versions of accountability policy attracted support in the 106th Congress, the ESEA was not reauthorized until the 107th Congress, after President George W. Bush took office. By making a few apparently technical changes to the definition of adequate yearly progress and the range of options for corrective action, the 107th Congress began a revolution in intergovernmental relations and education policy.

The Accountability Provisions of the No Child Left Behind Act

NCLB expands required state assessments. Instead of testing students in English and mathematics at three points in their K–12 careers, states now must annually assess the performance of all students in grades 3–8 and one high school grade, and must add a science test. Under NCLB, states retain the power to set standards, design or choose assessments, and determine what level of performance on the assessments should constitute a "proficient," "basic," or "advanced" score. However, states have far less discretion over defining AYP and determining how to intervene in schools and districts.

In the area of AYP, NCLB identifies the starting point from which progress is to be measured, as well as the goal toward which the progress is to be made: 100 percent of students scoring at the "proficient" level on state tests by 2014. States must identify the amount of annual increase in percent proficient that would move a school from the starting point to the 100 percent proficiency goal within twelve years. In order to make AYP, a school or district must achieve this incremental improvement for its student population as a whole, and for each major racial and ethnic group, students living in poverty, students with disabilities, and students with limited proficiency in English. A "safe harbor" provision states that if the percentage of students in a subgroup that did not achieve at least a proficient result decreased by "10 percent of that percentage" over the previous year, the group would be classified as making AYP [P.L. 107-110, Sec. 1111b(2)(I)].

NCLB also reduced states' choices of corrective actions. NCLB begins market-oriented accountability for schools as soon as they enter improvement status. In the first year of improvement status, students may transfer to other schools that are making adequate yearly progress. In the second year, the school district must allow parents to choose "supplemental education services" for their children, provided by public, private, or religious organizations and paid for with district Title I funds (P.L. 107-110, Sec. 1116b).

The list of corrective actions that a district may take in a school after two years of improvement status has been narrowed. The law now requires "governance changes" to be made in a school after it has been in improvement status for three years. The options for governance changes are reopening the school as a charter school, replacing all or most of the school staff, contracting out school management, turning management over to the state education agency if state law permits, and "any other major restructuring of the school's governance arrangement that makes fundamental reforms" (P.L. 107-110, Sec. 1116b.8.B.). If a district remains in improvement status for two years, NCLB requires the state to take corrective action, which may include withholding funds, instituting a new "scientifically based" curriculum, replacing personnel, removing one or more schools from the district's jurisdiction, placing the whole district in receivership or trusteeship, abolishing or restructuring the district, and authorizing students to transfer to schools in other districts (P.L. 107-110, Sec. 1116c).

Although adequate yearly progress and corrective action were not new requirements of federal policy, a few key adjustments to them in NCLB made them much stronger mandates than they had previously been. Because the changes were, on paper, merely tightening of existing requirements, they fit the general tendency of U.S. policymaking to proceed incrementally. The changes also fit the general trend identified by Posner (1998), who concluded that it is easier to extend a mandate than to enact one in the first place (p. 62), and also that policy advocates tend to pursue policies that are uniform across states. According to Bardach and Kagan (1982), Congress tends to make regulations more stringent because of "the natural tendency to follow things to their logical conclusion" (p. 19) and also because they believe that, in the absence of strict statutory targets, regulatory agencies will be soft on enforcement. Beginning in the 1960s and 1970s, Congress began stating regulatory goals in "absolute, unqualified terms," such as the zero effluent standard in the 1972 Water Pollution Control Act (p. 47). Tracing how Congress got from the fairly broad regulations of IASA to the strict mandates of NCLB shows how incremental change can produce a revolution in intergovernmental relations.

Beginning the Incremental Revolution: The 106th Congress

During President Clinton's second term, when ESEA was due to be reauthorized again, Assistant Secretary for Elementary and Secondary Education Michael Cohen (formerly of NGA) argued for putting more pressure on the states to enact standards-based reform. Preparing President Clinton to meet with governors, Cohen counted the number of states that had policies enabling them to identify and intervene in some way in underperforming schools:

> By '99, according to Ed Week, there were about 20 states that had that kind of policy in place, right? Which turns out to be, over a 13-year period [since *Time for Results*], a growth of one state per year. And Clinton's message to the governors was, at this rate, it will be another 30 years before we get this agenda enacted. We don't have time to wait. That's why the feds have to take a stronger role. And they didn't have a good answer for that. Now I think, and again, I think that argument is exactly what led to what's in No Child Left Behind now. (M. Cohen, interview with K. McDermott, November 6, 2003)

Although Congress did not pass another ESEA reauthorization during Clinton's presidency, debate on education bills during the 106th Congress (1998–2000) laid the groundwork for eventual passage of NCLB by the 107th Congress during the first year of George W. Bush's term in office.

A bipartisan Title I working group in the 106th Congress began to meet in anticipation of the upcoming reauthorization, with the Center for Law and Education and the Education Trust as leading members. A paper by researchers Tammi Chun and Margaret Goertz (1999), commissioned by the Civil Rights Project at Harvard University, examined Title I plans and concluded that the Texas system of holding schools accountable for the progress of student subgroups should be considered for state plans.

The working group began to establish contacts with members of the House and Senate education committees. The Center for Law and Education worked particularly closely with the staff of Senator Jeff Bingaman (D-NM), while the Education Trust's lobbyist, Amy Wilkins, met with Representative George Miller (D-CA). As Charlie Barone, legislative director for Representative Miller, the ranking Democrat on the House Committee on Education and the Workforce, said during a 1999 interview:

> The requirements, you have an accountability system in place, that were put in '94, are just kicking in now. And it's clear that the Department needed—we think, that's from Miller's perspective—tighter guidance around what an accountability system looks like, that measures the performance of all kids. (C. Barone, interview with E. DeBray, 10/29/99)

The "tightening" idea gained support during the hearings. Members of Congress and their staffs were dismayed when state education officials could not identify the characteristics of the students who were failing to achieve proficiency on their state tests. Rep. Miller in particular became an advocate of disaggregated data, and a bill based on his idea passed the House in the fall of 1999. According to Christine Wolfe, then a professional staff member for the House Committee on Education and the Workforce's Subcommittee on Oversight and Investigations, many members who voted for the bill didn't understand the difference between simply requiring states to disaggregate data on student performance and the much more far-reaching requirement to make such disaggregated data the basis of their accountability systems:

> people didn't even really talk about the Title I bill in those terms: "Hey, this is now requiring subgroup accountability at the school level!" But that was a major change in the Title I legislation. . . . A lot of people don't understand it! It's confusing to a certain degree, because since 1994 Title I has required disaggregated data, and the ability to examine test data by subgroups, but didn't require a state's accountability system to be built on that, and the achievement of all those groups. (C. Wolfe, interview with E. DeBray, 10/31/99)

Even though subgroup accountability was very important to a few members, hearings on Title I in the 106th Congress divided its focus between disaggregating data by subgroups, increasing state and local flexibility in spending federal funds, and making Title I funds a student-level entitlement that would be "portable," following students who changed schools. (The portability idea continued on the agenda into 2001, ultimately becoming the "supplemental services" provision of NCLB.)

While Representative Miller pushed for subgroup accountability, another Democrat, Senator Jeff Bingaman of New Mexico, was working on a proposal to tighten sanctions for low-performing schools. Based on recommendations from the staff of the Center for Law and Education, Bingaman's position was that states would have to make direct interventions to aid schools in "improvement" or "corrective action" status, and he offered language that was very specific about what some of those interventions had to be. The senator drew on governance ideas that had been supported by the Clinton administration, such as charter schools, creation of smaller schools, replacing school staff, and reconstitution of failing schools. In the case of a school where three years had gone by without making the gains needed under the state's definition of adequate yearly progress, Bingaman said the corrective action had to do two things. First, it had to change the school's administration or governance by the means described above (i.e., reconstitution, or creation of a charter school). Second, the corrective action had to provide for all staff professional development that was supported by reliable evidence of effectiveness and was related to the state's content and performance standards.

Bingaman's amendment was voted down in the Senate Health, Education, Labor, and Pensions committee along party lines in the spring of 2000. However, he was successful in advancing the issue of specific state and district interventions for Title I schools not making academic progress. Most significant, in terms of the policy idea's ultimate persistence, was that Bingaman shared it with Senator Joseph Lieberman, who was at work on a compromise bill proposing to consolidate many categorical ESEA programs while strengthening accountability and funding in Title I.

In the 106th Congress, as when IASA was passed in 1994, the NGA was a major participant in the legislative process, even though it is often difficult for the membership of the NGA to agree on what position to take on pending legislation since the group is ideologically diverse and must approve its positions by a super-majority vote (DeBray, 2006). According to Patricia Sullivan, then the NGA's director for education legislation, the group wanted Congress to "fix some of the obvious errors" in the IASA, but "stay out of the way" and "keep supporting the good work we do" (DeBray, 2006, p. 69). Individual Republican governors were critical of some elements of federal policy in a hearing before the Senate Committee on Health, Education, Labor, and Pensions. Governor Christine Todd Whitman of New Jersey asked the senators to give the states more flexibility that would facilitate her state's work with whole-school reforms (U.S. Senate, Committee on Health, Education, Labor and Pensions, 1999, p. 20). Governor John Engler of Michigan called for making all of Title I into a block grant, and asked the senators to "do for education what the 104th Congress did for welfare reform" (U.S. Senate, Committee on Health, Education, Labor and Pensions, 1999, p. 26). Senator, and former governor, George Voinovich of Ohio said flatly, "a lot of things that come out of the Department of Education are more appropriate for the State level" (U.S. Senate, Committee on Health, Education, Labor and Pensions, 1999, p. 6). The 106th Congress failed to reauthorize ESEA, but the legislation that would be considered in the 107th Congress borrowed heavily from Senator Lieberman's compromise proposal.

Making the Incremental Revolution: No Child Left Behind in the 107th Congress

Compared with other issues, such as school vouchers and the "Straight A's"[6] block grant proposal, the tightening of AYP and corrective action language received relatively little debate or publicity when Congress considered the No Child Left Behind Act in 2001. Despite claims by academic researchers and educators in the field that the stricter AYP definition would overidentify schools as failing, and the doubts of a few senators, Congress ultimately approved the more stringent measures. According to David Shreve of the NCSL, the law was "packaged" as an "incremental change" (D. Shreve, interview with K. McDermott, 11/7/03). While the AYP and corrective action provisions have posed major challenges to states and school districts (as some policymakers had predicted they might), the fact is that many members of Congress were largely unaware of the sudden and logarithmic expansion of the federal role in school accountability for which they had voted. Time pressure, the settling of technical details in conference, and partisan support among the Republicans to pass a president's program all contributed to the provisions' hasty adoption without much objection.

The model of subgroup accountability within schools was one that had been introduced to Texas schools in the late 1990s. President Bush's campaign had repeatedly stressed the claim that testing and accountability reforms in Texas had "narrowed the gap" in test scores between white children and black and Latino children in Texas public schools. Texas' education policies were a cornerstone of Bush's campaign claims to be a "compassionate conservative" and a reformer who could work effectively with Democrats. The ESEA reauthorization offered Bush a crucial opportunity to produce a federal law based on the Texas model.

President Bush's legislative blueprint required that adequate yearly progress be made by "disadvantaged" students within any school receiving Title I funds. As Andrew Rudalevige noted in his account of the development of No Child Left Behind accountability (2002, p. 20), "the blueprint did not explicitly mirror the level of disaggregation required in the school report cards." Nor did it specify the actions a district or state had to take for schools not making AYP, but it listed public school choice, "exit vouchers" for private schools, and supplemental services as alternatives.

The House and Senate both passed versions of the No Child Left Behind Act in May 2001. The Senate version of the accountability provisions was less stringent than that of the House. Senator James Jeffords (R-VT), who chaired the Committee on Health, Education, Labor, and Pensions, was not enthusiastic about the model of subgroup accountability with a specified timeline. Jeffords' staff committee director analyzed assessment data from several states and concluded that a majority of schools in those states would be identified as "failing" according to the Senate committee's draft version of the bill. A study by Thomas Kane of UCLA and Douglas Staiger of Dartmouth College concluded that more than 98 percent of the schools in Texas and North Carolina would have failed to meet the requirements in the bill, if they had been in effect between 1994 and 1999 (Kane & Staiger, 2002). Senators Judd Gregg (R-NH), Christopher Dodd (D-CT), Hillary Clinton (D-NY), and Tom Harkin (D-IA) shared Jeffords' concern about the results of the more stringent accountability formula. The Senate adopted a more lenient version that required all subgroups' performance to increase by at least one percentage point per year, but also would not have labeled schools as needing improvement simply because students of color did not have test score increases.

The House bill, on the other hand, required schools to make steady progress toward the goal of proficiency for all students in reading and math within twelve years. It required increasing percentages of students in the racial and economic subgroups to make the same amount of progress as all students in the school. The House's fidelity to this model was mainly the result of Representative George Miller's insistence. As it had in the 106th Congress, the Education Trust continued its aggressive advocacy of the tougher accountability provisions.

The White House sent mixed messages about its position on AYP, according to aides. Staff members recognized the political danger of labeling too many schools as failures, which might alienate suburban voters and squander limited federal resources. At the same time, the administration had political reason to want to see failing schools identified so that initial enactment of the public school choice and supplemental services sanctions could produce visible results of Bush's educational initiatives in action in the first term. Thus, they needed the law to identify some failing schools, but not too many. Before the conference committee began reconciling the differences between the House and Senate versions of the bill, Senator Jeffords left the Republican party, thus shifting control of the Senate to the Democrats. Consequently, Senator Edward Kennedy (D-MA) took over as chair of the Health, Education, Labor, and Pensions committee. Unlike Jeffords, Kennedy supported the more stringent accountability model.

In many ways, it was not until the conference committee began its work that members began to really grapple with the workability of the accountability provisions. Up to that point, the definitions of AYP and the corrective action requirements had been overshadowed by more politically volatile issues, including vouchers, annual testing, and the "Straight A's" proposal. Sally Lovejoy, chief education aide to House Education and Workforce Committee chair John Boehner (R-OH), recalled that in the 106th Congress, "no one paid any attention to" the issue of AYP, and that in the 107th Congress, the committee "pretty much took that same language that we had" (S. Lovejoy, interview with E. DeBray, 1/28/02). Conferees became concerned that all schools were going to be labeled "failing." Though conferees' education aides convened to agree on core principles of Adequate Yearly Progress, the final definition was ultimately resolved by the leadership, mainly Representatives Boehner and Miller, closely assisted by Senator Bingaman. The education aide to a Democratic senator on the HELP committee called Miller and Bingaman the committees' "two real hawks" on accountability (Interview with E. DeBray, February 1, 2002). The conference committee report kept the strict accountability measures from the House bill, but added the "safe harbor" provision.

Once it became clear that Congress was determined to enact stiffer accountability provisions, researchers and educators expressed concerns about what their effects might be. In a *New York Times* guest editorial, Kane and Staiger identified the emphasis on year-to-year growth as the "central flaw" in both the House and Senate bills. Another concern was the assumption that all students could be moved to proficiency within ten or twelve years. In interviews with the *New York Times*, Missouri's assistant commissioner of education, Stephen Barr, called it "an impossible dream," while Charles Zogby, the chief state school officer in Pennsylvania, said, "It's unrealistic to think that in some places where 90 percent of the children are below basic that we're going to turn this around in ten years. And then everybody is going to throw up their hands and say none of this is possible" (Wilgoren, 2001).

Letters sent by the NGA's leaders to House and Senate leaders make it clear that NGA understood the magnitude of the proposed changes to AYP and corrective action. Two different letters from NGA leaders to congressional leaders, dated April 13 and August 17, said,

> It is critical that the federal government not create new accountability systems, but utilize the existing systems in states. Any system of bonuses and sanctions should be based on state performance over time as indicated by the existing state assessment and accountability system. (Engler & Patton, 2001; Hodges & Taft, 2001).[7]

The August letter also suggests that the goal of 100 percent proficiency on a test can only be reached "if the test were made so simple as to underrate its purpose," and states, "It is imperative that a workable solution be found to hold schools, districts, and states accountable that does not throw a majority of Title I schools into school improvement as a result of impossible federal goals" (Engler & Patton, 2001). The National Conference of State Legislatures sent a letter to Congress on September 26, 2001, criticizing the testing requirements of NCLB as "an egregious example of a top-down, one-size-fits-all federal reform" (*Education Week*, 2001, p. 31).

The NGA was not as closely involved in the legislative process for NCLB as it had been in the previous Congress, and there was not much opportunity for other intergovernmental lobbying groups to participate. There had been no opportunity to raise these issues at the beginning of the legislative process because the legislation had moved through the House and Senate the previous winter without lengthy hearings. The conference committee negotiations were a tense affair, during which the AYP definitions were just one of hundreds of differences between the House and Senate versions of the bill that had to be negotiated. According to the education aide to a Senate HELP committee Democrat involved in the negotiations, staff for Senator Bingaman and Representative Miller "developed the proposal that's basically law now and brought it back to us, and there was a lot of hand wringing, lots of arguing. It was not a good situation."

In late summer of 2001, the negotiations deadlocked. President Bush put pressure on the conferees to finish their work, and was making an appearance at a school in Florida when terrorists attacked the World Trade Center and the Pentagon on September 11, 2001. After September 11, passing the education bill became even more of a political imperative. Bush said it was his highest priority other than the response to terrorism, and that passing the bill would show that business as usual continued despite September 11 and the anthrax attacks on Senate offices (Manna, 2004). Needless to say, the atmosphere was not conducive to rethinking the accountability provisions even if Representative Miller and Senator Bingaman had been willing to allow it.

To anybody who was not following the debate closely, it seemed like a tempest over a technicality. A July 2001 *New Yorker* article was one of the few extended discussions of the AYP formula in the general press. Its author, Nicholas Lemann, noted that most of the media's coverage of the bill had concerned whether or not it would include education vouchers. In contrast, although the AYP formula would have far-reaching consequences, members of Congress debated it "while the world slumbered on" (Lemann, 2001, p. 32). Looking ahead to the conference committee's decision about AYP, Lemann declared, "The whole world will not be watching. The whole world will be too confused to follow the action" (Lemann 2001, p. 34).

Members of Congress also could easily have believed that the law would not put much pressure on states to change their policies. NCLB contains language explicitly saying that it does not authorize "an officer or employee of the Federal Government to mandate, direct, or control a State, local educational agency, or school's curriculum" (P.L. 107-110, Sec. 9507a), and that no funds provided to the U.S. Department of Education under NCLB may be used to "endorse, approve, or sanction any curriculum designed to be used in an elementary school or secondary school" (P.L. 107-110, Sec. 9507b). It also clearly states that all corrective actions in schools and districts are to be "consistent with State law," (P.L. 107-110, Sec. 9507b), and its requirement for a single state assessment includes an exemption for some states. Under Section 1111(b) (5) of NCLB,

> If a State educational agency provides evidence, which is satisfactory to the Secretary [of Education], that neither the State educational agency nor any other State government official, agency, or entity has sufficient authority, under State law, to adopt curriculum content and student academic achievement standards, and academic assessments aligned with such academic standards, which will be applicable to all students enrolled in the State's public elementary and secondary schools,

then the state may comply with NCLB's standards and assessment requirements either by administering the statewide assessment only to students receiving Title I services or by ensuring that school districts receiving Title I grants have local standards and assessments in place that meet all the NCLB criteria for statewide assessments.

Despite the apparent incrementalism and nods in the direction of state autonomy, the NCLB provisions on AYP and corrective action have major implications for state authority over education policy. The "loopholes" closed by NCLB were in fact a recognition that state education policy responds to state conditions and priorities, as well as to continued uncertainty about the best way to hold states and districts accountable for student performance. Some approaches to educational accountability, such as holding schools accountable for the achievement growth of a cohort of students over time rather than comparing one year's students at a given grade level with the previous year's, are arguably better policies than the ones required in NCLB, but are now out of compliance with federal law. According to David Shreve of the National Council of State Legislatures, Congress often focuses on eliminating the most egregious examples of bad state policy, without regard for the effects of its enactments on states with better programs. Shreve says, "one of the things they lost sight of with No Child Left Behind, is that you brought a half a dozen states up from sub-basement to basement level, and you brought about 40 states from the second floor down to the basement level along with them" (K. McDermott interview, 11/7/03). Even though the U.S. Department of Education demonstrated some flexibility by approving changes to some states' NCLB plans in 2004, the fact remains that states must, in effect, ask federal permission before enacting certain kinds of policies over which they would previously have had sole authority.

Conclusion

The No Child Left Behind Act, which extends federal power over states' assessment and accountability policies, paradoxically had its origins in the extension of *state* power over education. Congress enacted the basic policy template of defining "adequate yearly progress" and requiring "corrective action" in schools and districts that do not make progress in the 1994 Improving America's Schools Act. The 1994 law was an outgrowth of the movement for state-level accountability policies. It was intended both to make federal law consistent with the new state laws and to push states without any accountability policies to enact them.

With respect to this second goal, the Improving America's Schools Act did not live up to its advocates' expectations. When Congress next took up a major education bill, accountability advocates made sure that it included a stricter definition of adequate yearly progress and more specific requirements for corrective action. It built on the provisions already enacted in 1994 in a way that appeared incremental, but actually had profound implications for states' policies. One reason why the changes were treated as incremental was the need to persuade conservative Republicans, generally ideologically opposed to a strong federal role in education, to back the president's efforts to expand federal mandates in this area.

As Lorraine McDonnell argues in a summary of the history of Title I (McDonnell, 2005), NCLB moves federal policy closer to the core of teaching and learning and, for that reason alone, it deserves to be seen as revolutionary. In addition, NCLB wrote a particular kind of relationship between state and local authorities into federal law. It is difficult, though, to generalize about the extent to which NCLB forced *change* in states' school accountability policies. Some states, like Texas and Massachusetts, already had policies in place that were consistent with NCLB. For others, meeting NCLB requirements meant departing from previous state policies, and state officials resented the federal mandates.

The most dramatic resistance thus far has come from Connecticut, which wanted to continue administering its state Mastery Test only in fourth, sixth, and eighth grades rather than testing annually between third and eighth grades. Connecticut officials argued that expanding the Mastery Test program would be prohibitively expensive, and would run afoul of a 2003 state law that forbade the use of any state funds to satisfy NCLB requirements. U.S. Secretary of Education Margaret Spellings countered that the state could expand testing within its existing budget by dropping the writing portion of the Mastery Test, which was not required under NCLB, and using less expensive, machine-gradable examinations. Resisting the idea of changing state testing policy to comply with federal law, the state filed a federal suit against Spellings in 2005. The Connecticut NAACP petitioned the court to enter the case on the side of the federal government, arguing that states should not be allowed to opt out of equity mandates just because they are expensive (McDermott, 2007). John Brittain of the Lawyers' Committee for Civil Rights Under Law, previously the lead attorney for the *Sheff v. O'Neill* plaintiffs, pronounced the state's resistance to be "very bad policy" (Frahm, 2006).

We believe that, in general terms, expanding state control over education has improved educational opportunities for all students. However, the particular testing and accountability mandates of NCLB, which have brought about the national policies we have described, deserve careful scrutiny as Congress begins its deliberations for the law's reauthorization. For instance, it is clear that the quality of states' assessment systems varies considerably; the limited federal contribution for compliance with the testing mandates has resulted in a set of incentives for many states to adopt more cost-effective but lower-quality tests. Likewise, it is possible that NCLB's mandated testing in the early grades has had a corollary effect of spurring state-level policies to retain students in grade, a practice increasingly linked to dropout in the upper grades. Finally, the subgroup accountability model in Title I has resulted in a school classification system that does not lead in any clear way to the effective targeting of state-level resources to build capacity in the schools that need it most. We think that the policies of the mid-1990s IASA, by which states could opt to administer higher-quality assessments in fewer grades and at lower expense, deserves at least some public debate as to its merits; we further consider that state capacity to intervene in schools that are clearly struggling should be just as high a fiscal priority in Title I as testing all students statewide in grades 3 through 8.

Notes

The authors gratefully acknowledge financial support from the Spencer Foundation and the William and Flora Hewlett Foundation, through the Advanced Studies Fellowship Program at Brown University. The data presented, statements made, and views expressed in this chapter are solely the responsibility of the authors.

1. This chapter draws on two related research projects. The first is Elizabeth DeBray's book on the enactment of federal education policy in the 106th and 107th Congresses, *Politics, ideology, and education: Federal policy during the Clinton and Bush administrations* (New York: Teachers College Press), 2006. This work was begun as her doctoral dissertation at Harvard University and completed with support from the Advanced Studies Fellowship Program at Brown University. The second is Kathryn A. McDermott's project for the Advanced Studies Fellowship Program, which analyzes the evolution of states' accountability policies prior to NCLB.

2. The U.S. Office of Educational Research and Improvement did, however, fund voluntary standards in several subject areas.

3. Subsequently, the idea of a unitary assessment system was extended to students in special education programs by the Individuals with Disabilities Education Act of 1997 and to students participating in vocational education by the Perkins Vocational-Technical Act of 1998.

4. "Reconstitution" refers to the replacement of most or all of a school's staff, including its principal.

5. In Figure 10.1, states with each of the policies were identified using sources such as *Education Week*'s annual "Quality Counts" report and state-by-state summaries from the Education Commission of the states. The author then searched legislative and state Board of Education records to secure the text of the policies, verify their content, and determine when they were enacted. In many cases, these searches could be performed online using LEXIS-NEXIS and state legislative resources. When this was not possible, information was drawn from microforms of legislative materials or direct contact with state libraries.

6. The "Straight A's" block grant proposal was first proposed by Republicans in the 106th Congress, where it was also approved as part of the bill that passed in that Congress. It was a pilot program to be awarded competitively to ten states by the U.S. Secretary of Education. Straight A's in its purest form would have given the states latitude to consolidate federal categorical program funding streams and set goals for improving performance for those programs over a five-year period, at which point they would be held accountable for results. It was opposed by congressional Democrats who argued for the preservation of categorical programs, particularly Title I. The final No Child Left Behind Act contains a modified but weakened version of Straight A's, with provisions for pilot programs for districts to experiment with consolidation of federal program funds.

7. The April 13 letter, signed by NGA Human Resources Committee chair Governor Jim Hodges (SC) and vice-chairman Governor Bob Taft (R-OH), was addressed to Senators Lott, Jeffords, Daschle, and Kennedy. The August 17 letter, signed by NGA chair Governor John Engler (MI) and vice-chairman Paul Patton (KY), was sent to Representatives Boehner and Miller

and to Senators Kennedy and Gregg, the chairpersons and ranking members of the House and Senate committees dealing with education.

References

Bardach, E., & Kagan, R. A. (1982). *Going by the book: The problem of regulatory unreasonableness.* Philadelphia: Temple University Press.

Chun, T., & Goertz, M. E. (1999). Title I and state education policy: High standards for all students? In G. Orfield & E. H. DeBray (Eds.), *Hard work for good schools: Facts not fads in Title I reform* (pp. 120–129). Cambridge: The Civil Rights Project, Harvard University.

Cohen, M. (2002). Implementing Title I standards, assessments, and accountability: Lessons from the past, challenges for the future. New York: Thomas B. Fordham Foundation.

DeBray, E. (2006). *Politics, ideology, and education: Federal policy during the Clinton and Bush administrations.* New York: Teachers College Press.

Derthick, M. (1999). How many communities? The evolution of American federalism. In M. Derthick (Ed.), *Dilemmas of scale in America's federal democracy.* New York: Cambridge University Press.

Education Week. (2001, October 10). Letter from National Conference of State Legislatures to Congress of September 26, 2001.

Engler, J., & Patton, P. E. (2001, August 17). Letter to Representative John A. Boehner, Representative George Miller, Senator Edward M. Kennedy, and Senator Judd Gregg.

Frahm, R. A. (2006, March 23). NAACP details opposition to 'No child' lawsuit. *Hartford Courant*, p. B1.

Goertz, M., Duffy M., & LeFloch, K. C. (2001). *Assessment and accountability systems in the 50 states: 1999–2000.* Philadelphia: Consortium for Policy Research in Education, Research Report Series RR-046. Available: http://www.gse.upenn.edu/cpre/Publications/rr46.pdf.

Hodges, J., & Taft, B. (2001, April 13). Letter to Senators Trent Lott, James M. Jeffords, Thomas A. Daschle, and Edward M. Kennedy.

Jennings, J. F. (1998). *Why national standards and tests? Politics and the quest for better schools.* Thousand Oaks, CA: Sage.

Kane, T. J., & Staiger, D. O. (2002, June 10–11). *Racial subgroup rules in school accountability systems.* Paper presented at the Kennedy School of Government, Harvard University, Cambridge.

Lemann, N. (2001, July 2). Testing limits: Can the President's education crusade survive Beltway politics? *The New Yorker*, pp. 28–34.

Manna, P. (2004). Leaving no child behind. In C. Cross (Ed.), *Political education: National policy comes of age*. New York: Teachers College Press.

Mathis, W. J. (2003, May). No Child Left Behind: Costs and benefits. *Phi Delta Kappan 84*, 679–686.

McDermott, K. A. (2003). What causes variation in states' accountability policies? *Peabody Journal of Education 78*(4), 153–176.

McDermott, K. A. (2007). A national movement comes home: State politics and educational accountability in the 1990s. In C. Kaestle & A. Lodewick (Eds.), *To educate a nation: Federal and national strategies for school reform*. Lawrence: University Press of Kansas.

McDonnell, L. M. (2005). NCLB and the federal role in education: Evolution or Revolution? *Peabody Journal of Education 80*(2), 19–38.

Peterson, P., Rabe, B., & Wong, K. (1986). The maturation of redistributive programs. In *When federalism works*. Washington, DC: Brookings Institution, 1986. Reprinted in A. R. Odden (Ed.), *Education policy implementation* (pp. 65–50). Albany: State University of New York Press, 1991.

Posner, P. L. (1998). *The politics of unfunded mandates: Whither federalism?* Washington, DC: Georgetown University Press.

Public Law 103-382 (1994). *The Improving America's Schools Act of 1994*.

Public Law 107-110 (2001). *The No Child Left Behind Act of 2001*.

Robelen, E. W. (2001, November 28). States sluggish on execution of 1994 ESEA. *Education Week*. Retrieved from www.edweek.com/ew/newstory.cfm?slug=13com-ply.h21.

Rudalevige, A. (2002). *Managing the president's program: Presidential leadership and legislative policy formulation*. Princeton: Princeton University Press.

Teaford, J. C. (2002). *The rise of the states: Evolution of American state government*. Baltimore: Johns Hopkins University Press.

Timar, T. (1997). The institutional role of state education departments: A historical perspective. *American Journal of Education 105*, 231–260.

U.S. General Accounting Office (2002). Title I: Education needs to monitor states' scoring of assessments. GAO-02-393.

U.S. Senate, Committee on Health, Education, Labor, and Pensions (1999, February 23). *Education reform: Governors' views* (Hearing). Washington, DC: U.S. Government Printing Office.

Walker, D. B. (2000). *The rebirth of federalism: Slouching towards Washington*. New York: Chatham House.

Wilgoren, J. (2001, July 17). State school chiefs fret over U.S. plan to require testing. *New York Times*.

Chapter 11

Reading from the Top

State Impact on Reading Curriculum and Instruction

Mengli Song

The 1980s saw the emergence of "a new context for governance" of education policy in the United States, with states assuming an increasingly proactive role in charting the course of education (Fuhrman, 1987). Spurred by a series of major federal reading legislations enacted during the decade, the policy activism of the state has been particularly salient in reading, an essential area of schooling and the battlefield of diverse interests for almost a century. In this chapter, we review recent activities and developments in the reading policy domain in nine states, and highlight the dominant role of the state in developing reading policies. We focus particularly on the loss of local control to state authority over curriculum and instruction—the core of teaching and learning.

Data for this chapter came from structured interviews with 366 individuals and analyses of policy-relevant documents conducted as part of the State Reading Policy Study at the University of Michigan between 1999 and 2002 (Miskel, Coggshall, DeYoung, Osguthorpe, Shepley, Song, & Young, 2003). Before examining the power of the state in setting reading policy, an overview of the recent context of the state reading policy domain is in order.

Context of the State Reading Policy Domain

With the century-long "reading wars,"[1] reading has always been an area of interest to academics, educators, and even policymakers. It is not until the 1990s, however, that reading truly aroused widespread concerns and garnered unprecedented political attention across the nation. In most, if not all, states, low reading achievement has been recognized as a grave problem in need of immediate policy action. Such recognition has often been triggered by widespread dissatisfaction with student test scores. In all nine states that we studied, students' performance on standardized reading achievement tests served as a major "problem indicator" that led to heightened agenda status for reading (Kingdon, 1995). Reflecting on what brought reading to the top of Utah's policy agenda, for instance, a higher education representative remarked,

> The single biggest event was declining reading scores of our students. . . . There were only two states between 1992 and 1998 that continuously declined. Only two states in the country! One was Wyoming and the other was Utah! So it was the declining reading test scores that have sparked the interest, the money, the legislative attention.

Even in Connecticut, a state praised as a "shining star" in terms of early reading achievement (National Education Goals Panel, 1999), reading test scores were seen as a cause for concern. A Connecticut House representative observed:

> I think that testing has had an impact, because I think it has identified the problems. I think it is what drove the change ultimately. . . . I think the change came legislatively . . . probably in response to the Mastery Tests. You know, once you start testing and people are failing the tests, people were looking for solutions to that.

For many, more troubling than the failing rates was the persistent achievement gap. A Connecticut State Department of Education official lamented, "The concept of two Connecticuts is becoming more and more apparent in the Mastery Test scores, and while we are seeing improvements uniformly, the gap is not narrowing." A state legislator in Michigan similarly noted, "The problem in Michigan, of course, is the achievement level is not spread evenly."

In addition to powerful problem indicators such as low test scores, a favorable political environment in recent years has also helped to bring reading to the top of the state policy agendas (Kingdon, 1995). Under a national mood that has placed strong emphasis on education in general and reading in particular, politicians on both sides of the political fence have identified themselves as supporters of education reform and considered reading a good political issue. For policymakers, advocating policies to improve reading achievement has offered them an opportunity for political accomplishment that is likely to be achieved with minimum opposition and little political risk. As a member of a teacher union in Michigan aptly put it, "You know being against . . . sound reading policy is like being against motherhood or democracy." A Michigan business leader likewise remarked that the issue of reading was like "mom, American flag, and apple pie." It is thus no wonder that many "education governors" or even "reading governors" have emerged in recent years, and that reading has become a top priority not only for the nation, but also for the states.

The recognition of reading as a pressing problem in need of a solution combined with a favorable political environment led to the opening of a "window" for policy change in many states in the 1990s. A "policy window," according to Kingdon's (1995) multiple streams theory of policymaking, opens at critical junctures of the policy development process, and represents a propitious time during which policy entrepreneurs are most likely to successfully couple their pet solutions to compelling problems. With the opening of policy windows in the state reading policy domain in the late 1990s, the reading policy communities were galvanized into action. Just within a few years, flurries of reading legislations and initiatives had been launched across the states. By the year 2002, thirty-five states had created or were developing major reading initiatives (Manzo, 2002). All the nine states that we studied (Alabama, California, Connecticut, Indiana, Maine, Michigan, North Carolina, Texas, and Utah) enacted statewide reading initiatives in late 1990s. Examples include the Alabama Reading Initiative of 1998, the Reading Plan for Michigan of 1998, and the Texas Reading Initiative of 1996, to name just a few. Although these initiatives often resulted from concerted efforts by policy actors both in and outside of the government, state government agencies clearly dominated the policy processes in virtually every state that we studied.

Dominance of the State in Reading Policy Development

As Mawhinney (2001) notes, underlying policymaking and politics are two fundamental issues: who wields power and influence and whose views are represented in a democracy. Our investigation of reading policy developments in nine states generated unequivocal and consistent answers to these questions. Employing both the traditional reputational approach and the formal network analytic methods (Wasserman & Faust, 1994), we found that the development of state reading policy was largely dominated by state government agencies, in particular, state departments of education, governor's offices, and state legislatures. Nongovernment actors—interest groups and individuals acting on their own—typically played only a marginal role.[2]

Specifically, in our cross-state study, we measured policy actors' influence using three types of indicators: perceived influence, actor centrality, and actor prestige. For each actor, perceived influence was measured as the number of nominations that the actor received from other actors in the state as being most influential on the state's reading policy. Actor centrality and actor prestige are both measures of influence based on the relationships among actors within the state reading policy network. From the social network perspective, a central actor is one involved in many relationships (Freeman, 1979; Wasserman & Faust, 1994), and centrality is commonly defined as the number of direct ties that an actor has with other actors in a network.[3] Knoke (1990) asserts that network centrality is synonymous with influence, for the extensive network ties empower central actors by giving them greater access to and control over valuable information on conditions, opportunities, and constraints. The measure of prestige takes into account the direction of the relationships and is defined as the number of relationships received rather than initiated by an actor. The idea is that relations are often asymmetric, and that powerful and prestigious actors tend to be the objects rather than sources of communication (Knoke & Burt, 1983). The asymmetry of relations reflects authority and deference produced by inequalities in control over valued resources as well as the distinction between leaders and followers.

Comparisons of government and nongovernment actors on the three influence indicators revealed that government actors were more influential than nongovernment actors based on both centrality and prestige in all the eight states where network data were available (Table 11.1). Despite the relatively small sample sizes, the differences were statistically significant in most cases. The difference in perceived influence between the two types of actors was also statistically significant in six states, marginally significant in Connecticut and Texas, and not significant only in Indiana. These results are consistent with the findings from Marshall, Mitchell, and Wirt's (1989) study of the state education policy domain and Mazzoni's (1993) longitudinal study of education policymaking in Minnesota, among others.

TABLE 11.1. Results of Independent-Samples T-Tests Comparing the Influence of Government and Nongovernment Actors on State Reading Policy, by Influence Indicator and State

State	Perceived Influence	Centrality	Prestige	Sample Size
Alabama	*	*	**	18
California	*	***	**	38
Connecticut	~	*	**	26
Indiana	NS	***	***	28
Maine	**	*	*	19
Michigan	**	**	***	29
North Carolina	*	NA	NA	24
Texas	~	***	**	29
Utah	**	*	*	21

Note. Sample size refers to the number of policy actors (i.e., government agencies, interest groups, and individual policy actors not affiliated with any groups or organizations) instead of number of individuals that we interviewed in a given state.

NA: not available; NS: not significant; $\sim p < .10$; $^{*}p < .05$; $^{**}p < .01$; $^{***}p < .001$.

With regard to the influence of government actors, the most notable finding from our study was the prominence of state departments of education. In eight of the nine states (with the exception of Alabama), the state departments of education ranked among the top three in terms of influence on reading policy based on both network and reputational measures. In four states (Connecticut, Indiana, Maine, and Utah), they ranked highest on all three influence indicators. A citizen's group representative, for example, thus described the influence of the Connecticut State Department of Education: "I really do see it as a top-down system in Connecticut. [The real influential actor] would be the state department of education. They are the policy developers. Certainly not the teacher unions or something like that."

The influence of other state government agencies, such as the governor's offices, state legislatures, and state boards of education, varied more widely across the states. Nevertheless, they were generally more powerful than groups outside of the government in the state reading policy domain. Governor's office, for instance, ranked highest in terms of perceived influence in both Michigan and Texas, and second highest in California and Indiana. It was also the most prestigious actor in Alabama, and the second most prestigious actor in both Michigan and Utah. A former Texas Education Agency official thus commented on the influence of the governor's office on Texas' reading policy: "There wasn't the push for literacy until George Bush was in office." An interest group representative concurred:

> If I could name four individuals who had the most to do with [Texas' reading policy], it would start with Governor Bush and [Commissioner] Mike Moses, and then closely followed by Margaret LaMontagne and Robin Gilchrist as their chief staff people involved in this area.

Obviously, the high levels of political activism and policy involvement of the state government accounted in a large part for their strong influence over state reading policy. Since the 1990s, numerous reading legislations and programs have been initiated by the state governments, which have greatly enhanced their visibility in the reading policy arena. The various government agencies were not only active in proposing new policy ideas, but also actively engaged in collaborations with one another on reading-related issues. In addition to his role as Connecticut's Commissioner of Education, for example, Ted Sergi also served as the secretary of the Connecticut State Board of Education and the education aide to Governor Rowland. An official of the Connecticut House of Representatives observed:

> The governor has complete faith in Commissioner Sergi. They have a very good relationship. . . . He truly delegated educational policy to his commissioner. . . . And there really is no gap between the two. There's no tension at all. So when Commissioner Sergi says something, it's as good as getting it from the governor.

Similar alliances between government agencies, particularly between the governor's office and state department of education, were also formed in other states. In Utah, for example, many of our respondents noted that most of the work coming out of the governor's office in relation to reading was done in concert with the state department of education, and that the combination of the two had the strongest influence on Utah's reading policy. Undoubtedly, effective alliances between the powerful made the powerful even more powerful.

In addition to policy activism, another source for the political clout of the state government was its control over or the ability to secure funding. As a professor in Connecticut put it plainly: "We have to say that the general assembly has impact because of money." In 1998, the Connecticut General Assembly passed PA 98-243: An Act Concerning Early Reading Success, which established a $20-million-per-year Early Reading Success Grant to help fourteen most needy school districts in improving the reading skills of their students. In the same year, the General Assembly also enacted a supplementary grant program (PA 98-168) to provide grants for twelve additional districts. In Texas, the state legislature passed House Bill 1 in 1997, which appropriated $32 million for the Texas Reading Initiative proposed by Governor Bush. Bush also successfully secured an additional authorization of $200 millions to fund the accountability measures he added to the Texas Reading Initiative in 1998. The millions of dollars behind these policy initiatives have certainly bought a great deal of political clout for their initiators. In this respect, interest groups outside of the government clearly were at a power disadvantage.

A more important reason for interest groups' lack of influence on state reading policy, however, was their lack of focus on the issue of reading. We heard repeatedly during our interviews that the focus for many educational organizations was on issues other than students' achievement. A Texas teacher organization representative, for example, admitted that reading was not an important issue for them, stating, "Our primary issues have been along the lines of salary and benefits and retirement and class size." A professor in Texas was obviously well aware of that.

> What's true about most of these [educational] organizations, including the university, is that they've been . . . remarkably acquiescent and silent on most of the initiatives related to reading. And most often, they are covering their own butts. . . . "We're looking for teacher raises next year." "We're looking for these benefits." . . . Well, get in line, folks!

Further, interest groups' passiveness was also believed to result from their focus on the implementation rather than the development of reading policy, as indicated by the following observation from a teacher organization representative in California:

> Many of [the interest groups] are more in terms of implementation level. They take whatever the state does and then translate it for teachers. . . . I don't think they really go up there and fight . . . or influence policy that way. I mean I don't know for sure that they in the networks lobby.

In sum, our examination of the influence structure of the state reading policy domain suggests that although with the "advocacy explosion" (Berry, 1997; Knoke, 1986, 1990), interest groups have grown rapidly in both number and diversity, their influence did not match their number at least in the state reading policy domain. With a few exceptions (e.g., the Alabama A+ Education Foundation and the University of Maine), reading interest groups typically played the role of passive followers and supporters. State government agencies, on the other hand, were the true movers and shakers in the reading policy processes, whose influence manifested not only in the sheer number of bills introduced and the amount of funding secured, but also in their firm control over the core of schooling: curriculum and instruction.

State Impact on Reading Curriculum and Instruction

The state reading legislations and initiatives enacted in recent years were broad in scope, running the whole gamut from standards and assessment, pedagogy, and accountability, to remedial programs, in-service professional development, and teacher education. Among the array of issues, curriculum and instruction have clearly been the foci. In every state that we studied, the reading policy initiatives not only expressed their grand goals in broad terms, but also stipulated in explicit language what specific reading skills students are expected to master and how reading should be taught in schools, depriving teachers and schools much of their authority over local decision-making.

Given the recent federal emphasis on scientifically based research, it came as no surprise that just about every state has resorted to research to guide policy development, particularly with regard to curriculum and instruction. With the exceptions of North Carolina and Utah, for example, the state departments of education in seven of the nine states in our study convened some kind of expert panel or task force to examine research-based evidence for effective reading instruction and to make recommendation for state reading policy. The list includes: Alabama Reading Panel (1996), the Superintendent's Reading Task Force of California (1995), Connecticut Early Reading Success Panel (2000), Indiana Phonics Task Force (2000), Maine Early Literacy Workgroup (1998), Michigan Early Literacy Committee (1998), and the group of top reading educators convened by the Texas Commissioner of Education in 1996 to address issues in reading instruction. Similar efforts also stemmed from governor's offices, such as the Governor's Advisory Council on the Reading Plan for Michigan (1998), and the Governor's Focus on Reading Task Force (1996) and the Governor's Business Council reading summits (1996) convened by the Texas governor.

With high levels of credibility, these expert panels and task forces provided valuable input as well as explicit language to the policy decisions that states have made regarding reading curriculum and instruction. The resulting state reading policies and policy guidance were often highly prescriptive in nature. California's 1999 reading/language arts curriculum framework, for instance, states that the K–3 reading/language arts curriculum should provide explicit and systematic instruction and diagnostic support in eight specific areas: phonemic awareness, phonics, decoding, word-attach skills, spelling, vocabulary, comprehension skills, writing skills and strategies and their application, and listening and speaking skills and strategies (California State Board of Education, 1999, p. 21). Similar levels of policy prescriptivism were also seen in other states as will be shown in the following sections. The means through which state governments imposed their control over curriculum and instruction were various: through specifications in curriculum standards and frameworks, through teacher training, and through teacher licensure regulations, among others. In the remainder of this section, we examine in detail how reading curriculum and instruction has been shaped in each of the nine states included in the State Reading Policy Study.

Alabama

The spotlight in the Alabama reading policy arena mostly fell on the Alabama Department of Education (ADE). What earned the department most credits within the state and even a national reputation was the development and implementation of the Alabama Reading Initiative (ARI) in 1998 under the leadership of Katherine Mitchell, the director of ARI.[4] As a precursor to the initiative, Mitchell convened the Alabama Reading Panel in 1996 at the behest of the state board of education and served as the chair of the panel. The panel was remarkable in that it brought together a diverse array of potentially contentious organizations from opposite sides of the "reading wars," and yet was able to reach a consensus on a statewide plan for literacy education. Based on a review of over seventy articles and books over a twelve-month period, the panel concluded, "The most pervasive finding is that approaches to teaching beginning reading must be balanced" (ADE, 1998b, p. 2). Members of the panel later termed their approach as "research-based integration" to capture the idea that some elements of effective reading instruction put emphasis on code skills, while others put emphasis on the comprehension strategies.

The panel's work was documented in two influential reports: *Report on the Review of the Research* (ADE, 1998b) and *Knowledge and Skills Teachers Need to Deliver Effective Reading Instruction* (ADE, 1998a). Both publications call for an integrated approach to reading instruction that emphasizes: phonemic awareness; systematic, explicit phonics instruction; explicit reading comprehension instruction; language and vocabulary development; a reading/writing connection; fluency instruction; ongoing assessment of student progress; and provisions for intervention based on scientifically based reading research. These two reports formed the basis of the teacher professional development program that was at the center of the ARI launched in 1998.

The goal of the ARI was to attain 100 percent literacy among all Alabama's schoolchildren. The ADE first implemented the initiative in sixteen pilot schools with private funds in 1998, and expanded to 424 schools by the year 2001–2002. In 1999, the Alabama state legislature appropriated $6 million for the ARI and an additional $10 million in 2000. Despite the state's budget crisis, advocates of the initiative managed to maintain its funding level at $10 million for 2001.

The accomplishments of the reading panel and the ADE were in a large part attributed to the entrepreneurship of Mitchell. For many Alabamians, the state department of education was synonymous with the name of Katherine Mitchell. A reading association representative opined, "Katherine Mitchell is a goddess [laughs], a reading goddess." Her influence, according to an administration official, stemmed partly from the support from the governor: "The governor really considers Katherine Mitchell the reading czar. And anytime anybody comes to ask for funding for reading programs, if it doesn't fit with the approach that Katherine is taking, the governor is very hesitant to support it." The observation attests to with our earlier point about increased power resulting from the alliance among the powerful.

The power of the "reading czar," however, could be a little overwhelming for some. A university respondent, for instance, indicated that despite the popular support for ARI, there was a certain degree of resistance among some of the faculty to the initiative, particularly to Mitchell's "her way or no way" philosophy:

> There may be certain faculty who may not agree with some of her positions. And to a certain extent Katherine is one of these people—"Don't confuse the issue with the data. We know what's best." And that also doesn't resonate real well in a research university. I think a lot of people buy that in the schools, but it doesn't resonate well with faculty.

Such sentiment, however, did not represent the mainstream. For many, Mitchell's leadership was highly regarded and her accomplishments were amazing, particularly "given the historical reading wars," according to a university professor. Serving as the director of the Alabama Reading First Initiative as of 2006, the reading czar continues to hold the reins to the reading curriculum and instruction in the Camellia State.

California

Defying the common view about the weak policy influence of state boards of education (e.g., Marshall et al., 1989; Mazzoni, 1993), the California State Board of Education (CSBE), appointed by the governor and spearheaded by the "one-woman gang," Marion Joseph, took a strong role in shaping the state's reading policy and ranked by far the highest in terms of perceived influence among all reading policy actors in the state. The most significant impact of the CSBE on the state's reading policy came from their adoption of the *English-Language Arts Content Standards for California Public Schools: Kindergarten Through Grade Twelve* in 1997, and the subsequent adoption of the *Reading/Language Arts Framework for California Public Schools* in 1999 that aligned the new standards with classroom instruction. The 1997 standards marked a significant shift in the direction of California's reading policy, as a policy researcher explained, "[Governor] Pete Wilson and his state board of education . . . decided that in the state reading standards . . . there would have to be a very strong phonics emphasis. And so therefore, you had this . . . policy turnaround." Although overall policy actors in the state were supportive for the new standards, some were concerned that the standards were too restrictive and represented a "relatively narrow pedagogical view," according to a teacher organization representative.

Ranking next to the CSBE in perceived influence was the California Office of the Governor, which was also actively involved in reading policy development. Following a State Assembly informational hearing on reading instruction in May 1996, eight major pieces of legislation were signed by Governor Pete Wilson and enacted in July and September 1996. They deal with reading instruction, class-size reduction, professional development, and teacher credentialing. This set of legislation, together with two bills passed in 1995 related to instructional materials, has been collectively referred to as the California Reading Initiative.

The two bills from 1995, Assembly Bills 170 and 1504, nicknamed the "ABC bills" for their sponsors (Alpert, Burton, and Conroy), were of particular importance, as they marked the beginning of tight legislative control over reading curriculum and instruction in California. The ABC bills mandate that reading instructional materials in grades K–8 should include "systematic, explicit phonics," and that instructional materials purchased by school districts with state funds must also contain "systematic, explicit phonics." Similar prescriptions also appear in Assembly Bill 3075 enacted in 1996, which stipulates that the reading requirement for teaching credential shall include satisfactory completion of a reading instruction program that is research-based and that include both a comprehension component and a component of direct, systematic, explicit phonics.

As could be expected, state control over reading pedagogy was also extended to teacher professional development. Assembly Bill 1086 passed in 1997 requires school districts to certify that no less than 90 percent of employees who provide direct reading instruction in grades K–3 have received specified in-service training in reading. The training must be provided by approved SBE instructors, and must include twelve components. The list, not surprisingly, starts with "phoneme awareness instruction," and "systematic explicit phonics instruction."

While the CSBE, Office of the Governor, and State Assembly all demonstrated a clear preference for phonic instruction, the California Department of Education (CDE) was trying to keep to the middle ground. In 1995, the Reading Task Force convened by the department attributed students' low reading achievement directly to the 1987 English-Language Arts Framework, and declared in *Every Child Reader* that the 1987 framework "did not present a comprehensive and balanced reading program and gave insufficient attention to a systematic skill instruction program" (CDE, 1995, p. 2). To supplement *Every Child a Reader,* CDE published a reading program advisory in 1996: *Teaching Reading: A Balanced, Comprehensive Approach to Teaching Reading in Pre-kindergarten Through Grade Three.* It states that reading instruction should follow a balanced and comprehensive approach, and should include three major components: a broad language-rich program, appropriate instructional materials, and diagnostic tools and intervention. The broad language-rich program further includes an organized explicit skills program (phonemic awareness; letter names and shapes; systematic, explicit phonics; and spelling), vocabulary development, and comprehension and higher-order thinking.

Clearly, the CDE's stance on reading pedagogy was not in total agreement with that of the pro-phonics CSBE, state legislature, and office of the governor. During our interviews, quite a few participants mentioned the tension between the CDE and the CSBE, as indicated by a representative of a citizens association:

> There's . . . a constant conflict between the department of education and the state board of education . . . because there's a greater desire on the part of the department to have a very balanced curriculum. And there's a greater desire on the part of the state board of education to really put the emphasis on the phonics.

In fact, the tension between the two could probably be traced back to the 1993 lawsuit filed by the CSBE against the State Superintendent of Public Instruction, which established the CSBE as the foremost education policy-making authority in California. The primary role of the CDE has since then been relegated to administering and implementing policies established by the CSBE instead of creating policies. The political feuds and the ideological disagreements between the CSBE and CDE, combined with the alliance between the CSBE and the office of the governor by virtue of the political structure of the state (i.e., the governor appoints the CSBE), made California the only state among the nine states we studied where the state department of education was overshadowed by the state board of education in terms of influence on state reading policy. Attesting to the influence of the pro-phonics CSBE, almost half (49 percent) of our respondents in California expressed a preference for phonics-based approach to reading instruction and only 30 percent supported a balanced approach, which makes California the most phonics-heavy state among the nine states in our study.

Connecticut

While taking great pride in being the highest-ranking state on the 1998 NAEP fourth-grade reading, educators and policymakers in Connecticut were deeply troubled by the persistent achievement gap in what a reading professor called "a two-tiered state." Starting with Public Act 97-256: The School Readiness Act, the Connecticut General Assembly has demonstrated its strong commitment to the goal of early reading success for all children, especially low-achieving and at-risk children, with a slew of reading legislation. The list includes: An Act Concerning Early Reading Success (PA 98-243), The Early Reading Success Grant Program of 1998, A Special Grant Program for Transitional Districts (PA 98-168), An Act Concerning a State-wide Early Reading Success Institute (PA 99-227); and An Act Concerning the School Readiness and Early Reading Success Grant Program (HB No. 68876).

The single most significant reading legislation in the history of Connecticut is PA 99-227: An Act Concerning a Statewide Early Reading Success Institute, also known as the Early Reading Success Initiative. The act requires the Connecticut State Department of Education (CSDE) to convene a panel to review research on how people learn to read and to identify professional development and competencies for effective reading instruction required for K–3 teachers, school administrators, and librarians. In compliance, the CSDE established the thirty-two-member Early Reading Success Panel in 2000, chaired by Commissioner Ted Sergi and featuring Marilyn Adams as an active panel member. Other prominent national experts, such as Isabel Beck, Barbara Foorman, Bill Honig, David Pearson, and Joseph Torgesen, were also invited to address the panel.

Although members of the Early Reading Success Panel brought with them diverse ideologies, viewpoints, and personal experiences, they were able to reach the consensus that "reading instruction in the primary grades must be comprehensive—that is, it must effectively develop a wide range of competencies in children" (CSDE, 2000, p. 2). The so-called reading wars, the panel asserts, involve a false dichotomy: "There is no opposition between phonics instruction and teaching higher-level comprehensive abilities, or between teaching basic skills and fostering motivation to read—all of these must be part of a high-quality primary reading curriculum" (p. 2). The panel report, *Connecticut's Blueprint for Reading Achievement: A Report by the Early Reading Success Panel*, was published in 2000 and has been distributed to educators and parents throughout the state.

Despite the panel's emphasis on a balanced or, in CSDE's terminology, a comprehensive approach to reading instruction, some policy actors that we interviewed did not feel the panel report represented a truly balanced view; rather, it was considered "phonics-heavy," as indicated by the following comment on the panel report made by a newspaper reporter:

> It's very heavy on language development. And they will tell you, they will argue to the end that this is a balanced approach, and it is, but it's very heavily influenced by the folks at Yale and U Conn. . . . I was struck by how phonics-heavy the state's new report on teaching reading is.

Although policy actors in Connecticut held different perceptions about the panel report, the report certainly represents the most important piece of guidance for reading instruction in classrooms across the state. The conclusions and recommendations made by the panel served as the basis for the design of statewide professional development provided through the Early Reading Success Institute that began operation in 2000, and for the establishment of state literacy standards and competencies necessary for teacher certification. They also set the stage for the use of Connecticut's 2001 Reading Excellent Act grant and the more recent Reading First grant.

Another major accomplishment of the CSDE in the field of reading was the release of *The Connecticut Framework: K–12 Curricular Goals and Standards* in 1998. In the subject area of reading, the CSDE adopted the *Standards of Reading Competency for Students in Grades K–3* in 1998, which specifies essential reading skills and abilities for K–3 students, lists expectations for each grade level, and recommends assessments to continually document students' progress toward the expected skills and abilities. The SDE also updated the statewide assessments (Connecticut Mastery Tests) to align the tests with state standards and curriculum framework. A third generation of the tests was introduced in fall 2000, and a fourth generation was administered in spring 2006.

The state's impact on curriculum and instruction was not only felt in the area of early literacy, but also in the area of pre-literacy. One year after the release of Connecticut's blueprint for early literacy, the Connecticut General Assembly passed An Act Concerning the School Readiness and Early Reading Success Grant Programs (HB No. 6876, 2001). Endorsing the findings of the Early Reading Success Panel, the act requires the establishment of standards for pre-literacy development, and school readiness plans that includes pre-literacy practices and teacher training in pre-literacy development. It also requires a specification of the components of comprehensive reading instruction programs and an expansion of the requirements for the Early Reading Success Grant Program.

The CSDE's policy activism has continued since our study ended. It released the *Connecticut's Preschool Curriculum Framework* in 2004, and more recently approved the *2006 Connecticut English Language Arts Curriculum Framework*. It has also scheduled to release *Connecticut's Beyond the Blueprint: Literacy Instruction and Literacy Across the Content Areas, 4–12,* in 2006. The state's sustained commitment to reading improvement provides reason to believe that the "shining star" in early literacy will continue to shine in the years to come.

Indiana

Assuming primary leadership for state reading policy, the Indiana Department of Education (IDOE) has launched numerous initiatives and programs to improve early reading achievement in the Hoosier State. In 1997, the State Superintendent for Public Instruction, Suellen Reed, announced the state's first reading initiative: Reading and Literacy for a Better Indiana. It covers three areas, two of which, the Early Literacy Intervention Grant Program and the School Library Printed Materials Grant, deal specifically with early reading. With biennium funds of $8 million, the Early Literacy Intervention Grant Program has been divided almost evenly to fund Reading Recovery and Other Early Literacy Intervention (OELI) programs.

Another important effort of the IDOE was to improve state reading standards. Viewing existing standards as lacking focus and rigor, Suellen Reed established a thirty-member Phonics Task Force to update the existing standards by incorporating phonics and phonemic awareness in grades K–3 standards. Further, in order to help teachers to align instruction with the new standards, the Phonics Task Force developed the Phonics Took Kit. Made available to all K–3 teachers in the state in 2000, the tool kit was designed to "provide teachers with current information about the importance of phonics knowledge. . . . It highlights best practices and encourages effective professional development in phonics" (IDOE, 2000, p. i). In addition, the department, with the assistance of Indiana University, also produced an online staff development course, Phonics Online, to help teachers better utilize the Phonics Tool Kit.

The focus on phonics, an IDOE official explained, was a move away from the state's whole language tradition to a balanced approach to teaching reading. Another member of the IDOE also expressed the department's support for a balanced approach with an emphasis on phonics, stating:

> We believe in a balanced approach to reading, but we do believe that that a balanced approach begins with a heavy emphasis on the sound/symbol relationship, and that you need to start with phonics. . . . For most kids most of the time, phonics works.

The IDOE's emphasis on phonics was also shared by the Indiana General Assembly, particularly Senator Murray Clark (R-Indianapolis), whose efforts were widely recognized as instrumental to putting reading on the state's policy agenda. What is most worthy noting is that, in 2000, Senator Clark sponsored an amendment, as part of Senate Bill 352, to the state's teacher licensure law, which went into effect in July 2001. The amendment requires all elementary teacher certification candidates to demonstrate proficiency in comprehensive reading instruction skills, including phonemic awareness and phonics instruction. This proficiency must be demonstrated through a written exam or through other procedures as outlined by the Indiana Professional Standards Board. Given all these efforts to sharpen the focus on phonics in both teacher professional development and teacher licensure, it seems likely that what teachers do behind the closed doors may indeed be changing.

Maine

With the state's long-standing tradition of local control, the Maine state legislature has not been as active as that in many other states in mandating education policy. Nevertheless, Maine's Education Reform Act of 1984 and the more recent concerns about students' reading performance on NAEP and the Maine Education Assessment prompted a number of highly visible policy activities related to reading. In 1993, Maine's legislature formed the Learning Results Task Force to develop "long-range education goals and standards for school and student performance to improve learning results and recommend to the commissioner and to the Legislature a plan for achieving those goals and standards" (MEDE, 1997a, p. 1). Based on the recommendations of the task force, the legislature adopted six Guiding Principles that describe the characteristics of a well-educated person, and required that the state department of education, along with the state board of education, develop *Learning Results Standards* in eight subject areas, including English language arts.

The *Learning Results Standards* were passed by the Maine state legislature in 1997 and were to be fully implemented by the 2002–2003 school year. Partly out of the consideration for local independence, the 1997 standards were fairly broad and ranked twenty-eighth in "specificity" according to the 2000 Quality Counts survey by *Educational Week*. What is notably missing from the eleven-page English language arts standards are the terms "phonics" or "phonemic awareness," although the phrase "letter–sound relationships" does appear in three places (MEDE, 1997b, pp. 1, 3, and 6).

In adopting the *Learning Results Standards* in 1997, the Maine legislature also provided for a review of the standards to start in 2004 and be completed in 2007. The review is intended to identify "only the essential knowledge and skills of the content areas" and provide a basis for the development of local curriculum (MEDE, 2006). With the assistance of national consultants and content area panels, the MEDE has reviewed and revised the 1997 standards, and began to elicit broad-based feedback on the proposed revised standards in January 2006.

The revised reading standards as currently proposed are organized into five categories: (1) Phonemic Awareness, Phonics, and Fluency; (2) Vocabulary; (3) Comprehension Strategies; (4) Reading Comprehension: Literacy Text; and (5) Reading Comprehension: Informational and Persuasive Text.

Compared to the 1997 standards, the revised reading standards are more concrete, and feature phonemic awareness and phonics much more prominently among "a variety of strategies" that students need to master. The emphasis on "a variety of strategies" in the revised standards could be largely attributed to the work of the Early Literacy Workgroup convened by the MEDE in 1998. The workgroup was charged to examine effective early literacy practices occurring in Maine schools. The resulting report, *A Solid Foundation: Supportive Contexts for Early Literacy in Maine*, identifies the common characteristics of the contexts that support high literacy achievement (MEDE, 2000). Interestingly, the characteristic concerning pedagogy is labeled "Various Resources Are Used to Respond to Students' Needs" and listed as the last of the six characteristics identified. Without careful reading, one could hardly recognize that the five-page section in the eighty-seven-page report is actually about reading instruction. Nonetheless, the message is clear: "No single program—whether literature-based on phonics-based—will work for all students" (p. 44). Instruction should be "balanced," and teachers need to use "a variety of instructional methods" grounded in assessments of students' needs (p. 44).

Providing a practical framework for schools to support literacy development, the *Solid Foundation* report has been widely disseminated throughout the state by the MEDE's Center for Inquiry on Literacy through daylong conferences and ongoing technical support and training. The center's efforts do seem to have had an impact—of the nine states in our study, Maine had the highest level of consensus (72 percent of respondents) on balanced approaches to reading instruction. With the next version of the *Learning Results Standards*, which will be presented to the legislature for approval in 2007, state guidance on reading curriculum and instruction is likely to be more direct and focused with a strengthened impact on Maine's schools.

Michigan

Michigan has a long history with standards and assessment. It introduced the Michigan Educational Assessment Program (MEAP) as early as 1969, and was among the first in the nation to establish statewide standards in 1973. Reading, in the 1973 standards, was simply defined as the ability to identify words and read fluently. In 1984, however, a group of reading professionals, led by Elaine Weber of the Michigan Department of Education (MIDE) and Karen Wixson from the University of Michigan, started an effort to redefine reading as "constructive, interactive, and dynamic, [with] a real focus on literature as well as comprehension strategies" (quote from a respondent). The group's efforts generated significant support for the new definition, and an updated version of MEAP based on a constructivist definition of reading was subsequently implemented in 1989.

In 1993, the Michigan State Board of Education awarded Karen Wixson and Sheila Potter a $1.3 million grant to develop standards and a language arts curriculum for the state. The process, however, turned out to be a bumpy one. Wixson and Potter's constructivist perspective on reading met with strong resistance from the newly elected president of the state board of education, Clark Durant, who called for a greater emphasis on direct phonics instruction. Despite the lengthy and widely publicized battles, Wixson and Potter managed to hold their ground. In 1995, the state board of education approved twelve English language arts content standards accompanied by benchmarks, which were included in the *Michigan Curriculum Framework* released in 1996. The language arts standards were general in concept and broad in scope, and set up under a balanced literacy framework with a focus on meaning and communication. The terms "phonics" and "phonemic awareness" were each mentioned only once in the standards (Michigan State Board of Education, 1996, p. 8).

An increased emphasis on phonics, however, recently emerged from the MIDE. Building on the 1996 *Michigan Curriculum Framework*, the department developed K–8 Grade Level Content Expectations in 2004 in response to the testing requirement of the No Child Left Behind Act of 2001, and were subsequently updated in 2005. While the terms "phonics" and "phonemic awareness" were nowhere to be seen in the original set of expectations, they were prominently listed as two essential skills in reading in the updated version.

A recent emphasis on phonics also occurred to the Michigan Literacy Progress Profile (MLPP), an early literacy assessment program developed by the MIDE as a key component of the multipronged Reading Plan for Michigan announced by Governor John Engler in 1998. The initial MLPP program contained a series of assessments covering five early reading milestones: oral language achievement, oral reading fluency and accuracy achievement, reading comprehension, writing achievement, and attitudes toward reading and writing. MLPP also includes "enabling skills assessments" in six areas, including phonemic awareness. Lacking explicit sections on phonics and vocabulary, the U.S. Department of Education did not deem MLPP an acceptable assessment tool for the Reading First grant it awarded to Michigan in 2002. As a result, the MIDE has been working to add to teachers' toolkits for assessment and instruction especially in the areas of phonics and vocabulary (Stevens, n.d.).

Indeed, as Putnam (2002) puts it, "the hook of dangling dollars in front of state officials is steering Michigan towards phonics or what's being called scientific-based reading research" (par. 6). The bulk of the $28.4-million-per-year Reading First grant would be used to purchase phonics-oriented textbooks and hire reading coaches to work with schoolteachers, and $3.7 million would be devoted to training teachers statewide in phonemic awareness, phonics, fluency, vocabulary, and text comprehension. Moreover, teacher-training programs at thirty-two colleges in the state were to be reviewed to make sure that they include phonics in the curricula for future reading teachers. Given Michigan's tradition in the constructivist perspective on reading that is often associated with whole language, the recent push toward phonics might actually make its "balanced" literacy framework a little closer to a true balance.

North Carolina

Soon after the release of the 1992 NEAP results showing that 44 percent of North Carolina fourth-graders read "below basic," North Carolina's *English Language Arts Standard Course of Study* became a target of criticism. It was blamed for lack of attention to basic reading skills and likened to California's whole language curriculum in the 1980s. Responding to the concern, the North Carolina General Assembly passed Senate Bill 1139 in 1996, which requires the state board of education to develop a comprehensive reading plan for the state. As part of the plan, the state board was to revise the *North Carolina Standard Course of Study* "so as to provide school units with guidance in the implementation of balanced, integrated, and effective programs of reading instruction" (Section 8.2.). The bill explicitly requires the revised *Standard Course of Study* to include early and systematic phonics instruction, stating,

> The General Assembly believes that the first, essential step in the complex process of learning to read is the accurate pronunciation of written words and that phonics . . . is the most reliable approach to arriving at the accurate pronunciation of a printed word. (Section 8.2)

Despite its purported endorsement for "balanced, integrated, and effective" reading instruction, the bill's mandate for early and systematic phonics instruction was viewed by many as reflective of the legislature's desire to promote phonics in the state. A member of a prominent reading interest group even called the bill the "phonics legislation." Nevertheless, the state board representative that we interviewed claimed that a consensus had been reached regarding reading pedagogy in the state:

> I think clearly where the reading wars have been resolved and where we resolved them in North Carolina when we last looked at our curriculum was that a balanced approach to reading was appropriate. . . . So balance is the keyword to our North Carolina reading curriculum, and we've attempted to make ourselves poster children for balanced reading instruction.

Whether or not North Carolina's revised reading standards ended the reading wars in the state remains open to debate. However, the state legislature clearly played a critical role in featuring phonics prominently in the Comprehensive Reading Plan for North Carolina adopted by the state board of education in 1997. In compliance with the legislative mandate, the North Carolina Department of Public Instruction revised the *K–12 English Language Arts Standard Course of Study* in 1997 to include more emphasis on early and systematic phonics instruction within a balanced reading program. The revised curriculum was approved by the state board of education in 1999, and has served as a framework that guides classroom instruction and assessment. It has also served as the ultimate guide for textbook selection and the foundation for the state's testing program.[5]

Texas

Where state reading policy is concerned, the Texas Reading Initiative (TRI) stood out not only because it has shaped reading curriculum and instruction in the second most populous state in the United States, but also because it has been the source of many key policy ideas that former Texas Governor Bush carried over from Houston to the nation's capitol. As the "education governor," Bush announced a comprehensive reading initiative, TRI, in 1996, and subsequently called a series of reading summits, organized by the Governor's Business Council, to discuss issues about the initiative. One thing in common among the expert speakers at the summits is that their names are often associated with phonics and the National Institute for Child Health and Human Development (NICHD): Marilyn Adams, Barbara Foorman, Jack Fletcher, Douglas Carnine, Reid Lyon, and Louisa Moats, among others. It is thus no wonder that a clear message from the summits was that the studies conducted by NICHD were the primary scientifically based research on beginning reading instruction, and were to be the driving force behind curriculum development, textbook selection, and staff development decisions under TRI (Patterson & Gerla, 1997). Governor Bush stated his position on this topic most openly and tersely in the October 17, 2000, presidential debate with Al Gore: "Phonics works, by the way, it needs to be part of our curriculum" (PBS, 2000, par. 41).

Although a strong supporter of the governor's reading initiative, the Texas Education Agency (TEA) took a more moderate stance on reading pedagogy. In 1996, Commissioner Moses convened a group of top reading educators for the purpose of generating a consensus on reading pedagogy. The consensus was documented in the report *Good Practice: Implications for Reading Instruction—A Consensus Document of Texas Literacy Professional Organizations* (TEA, 1997). The report calls for a "balanced and comprehensive" approach to reading instruction, an approach that recognizes "the importance of phonemic awareness, explicit letter–sound instruction, and word recognition practice, as well as, focused comprehension instruction and significant experience with literature" (p. 1). Those skills were also included in the new state standards—*Texas Essential Knowledge and Skills*—adopted by the Texas State Board of Education in 1997.

Also in 1997, the TEA published the famous "Red Book": *Beginning Reading Instruction: Components and Features of a Research-Based Reading Program*. With Jean Osborn serving as the primary consultant for its development, the booklet presents twelve essential components of reading instruction with eight supportive classroom features, and serves as the official statement of the principals underlying TRI. The TEA maintained that the Red Book calls for a balanced reading program, whereas some viewed the booklet as putting a greater emphasis on phonemic awareness and phonics. Although the definition for a balanced reading program is open to debate, no one would question the impact of the little red booklet. By the time the revised edition was released in 2002, over 250,000 copies of the Red Book had been distributed across the state, which "has served as a basis for professional development, the development of curriculum standards and instructional materials, as well as the establishment of research-based reading programs in schools" (TEA, 2002, p. 3). The TEA has also developed companion documents to the Red Book and referred them collectively as the "Red Book Series."

In addition to disseminating the "Red Book Series" as a basis for professional development, the TEA has also created Teacher Reading Academies under the provision of Senate Bill 4 proposed by Senator Tell Bivins (R-Amarillo) in 1999. The academies were intended to provide statewide professional development in comprehensive reading instruction aligned to state standards and assessments. The Texas legislature authorized $30,000,000 per year in 1999 to conduct training for all K–2 teachers in language arts, and authorized additional funding in 2001 for expanding the program to grades 3–4. A TEA policymaker proudly told us that those four-day training sessions offered through regional professional development centers had produced "a lot of changes" in Texas classrooms. Texas seems to be moving steadily toward the goal set by its former governor that all children read at grade level or higher by the end of third grade and throughout the rest of their schooling.

Utah

Since 1997, Utah has seen a flurry of legislations aimed at improving early reading achievement. Of particular importance was House Bill 67: Children's Reading Skills, which mandates the administration of a reading assessment in grades 1–6 to determine if instructional programs have resulted in students' mastering reading skills. It also mandates that reading instruction shall include: (a) early and explicit teaching of phonetic decoding skills, (b) exposure to a wide range of quality literature, (c) writing, and (d) regular and adequate time to read a variety of materials across the curriculum. Further, the bill requires districts to provide remedial assistance to students seriously deficient in these skills. Two years later in 1999, the state legislature passed House Bill 312, which provided an unprecedented $8 million to ensure that all Utah students read at grade level by the end of third grade, and which made it possible for the provisions set forth in House Bill 67 to produce a real impact.

While the Utah state legislature mandated reading assessment in grades 1–6 via House Bill 67, decisions over the implementation of the testing program were still in the hands of local school boards. In an effort to tighten state control over assessments, the state legislature enacted House Bill 177 in 2000, which stripped local school boards of their control over testing, and transferred the performance assessment duties entirely to the State Board of Education. Moreover, House Bill 177 established the Utah Performance Assessment System for Students (U-PASS) as the new statewide testing program.

Other than the state legislature, the Utah State Office of Education (USOE) has also been actively involved in shaping the state's reading policy. Under the Utah Reads project established by Lt. Governor Olene Walker in 1999,[6] the USOE developed the *Utah Reads K–3 Literacy Model*, which provides a conceptual framework incorporating three overlapping areas of literacy: curriculum and instruction, engaged practice, and literacy environment. Consistent with the provisions regarding reading instruction contained in House Bill 67, the area of curriculum and instruction in USOE's literacy model covers oral language practice, phonemic awareness, alphabetic knowledge, alphabetic principle, fluency, vocabulary, and comprehension as stand-along components. It also covers continuous assessment, read aloud, shared reading, guided reading, independent reading, decodable books, high-quality literature, and coordinated library and reading programs as shared components that also fall under the other two areas. This long list sheds light on how Utah, for the most part, avoided the reading wars: the USOE included almost everything in their literacy model and, consequently, the phonics versus whole language debate never fully reared its head in Utah.

Advertised as a balanced approach to reading, the all-inclusive *Utah Reads K–3 Literacy Model* defined reading pedagogy for the state and was instituted to guide reading instruction throughout the state. It also laid the foundation for the state's future work on curriculum and instruction. In 2003, the Utah State Board of Education adopted the *Utah Elementary Language Arts Core Curriculum: Kindergarten–Sixth Grade*, which consists of eight standards, with each standard representing one essential area of reading instruction: oral language, concepts and print, phonemic awareness, phonics and spelling, fluency, vocabulary, comprehension, and writing. This core curriculum became the central component of the *Utah Literacy Model*, which replaced the original *Utah Reads K–3 Literacy Model.* Although Utah's literacy model changed its label, its essence remains. The coherence and consensus that have been characterizing the state's reading policy will likely pay off in terms of improved reading achievement for Utah's schoolchildren.

Summary

Recent policy activism in the field of reading provided us with a unique opportunity to examine state impact on reading policy. Consistent with Kingdon's (1995) discussion of policy windows, our investigation of reading policy developments in nine states revealed that with reading achievement widely recognized as a compelling problem and with a political environment favorable to promoting solutions to the reading problem, a policy window opened in each of the nine states in late 1990s. This open policy windows mobilized a plethora of actors committed to ameliorating the reading problem. In the pluralistic arena of state reading policy, however, power was not distributed evenly across the plurality of actors. Although policy actors outside of the government outnumbered those inside, influence over reading policy clearly concentrated within the state governments.

Where government actors' influence was concerned, the most notable finding from our investigation was the prominence of state departments of education, which were clearly the most influential actor overall across the nine states. This finding is somewhat different from those obtained by Marshall et al. (1989). Marshall and her colleagues found that in all the six states that they investigated, state legislatures were perceived as the "insiders" in terms of influence on education policy, and state departments of education were in the "near circle," next to the insiders in the power hierarchy. Our study, however, indicates that state departments of education possessed greater policy influence than state legislatures in all nine states. This seeming inconsistency might be attributable to the increasing power of state departments of education during the past decade (Lewis & Maruna, 1999; Lusi, 1994), and might also has to do with the fact that Marshall et al. (1989) looked at influence on state education policy in general, whereas we focused specifically on the area of reading. Nevertheless, both studies spoke to the strong power of state departments of education, as well as state legislatures, in shaping education policy at the state level.

Once concerned primarily with school finance, state governments have extended their influence to a wide array of issues in education. In the field of reading, a common focus of state policymakers was on curriculum and instruction, the core of schooling. During the last decade, all nine states in our study have revised, more than once in some states, English language arts curriculum standards; the updated standards all include phonemic awareness and phonics as essential reading skills—within a purportedly balanced or comprehensive instructional framework. State reading policy actors, however, did not necessarily agree on what constitutes the right mix of ingredients for the "balance." Many of our respondents in California, Indiana, and North Carolina, for example, viewed the curriculum standards in their states as tilting appreciably toward the phonics end. Similarly, many state reading policies not focusing on standards also specifically prescribe explicit and systematic phonics instruction.

Although different states may not have arrived at the same definitions for a balanced literacy framework, they have all developed firm control over the curriculum and pedagogy that they defined for their states. The state impact on reading curriculum and instruction, from what we found, was exerted through a variety of channels. Other than revising existing curriculum standards in their desired directions, most, if not all, state education agencies, often with legislative support, made heavy investment in statewide professional development to help teachers to align instruction to new state standards. Moreover, some states (e.g., California and Indiana) have also added specific requirements regarding reading pedagogy to teacher licensure laws. Additional means through which states influenced what to teach and how to teach in early reading included updating state assessment programs to highlight the essential skills of reading, disseminating research-based reports on reading pedagogy drafted by expert panels, restructuring teacher education programs, and imposing restrictions on textbook adoptions, among others.

Concluding Observations: State Power versus Local Control

The rising power of the state has become an unquestionable reality in reading and in education in general. During the past decades, states have extended and strengthened their control over a wide spectrum of issues in education, particularly in the areas of standards and assessment, curriculum and instruction, and professional development. Overall, states' efforts in improving their education systems have received broad-based support from various stakeholders and constituencies. Our study of reading policy in nine states, for example, revealed that policy actors were generally supportive of state standards and assessments, and were also fairly confident that reading achievement was on the rise in their respective states.[7] A representative of a school administrators association in North Carolina, for instance, proclaimed, "A lot of progress has been made since 1998 because of our testing program and our accountability."

Amid these positive reactions, however, were voices of concern for the loss of local control. Two Texas reading researchers (Patterson & Gerla, 1997) lamented:

> We no longer assume that the primary decision makers are reading researchers and educators, that we can close our classroom doors and ignore statewide initiatives. . . . We no longer see top-down mandates as impotent, particularly when they are linked to competitive grant monies and high-stakes testing. (par. 23)

A member of a Michigan teacher organization more forcefully declared, "Our position is 'no' on [state reading tests]. We prefer that each individual school district would make that decision. . . . I think we're bound into the local control."

Although the practitioners' voices of concern from may not be loud, and their control over policy development not strong, their power over policy implementation is not to be overlooked. As McLaughlin (1987) reminds us, "Change is ultimately the problem of the smallest unit . . . and what actually is delivered or provided under the aegis of a policy depends upon the individual at the end of the line" (p. 175). Marshall and Gerstl-Pepin (2005) similarly observe that policy outcomes are often shaped by the so-called lowerarchy. Thus, in order for a policy to achieve its intended impact, local buy-in is essential. An effective way to achieve local buy-in is to include teachers and other practitioners in the decision-making loop, which would not only give practitioners a sense of ownership over the policy made, but also help top-level policymakers develop well-informed policies with the input from those with professional expertise and firsthand knowledge about teaching and learning.

Moreover, it is important to built local discretion and flexibility into policies imposed from top down to allow room for practitioners to exercise professional judgment in light of the unique local context. Much like the case with phonics versus whole language, a delicate balance needs to be struck between state authority and local control rather than fixating on one to the exclusion of the other. Also like the case with phonics versus whole language, balance does not necessarily mean equal weights for both parties. Given the heavy focus of the No Child Left Behind Act of 2001 on statewide accountability and the hefty sums of money attached, states are under both strong incentives and tremendous pressure to take firm control over their K–12 education systems. Thus, it seems safe to predict that the balance between state authority and local control will continue to weigh more heavily toward the former in the years to come—not just in the area of curriculum and instruction, and not just in the field of reading.

Admittedly, the optimal balance between state authority and local control is not easy to define, as it is contingent on a multitude of factors (e.g., policy content and history, and state social and political culture). Nevertheless, it is an important consideration to be taken into account in order to make sound education policies that will bring about desired policy outcomes. The optimal balance cannot be achieved through power struggles or turf battles; it can only be achieved when both the state and the local share the common focus on students and share the common commitment to making education right and good for students.

Notes

1. "Reading wars" refers to the relentless debate over the appropriate reading instruction methods between two ideological camps: phonics and whole language. Phonics advocates call for explicit and systematic skills instruction in the alphabetic principle, phonemic awareness, decoding, and sound–letter relationships (Adams, 1990; Chall, 1996). Whole-language proponents, in

contrast, emphasize literature-based reading, meaning construction for purposeful functions, child-centeredness, and teacher empowerment (Bergeron, 1990; Goodman, 1986, 1989).

2. In this study, interest groups refer to membership organizations, advocacy organizations not accepting members, businesses, and other organizations or institutions, whether formally organized or not, that try to influence public policy.

3. See Song and Miskel (2005) for a detailed discussion on the social network perspective, the notions of actor centrality and prestige, and the network analytic methods.

4. The ARI was awarded the 2002 Education Commission of the States Innovation Award, which recognizes a state for excellence in the policy area of literacy. Its potential for transforming reading instruction has also promoted two states (Massachusetts and Florida) to establish pilot initiatives modeled after the ARI.

5. The Standard Course of Study has been updated every five to seven years. The most recent version was revised and approved in 2004.

6. Utah Reads is no longer supported by the Utah State Office of Education and has been replaced by the STAR (Student Tutoring Achievement for Reading) program. See http://www.schools.utah.gov/curr/STAR/ for details about the STAR program.

7. The overall level of support for state reading standards among all respondents across the nine states was 4.44 on 1–5 scale, with 1 being "highly negative" and 5 "highly positive." The overall level of support for state reading assessment was 4.04 on the same scale. The overall belief about the trend of reading achievement among respondents across the nines states was rated as 1.51 on a 1–3 scale, with 1 being "improving," 2 "staying the same," and 3 "worsening." See Miskel et al. (2003) for details.

References

Adams, M. J. (1990). *Beginning to read: Thinking and learning about print.* Cambridge: MIT Press.

Alabama Department of Education. (1998a). *Knowledge and skills teachers need to deliver effective reading instruction.* Montgomery: Author.

Alabama Department of Education. (1998b). *Report on Review of Research.* Montgomery: Author.

Bergeron, B. S. (1990). What does the term whole language mean? Constructing a definition from the literature. *Journal of Reading Behavior, 22*(4), 301–329.

Berry, J. (1997). *The interest group society.* (3rd ed.). New York: Longman.

California Department of Education. (1995). *Every child a reader: The report of the California Reading Task Force*. Sacramento: Author.

California Department of Education. (1996). *Teaching reading: A balanced, comprehensive approach to teaching reading in pre-kindergarten through grade three*. Sacramento: Author.

California State Board of Education. (1997). *English-language arts content standards for California public schools: Kindergarten through grade twelve.* Sacramento: Author.

California State Board of Education. (1999). *Reading/Language Arts Framework for California Public Schools.* Sacramento: Author.

Chall, J. S. (1996). *Learning to read: The great debate*. (3rd ed.). Orlando, FL: Harcourt Brace.

Connecticut State Department of Education. (2000). *Connecticut's blueprint for reading achievement: The report of the Early Reading Success Panel.* Hartford: Author.

Connecticut State Department of Education. (2000). *Connecticut's Reading First Model.* Hartford: Author.

Freeman, L. C. (1979). Centrality in social networks: I. Conceptual clarification. *Social Networks, 1*, 215–239.

Fuhrman, S. H. (1987). Educational policy: A new context for governance. *Publius: The Journal of Federalism, 17*(3), 131–143.

Goodman, K. S. (1986). *What's whole in whole language?* Portsmouth, NH: Heinemann.

Goodman, K. S. (1989). Whole language research: Foundations and development. *The Elementary School Journal, 90*, 208–221.

Indiana Department of Education. (2000). *Phonics tool kit*. Indianapolis: Indiana Department of Education.

Kingdon, J. W. (1995). *Agendas, alternatives, and public polices*. (2nd ed.). New York: HarperCollins.

Knoke, D. (1986). Associations and interest groups. *Annual Review of Sociology, 12*, 1–21.

Knoke, D. (1990). *Organizing for collective action: The political economies of associations*. New York: Walter de Gruyter.

Knoke, D. & Burt, R. S. (1983). Prominence, In R. S. Burt & M. J. Minor (Eds.), *Applied Network Analysis* (pp. 195–222). Beverly Hills: Sage

Lewis, D. A., & Maruna, S. (1999). The politics of education. In V. Gray, R. Hanson, & H. Jacob (Eds.), *Politics in the American states: A comparative analysis* (7th ed) (pp. 393–433). Washington, DC: Congressional Quarterly Press.

Lusi, S. F. (1994). Systemic school reform: The challenges faced by state departments of education. In R. F. Elmore & S. H. Fuhrman (Eds.), *The governance of curriculum* (pp. 109–130). Alexandria, VA: Association of Supervision and Curriculum Development.

Maine Department of Education. (1997a). *Learning results, preface.* Retrieved May 5, 2006, from http://mainegov-images.informe.org/education/lres/preface.pdf.

Maine Department of Education. (1997b). *Learning results, English language arts.* Retrieved May 5, 2006, from http://mainegov-images.informe.org/education/lres/ela.pdf.

Maine Department of Education. (2000). *A solid foundation: Supportive contexts for early literacy programs in Maine schools.* Augusta: Author.

Maine Department of Education. (2006). *Proposed revised Maine Learning Results Standards: History of review/rationale.* Retrieved April 27, 2006, from http://www.maine.gov/education/lres/review/revised_mlr_history.htm

Manzo, Kathleen K. (2002). Federal program will test states' reading policies. *Education Week, 21*(41). 1, 16–17.

Marshall, C., & Gerstl-Pepin, C. (2005). *Re-framing educational politics for social justice.* Boston: Allyn & Bacon.

Marshall, C., Mitchell, D., & Wirt, F. (1989). *Culture and education policy in the American states.* New York: Falmer Press.

Mawhinney, H. B. (2001). Theoretical approaches to understanding interest groups. *Educational Policy, 15*(1), 187–214.

Mazzoni, T. L. (1993). The changing politics of state education policy making: A 20-year Minnesota perspective. *Educational Evaluation and Policy Analysis, 15*, 357–379.

McLaughlin, M. W. (1987). Learning from experience: Lessons from policy implementation. *Educational Evaluation and Policy Analysis, 9*(2), 171–178.

Michigan Department of Education. (1996). *Michigan Curriculum Framework.* Lansing: Author.

Michigan Department of Education. (2004). *Michigan's grade level content expectations in English language arts and mathematics, Version 6.04.* Lansing: Author.

Michigan Department of Education. (2005). *Michigan's grade level content expectations in English Language arts and mathematics, Version 12.05.* Lansing: Author.

Miskel, C. G., Coggshall, J. G., DeYoung, D. A., Osguthorpe, R. D., Shepley, T.V., Song, M., & Young, T. V. (2003). *Reading policy in the states: Interests and processes.* Final Report for the Field Initiated Studies Grant PR/Award No. R305T990369, Office of Educational Research and Improvement,

U.S. Department of Education and the Spencer Foundation Major Research Grants Program Award # 200000269. Ann Arbor: University of Michigan.

National Education Goals Panel. (1999). Shining star. *The NEGP Monthly, 2*(11), 1–10.

Patterson, L., & Gerla, J. (1997). *The Texas Reading Initiative: Continuing conversations about early reading instruction in Texas.* Retrieved April 29, 2006, from http://www.readingonline.org/critical/houston/leslie.htm.

PBS. (2000, October 17). *Presidential debate: Vice President Al Gore v. Gov. George W. Bush.* Retrieved April 29, 2006, from http://www.pbs.org/newshour/bb/election/2000debates/3rdebate2.html.

Putnam, J. (2002, August 19). Phonics finds favor in Michigan schools. *Booth Newspapers.* Retrieved April 28, 2006, from http://www.nrrf.org/article_putnam-8-19-02.htm.

Song, M., & Miskel, C.G. (2005). Who are the influentials: A cross-state social network analysis of the reading policy domain. *Educational Administration Quarterly, 41*(1), 7–48.

Stevens, F. (n.d.). *Reading first: Making reading first for Michigan and the Michigan Literacy Progress Profile (MLPP).* Retrieved April 28, 2006, from http://www.mireadingfirst.org/downloads/mlppvsrf.pdf#search='Michigan%20Literacy%20Progress%20Profile%20Reading%20First'.

Texas Education Agency. (1997). *Good practice: Implications for reading instruction-A consensus document of Texas literacy professional organizations.* Austin: Author.

Texas Education Agency. (1997). *Beginning reading instruction: Components and features of a research-based reading program.* Austin: Author.

Texas Education Agency. (2002). *Beginning reading instruction: Components and features of a research-based reading program, Revised edition.* Austin: Author.

Wasserman, S., & Faust, K. (1994). *Social network analysis: Methods and applications*: New York: Cambridge University Press.

Part III

Trends and Conclusions

Chapter 12

Improvement or Interference?

Reenvisioning the "State" in Education Reform

Lance D. Fusarelli

As Bonnie Fusarelli and Bruce Cooper assert in the introduction to this book, states—including governors, legislatures, courts, and state education agencies—play a crucial and increasingly influential role in education policymaking, despite a political tradition of local control that occupies (or at least used to) a privileged, sacred status in American thought (Fowler, 2000). Every classroom, school, and school district in the United States (over 14,000 districts nationwide) is significantly shaped by the actions of state policymakers. Once upon a time, "locally elected school board members had the last word on what and how your child was taught, how the district's money was spent, who graduated from high school, how teachers were trained, and who was hired or fired. Not any more" (Kossan, 2005, p. 1). State and federal policymakers, particularly legislators, jurists, and governors, have become major players in education reform (Fusarelli, 2005; Gittell & McKenna, 1999; Welburn, 2002).

Significantly, the rising state does not represent "an abrupt break with the past" but rather builds "on decades of more gradual state involvement" (Mazzoni, 2000, p. 181). The editors note that state governments determine "the way schools are organized, the standards for teacher certification, the nature of the educational experiences" of students, and the scope and content of the curriculum, as well as the "funding, operation, and structure of school districts." As Picus observes in his study of policymaking in California, "State control of education policy has been all encompassing, removing local influence over what is taught, and taking away local authority to determine how much is spent."

Further, with passage of the No Child Left Behind Act (NCLB), the national government has asserted its power and influence over both state and local education policy to an unprecedented degree,[1] although McDermott and DeBray-Pelot observe that the growing national role has not produced "a withering away of state governments." Manna (2006) refers to this process as "borrowing strength," in which one level of government (the national government) advances its agenda by utilizing or building on the policies, resources, and structures of other levels of government (in this case, state governments). In fact, one of the restructuring options for schools that persistently fail to make adequate yearly progress (AYP) is state takeover. Under the federal legislation, nearly 2,000 schools throughout the United States "have been ordered into radical 'restructuring,' subject to mass firings, closure, state takeover or other moves" (Feller, 2006b, p. 1).

Still, NCLB expands national authority and control over education at the expense of state and local polities and "puts federal bureaucrats in charge of approving state standards and accountability plans; sets a single nationwide timetable for boosting achievement; and prescribes specific remedies for under-performing schools" (Finn & Hess, 2004, p. 39). Remedies include permitting state education agencies to take over individual schools, reduce district funding, and even restructure the school district, including removing the superintendent and locally elected school board. Finn and Hess (2004) assert that despite its accountability and school choice provisions, NCLB "marks a radical break with conservative tradition, initiating a massive shift of education authority from states to Washington" (p. 53). As further evidence, Congress has recently gone so far as to mandate teaching about the U.S. Constitution, to be covered each September, the month of the final signing of the document, as well as requiring the U.S. Department of Education to evaluate the rigor of high school programs to determine whether students qualify for college aid in the form of math and science grants for poor students (Feller, 2006a; Sack & Trotter, 2005).

Notably, this expansion of national authority (or intrusion, depending on one's perspective) over education has occurred largely under Republican control of the presidency and Congress (Hoff, 2006). As a representation of the dominant ideology of national authorities, NCLB has provoked policymakers in several states to criticize the law as "an intrusion on their freedom to set educational policy" (McDermott & DeBray-Pelot) and, undeniably, that's exactly what it is—all in the name of equity. According to Murray (2006), "NCLB takes a giant step toward nationalizing elementary and secondary education," which he calls "a disaster for federalism" (p. 1). As McDermott and DeBray-Pelot note, "the fact remains that states must, in effect, ask federal permission before enacting certain kinds of policies over which they would previously have had sole authority." Ironically, NCLB "had its origins in the extension of *state* power over education. The 1994 law was an outgrowth of the movement for state-level accountability policies" (McDermott & DeBray-Pelot).

These events suggest that an important policy convergence has taken place between state and national policymakers. As Fusarelli (2002a) found in his research on gubernatorial elections, the striking similarities and commonalities among many of the education reform initiatives undertaken by state policymakers reflect an emerging elite ideological consensus among state and national policymakers on preferred education reforms. In fact, conservatives such as William Bennett and Rod Paige (both former secretaries of education) and Diane Ravitch have called for a national test tied to a national curriculum. Bennett and Paige argue that allowing states to define proficiency, instead of using a national standard such as the National Assessment of Educational Progress (NAEP), encourages states to lower standards (Bennett & Paige, 2006). For example, Tennessee reports 87 percent of its fourth graders are proficient in reading, yet the NAEP fourth-grade reading score is only 27 percent; in Maryland, the figures were 82 percent and 32 percent, respectively (Mathews, 2006). In Oklahoma, the number of schools needing improvement dropped by 85 percent, due in large measure to the state redefining how it calculates adequate yearly progress (Bennett & Paige, 2006). The key issue is whether increasing state and national control over local education has improved teaching and learning, enhanced equity, or actually harmed education by limiting the discretion, control, and flexibility of teachers, school leaders, and other school personnel (local experts) to do what they think is best for students.

In this chapter, I review the domains in which state and national control over local education has most expanded in the past three decades, drawing both from the research literature and from contributors to this volume—who provide extensive case histories of the growth of state control. I then examine efforts by scholars, primarily institutional theorists, who study state formation and expansion for the purpose of placing the growth of state power and control within a coherent, structural framework. As part of this analysis, I examine requisite elements of state institutional capacity to undertake and promulgate reform. The case studies presented in this volume shed light on whether increasing state control over education produces more policy coherence or simply more policy confusion within the educational system (i.e., does it produce better policies for better schools?), which is the key research question of concern to all the contributors to this volume. The chapter concludes with an assessment of the impact of increasing state control (and corresponding loss of local control) over education and offers a forecast for future directions for federalism and for education reform itself as this trend plays out in school systems nationwide.

Domains of State Control

Finance

Virtually every contributor to this volume noted that the trigger to the expansion of state control over education was school finance litigation. Picus traces the massive expansion of state control in California to the *Serrano* decision in 1968. In states that invest heavily in education, the demands of political accountability create conditions of intense oversight and control. In Kentucky, school finance litigation led to passage of the comprehensive Kentucky Educational Reform Act (KERA) in 1990 that restructured PreK–12 public education through significant changes in curriculum, governance, and finance and marked a major shift from local to state control over all aspects of education in the state (Browne-Ferrigno). Money matters, and, "Inevitably, school finance reform requires more money," which leads to the expansion of state control (Campbell, Cunningham, Nystrand, & Usdan, 1985, p. 58).

In California, as in most states, "the state exerts a tremendous amount of control over how education funds are allocated and used by local school districts" (Picus). Notes Picus, "It is not surprising, therefore, that as the state controls larger and larger portions of school revenues, it also has become more influential in the ways school systems operate, taking more control away from local school districts, either through the way funds are allocated to schools, or through direct legislative actions designed to elicit certain behaviors on the part of school districts." State control over school finance has grown to such an extent that, in New Jersey, local school boards are prohibited "from making simple budgetary decisions in response to district program needs" (Cooper & Nisonoff). According to Cooper and Nisonoff, "the state, in effect, does not trust locally elected school boards to make budgetary line-item transfers and so has relegated this responsibility to state bureaucrats." The researchers note that "the hand of the state" now reaches "into every school system, and curtails the authority of the school board, superintendent, and community to raise, allocate and spend money, including funds from local property taxes." However, as Brady and others point out, "As state control over school funding increased, state success toward minimizing fiscal inequities between high- and low-property wealth local school districts has been limited."

Curriculum, Instruction, and Testing

As McDermott and DeBray-Pelot observe, much of the growth of state power over education stems from efforts in the 1980s to implement standards-based reforms—reforms that are founded on "the idea that education policy should be made 'coherent' and organized around clear statements of what students should know and be able to do, coupled with assessments that would determine whether or not students were attaining the standards. Standards-based reform also includes expanding the state government's power to hold local schools and educators accountable for students' test results. This expansion of state control was intended to reduce variability among schools' curricula and students' experiences in school." As a result of these efforts, all states have developed systems of student assessment and accountability—many of which are quite comprehensive.

In addition, states now have curriculum frameworks and content standards clarifying what students are expected to know and be able to do. It seems that "everyone is telling teachers what to teach" (Teicher, 2005, p. 1). In 2005, Illinois legislators mandated an expansion of curriculum content on genocide (beyond the Holocaust) to include Armenia, Cambodia, Bosnia, Rwanda, and Sudan. When Maryland lawmakers wanted greater instruction about the Irish potato famine, their efforts conflicted with the state's long tradition of leaving curriculum issues primarily to local districts; as a compromise, schools were allowed to opt out of the suggested curriculum modification (Teicher, 2005). Cooper and Nisonoff note that New Jersey "led the nation in establishing comprehensive statewide educational standards (State Core Curriculum Content Standards or SCCCSs) that attempted to align cross-grade requirements and standards to local curriculum and teaching, to local tests, and more uniform consequences for failure." In her analysis of state reading initiatives, Song found that "the reading policy initiatives not only stated their grand goals in broad terms, but also stipulated in explicit language what specific reading skills students are expected to master and how reading should be taught in schools, depriving teachers and schools of much of their authority over local decision making." Several states are implementing more rigorous standards and student performance benchmarks, similar to what occurred with the standards movement of the 1980s, with exit exams determining promotion to the next grade level. Michigan's new high school graduation standards, which will affect the class of 2011, will be among the toughest in the nation. Reflecting the expansion of state power over local education, Representative Brian Palmer, Chair of the [MI] House Education Committee, stated, "This is the first time we have developed consistent standards across the board for schools" (Hornbeck, 2006, p. 2). In virtually every state, mandatory student testing occurs at nearly every grade level; in fact, NCLB's testing requirements, which opponents have criticized as overly burdensome and expensive, pale in comparison to the volume of testing required of students by state authorities. For example, in Kentucky, "students are tested at the end of each school year in seven content areas, with content focus and assessment type staggered across different grade levels, beginning in Grade 3 and continuing through Grade 12" (Poggio, 2000, cited in Browne-Ferrigno).

Some states such as Texas and California have even centralized the adoption of textbooks statewide, a process that often becomes politically charged (such as diatribes against "rainforest algebra"—using ecological word problems in algebra). Moreover, large markets such as California and Texas tend to limit options for smaller states because publishers produce a limited variety of textbooks to capture those markets (due to economies of scale). Since states require local districts to adopt texts from an approved list, and the only way to get on the approved list is to address state curriculum guidelines, the state has substantial control over the nature and content of the primary source of instructional materials (Malen, 2003).

In addition, several states, including most recently California, require students to pass exit exams before receiving a high school diploma. This represents the ultimate manifestation of the distrust state policymakers have of local school officials. Unwilling to take the word of local school officials that students who have successfully completed the standard course of study have received a sound, basic education, state policymakers demand proof by requiring passage of an exit exam. As Picus notes in his analysis of the growth of state control in California, nearly 47,000 high school seniors failed the exit test and were at risk of not graduating with their class. Other states such as Texas have experienced similar problems. Taken together, these efforts reflect a substantial usurpation of local control by state and national policymakers in the areas of curriculum, instruction, and testing.

Staffing and Governance

The growth of state and federal authority over education has also impacted the staffing and governance of schools. With the advent of high-stakes testing, many school districts have hired testing coordinators, testing coaches, and substitute teachers to free up classroom teachers to engage in test prep (Malen, 2003). Teachers, including veteran teachers, must now demonstrate that they are highly qualified. Through teacher and administrator licensure, states control who can teach and who can lead school systems. Most states have introduced measures to increase the length of the school day and school year and to increase minimum salaries for teachers. Many states such as Texas have created "comprehensive system[s] of external accountability" (Maxcy, Rorrer, & Aleman), including school report cards that assess individual school and school district performance. These report cards or performance indices are used by local and state officials in a variety of ways. In many states, principals and district leaders are subject to demotion, transfer, or termination for low school or district performance. Schools or districts labeled as failing are subject to a host of state sanctions, including reconstitution and state takeover—the ultimate expression of state power. Cooper and Nisonoff note that "on July 3, 1983, for example, New Jersey's state education department declared Newark's schools to be 'failing', dismissed the sitting elected board of education and its choice of a superintendent, selected a Special Master to oversee the district, and finally appointed a 'state superintendent' to run the district." Vergari notes that, in New York, failing schools or schools under registration review (SURR) "must adopt and implement corrective action plans" and "receive technical assistance from both the state and their respective districts. If improvements do not occur, SURR schools are subject to state takeover or closure." Vergari notes that, "Between 1989 and 2006, 280 schools had been placed on the SURR list. Forty-seven schools that did not meet their performance targets were closed."

Further, the slow spread of mayoral control over schools, particularly urban systems, has brought about unprecedented intrusion into local control. Heated political battles over efforts by mayors to assume control of schools (which represent by far the largest expenditure in municipal budgets) in New York, Los Angeles, and Washington, D.C., have pitted mayors against powerful teachers' unions, school administrators, parents, and even state legislators. In New York, Mayor Michael Bloomberg and his handpicked school chancellor, Joel Klein, cut administrative positions, mandated uniform reading and math programs, broke up large high schools into smaller learning communities, and ended social promotion, even going so far as to dictate how teacher bulletin boards should be designed (Helfand, 2006). Such examples, particularly the willingness of state officials to dismiss locally elected school boards, mandate the firing of school leaders, and take over school systems, demonstrate how powerful the state has become in its control over staffing and local education governance.

Theorizing State Control over Education

The contributors and editors of this volume share a common paradigmatic philosophy with scholars in political science and sociology—one emphasizing the utility of bringing the state back into models of policy change (Evans, Rueschmeyer, & Skocpol, 1985). However, whereas political scientists operating within the paradigm of institutional theory focus more broadly on national governments as "states," the contributors to this volume, with the exception of McDermott and DeBray-Pelot, focus almost exclusively on, literally, state governments. This is logical given James's (1991) review of the research on state authority over education where he asserted that "the state can be conceptualized in its broader meaning as the totality of public authority that constitutes the political system at all levels, or more concretely as American state governments, which have primary constitutional authority over formal schooling in the United States" (p. 173).

Another useful definition of "the state" proffered by Mawhinney (1994) has important implications for our understanding of the growth of state power over education. Mawhinney conceptualizes the state as "a set of institutions reflecting a system of norms that are founded on conceptions of political authority supported by historical traditions" (p. 18). With the growth of state (and national) control over virtually all aspects of schooling in the United States (to the point where conservatives such as Diane Ravitch are advocating a national curriculum), then, over time, the political authority and legitimacy of state and national control will become more and more an historical fact, leaving little room to question its legitimacy. I argue that with the expansion of control by the national government over local education, it is now conceptually useful to view the growth of "state" control over local education in a more broad sense than James' definition of the state; thus, the "state" is the totality of structures, processes, and institutions at both the state government level and the national level that influence and increasingly control education at the local level.[2]

A key issue is why the rising state has asserted and expanded its control over education at the local level. Institutional theorists generally believe that "states arise from the internal evolution of societies," meaning that as the public's expectations and demands for services increase, then states develop and become more complex in their functions and operations (Thomas & Meyer, 1984, p. 463). Further, external forces, such as global economic competition, play a major role in the development and expansion of the state apparatus (Fowler, 2000; Thomas & Meyer, 1984). As Florida governor Jeb Bush and New York City mayor Michael Bloomberg asserted in an editorial, "We believe in the role of sovereign states in our federalist system, but we also believe it is in our national interest to raise standards and expectations," through use of a uniform assessment tool such as the National Assessment of Educational Progress (Bush & Bloomberg, 2006, p. B07).

Although the impetus for increased state and federal involvement in education varies, common factors include pressure from the judicial system for greater equity in schooling inputs, economic concerns, the involvement of big business in education reform, impatience with ineffectual, incremental change, gubernatorial and legislative leadership, coalitional politics, the emergence of national policy networks, and an emergent institutional capacity to undertake reform (Fusarelli & Fusarelli, 2003; Mazzoni, 1995). Further, as Fowler (2000) observes, as state activism and involvement in local school affairs increase, states and the national government create programs and initiatives that themselves serve as springboards for more extensive state involvement.

As this process unfolds or evolves in society, it can lead to a "system-wide redefinition of persons as human capital and of education as a critical means to development" (Thomas & Meyer, 1984, p. 478), which explains in part why some prominent conservatives believe the conditions are ripe for conversations about creating national standards and national testing. Perhaps old notions about federalism and separation of powers over education, like the political tradition of local control, are outmoded and inadequate to effectively and efficiently educate future generations of Americans. Particularly since passage of NCLB, the unquestioned sovereignty and jurisdiction of states over education no longer remains—at the very least, the lines of authority are becoming blurred. In fact, one key finding from research on institutional development is that "the jurisdiction of the state in the West has tended to expand over time, as more and more aspects of social life have been incorporated into the general welfare function that is the essence of the Western state" (Thomas & Meyer, 1984, p. 468). These factors may be why Finn, Ravitch, and others believe that we are closer now than ever before to considering ideas such as national standards and national testing—which even a decade ago would never have been seriously entertained by policymakers.

The growth of state power has brought about a concomitant loss of local control that has been steady and ongoing for the past three decades (Wirt & Kirst, 2005). James (1991) found that there is a "growing state presence in shaping educational policy" (p. 190) made possible through an expansion in state capacity and "the use of law as an instrument for managing local schools" (p. 187). Campbell and Mazzoni's (1976) seminal research on early state efforts to control education found that, in the 1970s, state legislatures were beginning to exert their influence into local schooling processes. For the next two decades, states "engaged in a massive use of policy in seeking to reform their public schools, in the process becoming *de facto* as well as *de jure* policy-makers in education. Big business, governors, key legislators, the media, and national networks and organizations have become major players in the education reform movement" (Mazzoni, 1995, p. 53).[3] Picus notes that legislators often make explicit trades, such as in California, offering increased funding in exchange for education reform. As a result of the rising state, "the relationship of schooling to the state apparatus" has been changed in fundamental and significant ways, with greater state and national involvement in local affairs (Cibulka, 1995, p. 145).

Cooper and Nisonoff extend Picus's point and incorporate it into a six-step model of state power. In the first stage, school finance litigation brings forth increased state spending aimed at generating greater equity in the school system. With greater state spending comes increased oversight and regulation (stage two). With regulation and oversight comes more control (stage three). In the fourth stage, increased state control leads to greater standardization of the schooling process. In the fifth stage, having created greater equity, control, and accountability in the school system (and thus having achieved institutional legitimacy over the processes of schooling), the state seeks to expand its bureaucratic control, further decreasing local autonomy. However, in the sixth and final stage, the enormous costs incurred with achieving equity, shifts in judicial activism and intervention, and possibly frustration with the lack of educational improvement lead the state to reduce funding, requiring local school systems to do more with less, while still maintaining firm state regulatory control under the auspices of accountability. The authors see these steps as closely interrelated and in a steady progression since the 1970s.

McGivney's (1984) research offers a typology detailing the evolution of state politics of education for understanding changes in educational governance patterns. The four typologies detailing the developmental stages of state politics of education include: Stage I: localistic decentralized, where the decision-making process involves each local unit as well as the state legislature; Stage II: statewide monolithic, where the decision-making process involves state-wide coalitions; Stage III: state-wide fragmented, where the decision-making process involves the state governor, state legislature, and the courts; and Stage IV: state-wide bureaucratization, where the decision-making process involves bureaucracy. In McGivney's study of twenty-two states, these four stages were meant to classify "stages of evolutionary typology" in the state politics of education. Spring (2002) asserts that McGivney's typology needs to be modified to include a fifth stage: the nationalization of state educational politics.

Elements of these stages may be found in differences in state control and centralization. For example, research by Seashore, Gordon, Meath, and Thomas of differences in state educational policy in Oregon, New Mexico, and Missouri documents differences in the growth of state control over education. Despite some centralization of control in the form of state standards, Oregon and Missouri still manifest a firm commitment to local control—with local policymakers given significant discretion over the interpretation and implementation of education policies, including developing assessment measures. Centralization and state control tend to be limited to funding and accountability. New Mexico, on the other hand, under the leadership of Governor Bill Richardson and other legislative leaders, has centralized state control over education with new, comprehensive initiatives focused on systemic change and on building state capacity to implement and support those initiatives. Seashore et al. conclude that differences in state political culture are largely responsible for differences in the degree of state centralization and control over schooling, a finding supported by Spring (2002). Spring sees the emerging power of national governance organizations such as the National Governors' Association, the Council of Chief State School Officers, and the Education Commission of the States as key players in the nationalization of education policy by serving "as forums for the discussion of educational policies and for the coordination of state educational efforts" (p. 131). With the nationalization of education policy, we would expect less interstate variation in control over education in the next decade as the educational system gradually becomes more tightly coupled and aligned, particularly as national policymakers become more concerned about education.

Developing Institutional Capacity for Reform

The growing power of the state over virtually all aspects of schooling in the United States has been made possible because states have developed (and continue to expand) their institutional capacity to engage in systemic reform initiatives in education, particularly data collection and warehousing, assessment, and evaluation. The policymaking capacity of the state can be gauged on three dimensions: (1) the formal boundaries of legitimate government intervention; (2) government's fiscal ability; and (3) the professionalism and expertise of legislators and public administrators (Robertson, 1993). Factors associated with the expansion of state capacity include states' adoption of annual meetings, the movement toward single-member districts, unlimited sessions, pre-session organization, uniform rules, growth of professional staff, and legislative management improvements such as electronic voting, bill-introduction deadlines, and the installation of "electronic data-processing equipment to track bills and reveal their contents" (Reeves, 1990, p. 88).

Robertson and Judd (1989) note that "over time, Congress and state legislatures, the president and state governors, and bureaucracies at all levels of government have grown larger, and more professional" (p. 10). This has enabled actors operating within the state apparatus to be increasingly active in shaping education policy and initiating policy change. Murphy (1990) observed that there "has been a dramatic increase in the capacity of state governments to engage in educational issues," particularly as legislative and gubernatorial staffs have increased (p. 21; Campbell, Cunningham, Nystrand, & Usdan, 1985; Fowler, 2000). Legislatures and their staffs have become more professionalized and judicial interventions and gubernatorial initiatives have increased, enabling state governments to "use the means at their disposal to influence schooling at the local level" to a degree unprecedented in U.S. history (Firestone, 1990, p. 146). In many states, legislatures now operate as "big school board[s]" and make decisions affecting all areas of schooling (Campbell, Cunningham, Nystrand, & Usdan, 1985, p. 60).

One key issue is whether the increased involvement of the state in local education translates directly and proportionally to a loss of local control (what Malen, 2003, refers to as the high-impact view) or whether street-level bureaucrats (local educators) still retain considerable power with their ability to implement (or thwart) reform initiatives (the low-impact view). Drawing from Malen (2003), proponents of the low-impact view cite extensive implementation studies as evidence that local officials retain considerable influence over education policy, despite increasing state activism. According to Malen, proponents of this view note that "the large and loosely jointed [educational] system gives local units considerable wiggle room" to creatively interpret and implement state-mandated policy initiatives (p. 200). However, she cautions, the "low-impact view may equate ingenuity with autonomy" (p. 201). Malen believes the high-impact view of state control is more accurate, particularly when analyzing state-led decentralization initiatives, which she refers to as "the illusion of local empowerment" (p. 203). She notes that "the promise of greater local discretion" offered by decentralization was largely unfilled due to limitations on the scope of authority granted to local schools (particularly over budget, personnel, and instruction), overriding rule and resource constraints, and a shift of responsibility (for student performance) to the local level without a corresponding increase in local autonomy (p. 203). The general consensus from the research literature supports this high-impact view of the rising state over local education.

Policy Coherence or Confusion?

The rising state control over education leads to an important policy question: Has the growth of state and federal control over education actually improved schooling in the United States? Has it created a more coherent, tightly coupled educational system? Picus asserts that, in California, increasing state control has not produced greater policy coherence. The contributors to this volume are divided on this issue. According to Browne-Ferrigno, most educators and researchers believe that the quality of schools and student learning has improved significantly in Kentucky since enactment of KERA. In New York, Vergari observes that, "While some analysts lament what they perceive to be an unfortunate focus on 'teaching to the test,' others note that the state standards ensure greater equity and accountability across school districts." Maxcy, Rorrer, and Aleman comment that, in Texas, the standardization of curriculum, alignment of assessments, and specification of student- and school-level performance outcomes, coupled with a public reporting system providing demographic, programmatic, staffing and performance information, constitute a comprehensive educational system that "stands in stark contrast to the highly fragmented system it replaced."

Despite strong rhetoric about local control, Texas lawmakers passed massive education reform legislation in 2006 that gives the state education agency (SEA) power over school district spending, mandates how much student test scores must improve each year, gives the SEA the power to remove teachers and school administrators in low-performing schools (including replacing the entire staff), and establishes a uniform start date for all public schools (Stutz, 2006). Although some legislators dismissed the notion that local control was being eroded, the legislation marked a significant departure from the landmark 1995 reform legislation that decentralized many areas of responsibility and decision-making to the district and school level. Richard Kouri of the Texas State Teachers Association stated, "Things that were previously decided locally no longer will be. The pendulum has swung pretty far in the direction of more state control" (Stutz, 2006, p. 3).

State efforts to centralize and standardize schooling through regulation, support, and resource allocation—particularly through such mechanisms as curriculum alignment and well-developed accountability systems—have, in some states, created greater equity and improved state test scores (Fuller & Johnson, 2001; Grissmer & Flanagan, 1998; McDermott, 1999; Scheurich, Skrla, & Johnson, 2001). McDermott and DeBray-Pelot agree and assert that "in general terms, expanding state control over education has improved educational opportunities for all students." Song notes in her research on reading policy that policy actors "were generally supportive of state standards and assessments, and were also fairly confident that reading achievement was on the rise in their respective states." Vergari concurs, noting that, "As in other states, New York State policymakers determined that long-standing local power over public education had not yielded satisfactory outcomes. The active state has led to more rigorous requirements for all public school students, teachers, and leaders; the delivery of extra supports to lagging students; a new type of public school called a charter school; stepped-up attention to school safety issues; and large increases in funding for school facilities and other needs." She asserts that "substantial state power over education in New York promotes both accountability and equity in the school system, although there is variance in implementation quality across policies."

Picus, on the other hand, sees more policy confusion than coherence with increased state involvement in education. According to Picus, "Despite considerable rhetoric to the contrary, state policy in California is more a series of requirements and mandates than it is a system with clear policy goals and adequate support for schools to meet those goals in the ways they deem most appropriate." Baker and Green found that, in Kansas, the "legislature may have used centralized state control of school funding to maintain racially separate but equal educational systems. Moreover, the state legislature has consistently responded to judicial intervention by maintaining funding inequities through centralized state control." Baker and Green assert that "the Kansas saga paints a very different view from the common perception about judicial and legislative roles in state school finance and governance and the relationship between state control and equity. Kansas legislators themselves, through no prompting by the courts, made a bold power grab in the 1960s, first through statutes governing organization of schools then through revising the constitution to grant them more power and responsibility. Further, the legislature removed language requiring uniform treatment of the state's children. From that point forward, Kansas legislators actively used greater state control to create inequity in school funding, across school districts that they had actively organized to be racially segregated—even in the face of judicial opposition."

Cooper and Nisonoff agree, asserting that "we see little evidence that the rising power of the state in New Jersey has made a significant difference in either equalizing educational opportunity or improving the state's overall performance." Although state policymakers are mandating and implementing more rigorous curriculum frameworks, higher standards, and outcomes-based accountability systems, some states such as Georgia have such broad, often vague, standards and curriculum frameworks that many teachers "are left to pick and choose what they should teach and then hope their students are prepared for the state's curriculum-based exams" (Tofig, 2003, p. 1)—a situation that suggests that state-mandated curriculum and testing may not be as tightly coupled or aligned (at least from the perspective of street-level implementers) as it appears from the top.

Yet Browne-Ferrigno and others assert that, left to their own devices, many local school officials will do little to address or remedy inequities within the educational system. She asks, "Is there compelling justification for state control over public education when opportunity for learning is inequitable and inadequate?" and answers affirmatively. She notes that more than one-third of the school districts in Kentucky sought equitable funding through court action when they could not obtain redress elsewhere. However, Malen (2003) notes that "neither state governments nor local units have persistently mobilized on behalf of policies that might cut to some of the underlying causes of educational problems that are evident in our schools . . . neither state governments nor local units can assemble a policy history that makes a prima facie case for a particular division of duties or for an unflinching commitment to a comprehensive plan for education reform" (p. 211).

In fact, assert Finn and Hess (2004), the Bush administration justifies the extension of federal control over education "by wrapping its policies in the mantle of racial and social justice, arguing for federal intervention to protect poor children and minorities from the callous disregard of state leaders and local interests" (p. 54). In their historical analysis of the federal role in education, Hirschland and Steinmo (2003) argue that the institutional fragmentation produced by federalism "has often resulted in the empowerment of localist and reactionary interests who fear reform efforts" designed to change the status quo (p. 345). Hirschland and Steinmo assert that "at times, strong national policies on behalf of educational provision and reform have been required to make right the great inefficiencies and inequities promulgated by this very localism" (p. 345). Other scholars have reached similar conclusions. As McDermott (1999) argues, "In the United States, improving educational opportunities for poor children, and for children of color, has often required countermajoritarian exercises of state or federal power" in the name of equity (p. 50). While seeing the democratic virtue of local control, McDermott believes this same local control can "impede the pursuit of educational equity" (p. 121).

This raises more fundamental questions: If, as the contributors to this volume suggest, state governments differ to the extent or degree to which their involvement promotes greater systemic equity in the educational system, then would the national government need to be the driving force in ensuring or guaranteeing systemic equity? If increasing state control is justified in the name of equity, yet inequities exist between states, would greater national control not also be justified on the grounds that national citizenship requires a high-quality national education not dependent on differences in state standards and funding of education? What level of government would produce the most equitable system of schooling? Many of the contributors to this volume believe that only local control leads to inequities across various domains (curriculum, governance, finance, etc.) of the educational system and suggest that such inequities can be remedied at the state level. However, other scholars such as Hirschland and Steinmo (2003) hold a dim view of state interests, characterizing them as antiegalitarian, antidemocratic, regressive, and producing inherent inequalities, and believe that only the national government can craft policies to redress these inequities. Some of the contributors to this volume would agree. As Cohen and Spillane (1992) point out, the increasing involvement of the national government in state and local education has often been in the name of disadvantaged groups, including students with disabilities, at-risk students, non-English-speaking students, and females. For example, Congress and federal courts, not state government and certainly not local interests, were largely responsible for integration of schools (Beadie, 2000; James, 1991; McDermott, 1999). These questions need to be addressed as the state exerts itself evermore into education at the local level.

One important feature of the growth of state control over education is that several states appear to be following the pattern adopted in California whereby the state is responsible for developing standards and accountability measures, and local schools are responsible for the implementation of educational programs to meet those standards, with consequences for failure. Picus observes that, "to the extent that high levels of state control can focus schools on good instruction and high quality curriculum, influence from above can lead to improved student outcomes. The problem in California—despite highly regarded state curriculum guidelines—is that the overall governance from the state level has become incoherent, forcing local school officials to undertake many actions and activities that are counterproductive to student learning. Therefore it is not state control per se that is problematic, it is California's lack of a coordinated strategy that has bogged schools down in the morass of high state control."

This lack of coordinated strategy is reflected in the testing policies of some states. Despite increases in testing requirements, several states fail to assess students in all core areas every year, making it difficult to track and assess student growth. Browne-Ferrigno notes that while Kentucky is one of the states that do not assess in all core areas annually, some districts have initiated voluntary testing programs that assess students' annual yearly progress to meet the requirements in the No Child Left Behind legislation, which leads to more coherent, integrated educational policymaking. However, states differ markedly in their capacity to effect educational improvement and reform, with few states, principally state education agencies, possessing the capacity to provide support to increasing numbers of schools in need of improvement (Institute for Educational Leadership, 2001). Approximately 8,500 Title I schools nationwide are in need of improvement and are entitled, under NCLB, to technical support from the state (Archer, 2006). On average, 16 percent of Title I schools "need improvement," although in Alabama, Alaska, California, Florida, and the District of Columbia, more than 30 percent need improvement—an almost impossible support task for state education agencies (Archer, 2006).

Under NCLB, states must have a "system of intensive and sustained support" in place, including support teams "to work with schools and districts getting federal Title I aid" (Archer, 2006, p. S4). While all states offer support, few have the requisite capacity to provide the level of support required by the federal legislation. According to the Center on Education Policy (CEP), "leaders of 26 state education agencies felt they lacked 'sufficient in-house expertise' to help schools and districts identified for improvement" under NCLB (Archer, 2006, p. S11). Jack Jennings, president of the CEP, stated, "For the better part of a decade now, many state education agencies have been cutting back in personnel and funding, and the federal government hasn't made up the difference" (Archer, 2006, p. S11).[4] The Institute for Educational Leadership (IEL) places the blame on what Usdan calls the "theology of localism," which makes state lawmakers reluctant to vastly increase the size of the state education agency (commensurate with increased expectations and demands) (Institute for Educational Leadership, 2001, p. 2). Paul Reville, president of the Rennie Center for Education Research and Policy, stated, "In most state legislatures, the idea of building the bureaucracy with further investment is an unpopular one," despite organizational imperatives and evidence of institutional effectiveness (Archer, 2006, p. S12; Goodsell, 2004).

Thomas and Meyer (1984) observe that "one of the most prominent features in the history of the Western states has been its rationalization, i.e. the organization of social life within a unified frame of means and ends, often despite normative reactions against it" (p. 469). The reluctance of state and federal legislators (and the public) to adequately fund state education agencies commensurate with the increased expectations placed on them is an example of how some elements of the state (legislators) seek to create or impose rationality and functionality, while at the same time are reluctant to allocate requisite resources necessary to implement that same rationality, thus undermining state capacity. If state education agencies lack the requisite capacity to meet the demands placed on them by state and federal lawmakers, then we are much less likely to see the kind of state intervention and improvement that might otherwise occur.

The Institute for Educational Leadership is particularly critical of the lack of state capacity to effect reform, noting that state education agencies are "inhibited, even victimized, by inadequate budgets, staffs of uneven (sometimes diminishing) quality, outdated tax structures, indifferent populations, irrational political expectations, and, in many states, badly outdated operational systems" (Institute for Educational Leadership, 2001, p. 15). This situation may explain the reluctance of some state education agencies to use their power to intervene in or take over failing schools. It may also explain the mixed record of success of those efforts. Yvonne Caamal Canul of the Michigan Department of Education stated, "The good news is that we're being asked to step up to the plate and take on more authority. The bad news is we didn't hire people over the past 20 years or 15 years to think that way about their work" (Archer, 2006, p. S3). Furthermore, state education agencies "tend to pay less than many districts do, making it hard to recruit the new talent they require" (Archer, 2006, p. S11).

In addition, increasing federal authority and control over education has led to complaints by local and state officials about unwarranted federal intrusion into local policymaking. However, increasing state and federal control over education does not necessarily eliminate or reduce local control if flexibility in the form of opt-out or waiver provisions is included in state and federal regulations. For example, in 2003, Seattle became the nation's first school district to receive "red tape relief" under NCLB's "local-flex" initiative, which gives up to eighty school districts flexibility in spending federal education funds with very few strings attached (Committee on Education and the Workforce, 2003). However, many analysts assert that, "while money and control do not stand in a one-to-one relationship, it is difficult to envision added state funding without some increase in state control" (Campbell, Cunningham, Nystrand, & Usdan, 1985, p. 74).

Conclusions and Forecasts

As state and federal policymakers exert ever-greater control over all areas of schooling in the United States, significant policy questions are raised: Is this shift in power, authority, and control permanent or should it be viewed as a pendulum whereby power will shift back toward local control in the coming decade? Under what circumstances would such a realignment occur? Picus observes that, in California, the trend toward state centralization and control "continued through recessions and large state deficits and through good times when the state budget provided lawmakers with large annual surpluses to distribute throughout the state." Picus concludes that this growing control "shows little or no sign of abating, despite political rhetoric to the contrary." Vergari agrees, asserting that "this centralizing trend in education policy, reinforced by the requirements of the federal No Child Left Behind Act of 2001, is likely to continue for the foreseeable future." Song reaches a similar conclusion when she states that "with the heavy focus of the No Child Left Behind Act of 2001 on state-wide accountability and the hefty sums of money attached, states are under both strong incentives and tremendous pressure to take firm control over their K–12 education systems. Thus it seems safe to predict that the balance between state authority and local control will continue to weigh more heavily towards the former in the years to come."

As the idea of national standards and even national testing crosses party lines, this "federalism debate" in education will heat up (Gordon, 2006). Many prominent conservatives such as Chester Finn and Diane Ravitch argue that in a global economy, in which the nation's economic survival rests on a strong educational system, it makes no sense for different states to have different standards. Finn noted that the state standards themselves are diverse and vary from state to state and Ravitch has asserted that the strategy of "50 states, 50 standards, 50 tests" has not improved achievement (Manzo, 2006; Olson, 2005). Robert Wehling, former global marketing officer for Proctor & Gamble, observed, "We are the only developed nation in the world without, essentially, national standards and curriculum frameworks" (Olson, 2005, p. 24).

Significant in this reconceptualization of education is the view that education is a prerequisite of national citizenship (Gordon, 2006). Tying education to this more broad definition of citizenship necessitates a fundamental rethinking and expansion of constitutional rights and obligations. As societies evolve, and as the state apparatus expands its sovereignty and jurisdiction, people come to view society not as a collection of individual states (in the case of the United States) but rather as a collective entity with expansive responsibilities (Thomas & Meyer, 1984). The problem, of course, with extending this logic is that, like national standards and testing, the vast funding inequities within and between states would then become, as a prerequisite for national citizenship, also an area for redress through the federal government. Former U.S. Department of Education official Eugene Hickok commented that the push for national standards and testing "might force greater federal intrusion into related areas, such as school financing, curriculum, and scheduling" (Manzo, 2006, p. 14). However, the federal judiciary has to date had a long-standing opposition to such interventions.

The rising state control over education has significant implications for educational governance. Cooper and Nisonoff are correct in their observation that the governance model of schooling is changing from a loosely coupled system "to newer paradigms of more standardized state and federal interventions, ones that rest on the assumption that it's perhaps better to have less local autonomy and greater local equity and adequacy." As Brady observed, "States' efforts to enhance equity in public education through the improvement of student and teacher performance have considerably diminished local school district controls over school funding, testing standards, curricular reform, and accountability." However, as Cooper and Nisonoff note, these trade-offs are still being negotiated in a system with a long history of local school governance—which Usdan (2001) colorfully referred to as the "theology of localism."

However, even within the constraints of federalism, the national government could assert itself even more forcefully into local education if it so chooses. As Hirschland and Steinmo (2003) observe, national reformers "adapted their strategies to the constitutional system they lived within" (p. 354). In the pre-Civil War era, that meant taking advantage of the capacity and fiscal resources of the national government (through sale of federal lands) in support of education. Today, national influence is being exerted through often controversial and somewhat unpopular mandates and aid to states. If Congress so desired, it could exert even greater influence by dramatically increasing federal aid to education, which "could be used to lure local policies toward national agendas" (Hirschland & Steinmo, 2003, p. 359). However, state policymakers are not always willing to use all the tools at their discretion to micromanage schools. In Massachusetts, James Peyser, Chair of the State Board of Education, believes the state "has failed to take tough action to fix struggling schools. . . . I am afraid that we are not even trying to use the authority we have" (Jan, 2005, p. 1).

Several scholars note that NCLB and state education reform efforts (particularly neocorporatist reforms such as higher standards, testing, accountability, and performance-based systems) "represent top-down strategies to improve student achievement through tightened centralized control (in terms of mandated, targeted outcome measures), while ostensibly leaving the 'how you get there is up to you'" in the hands of local school officials (Fusarelli & Fusarelli, 2003,

p. 170; Fusarelli & Johnson, 2004). This notion of top-down mandates coupled with bottom-up flexibility is reiterated over and over by state and national officials. The key question is whether an energized and increasingly powerful state operating with tightened, centralized command and control systems will permit (or actively discourage) bottom-up flexibility (Fusarelli & Johnson, 2004). As Fusarelli and Johnson (2004) pose the question: "Do efforts to more tightly couple education through top-down, outcomes-based standards and accountability policies—with the federal and state governments assuming ever greater responsibilities for monitoring educational performance—weaken lay control of schools and pose a threat to democratic governance?" (p. 122). This question remains largely unanswered, although events in the post-NCLB era suggest clearly that local or lay control of schools has been significantly weakened.[5]

Occasionally, state policymakers attempt to centralize some parts of the educational system while decentralizing others—reflecting either a desire to find an optimal balance between state and local control, local resistance to a naked power grab by state and federal authorities, or conflicting views within state legislatures about how best to improve the educational system. One may see this conflicting tension in the efforts by state legislatures to create charter schools and pass voucher legislation—a trend that Cooper and Nisonoff term "radical decentralization." In some instances of decentralization, this decentralization occurs not at the state level (state policymakers ceding control to local officials) but rather state-mandated decentralization within the local level itself. For example, under KERA, "Individual schools gained greater local authority from local boards of education through the mandated installation of site-based management groups having legal authority over school matters" (Browne-Ferrigno). Notes Browne-Ferrigno, KERA empowered site-based decision-making councils "to make new principal selections that are binding and to approve hiring of new certified staff recommended by the principal. Superintendents' authority to select principals for the schools in their districts was minimized as a result of this governance change." In New York City, Mayor Michael Bloomberg has called for principals to be given "greater power over hiring, budgets, and curricula . . . in exchange for high performance" (Maxwell, 2006, p. 8). Bloomberg stated: "It moves us toward our long-held objective of putting more resources, autonomy, and accountability where they belong—in the schools" (Maxwell, 2006, p. 8). However, some districts, such as Wake County, North Carolina, have begun moving in the opposite direction by curtailing principals' power and local flexibility in response to audits that uncovered inequities in fundraising, special programs, and equipment (Hui & Epps, 2007). Furthermore, some scholars believe that efforts toward decentralization give the appearance or illusion of relinquishing power, while retaining authority with the state, since rules, regulations, mandates, and sanctions remain in place to structure education (Malen & Muncey, 2000).

Some researchers such as Spring (2002) do not believe the trend toward centralization at the state level contradicts "efforts to increase school autonomy through site-based management and [to] encourage greater teacher and parental involvement in local school decisions" (p. 116). Spring asserts that state efforts focus on "controlling the knowledge distributed by schools" (i.e., state standards) while local decision-makers continue to decide how best "to dispense that knowledge efficiently" (p. 116). Malen (2003) agrees and asserts that if the state determines "the ends and the standards by which those ends are assessed," then local officials can have the autonomy to determine "the means through which those goals and objectives" are realized (p. 209). She goes on to state that "upper levels of government (federal and state) are to decide the 'what' of schooling by setting standards, disseminating frameworks, and developing assessments; and local units are to decide the 'how,' the strategies to be used to accomplish these aims," although she points out that even this view "clearly privileges the state" (p. 209). Former U.S. Secretaries of Education William Bennett and Rod Paige (2006) suggest that a new model in which standards are set nationally and daily decisions are made locally "strikes the best balance" between state and local control (p. 2). However, findings from research on institutions are fairly clear and consistent: as states develop and expand, bureaucratic domination increases, "justified by ever broader notions of justice and progress that go beyond the boundaries of any individual state" (Thomas & Meyer, 1984, p. 470).

This confusing jumble of power, control, and authority in educational governance is symptomatic of the institutional structure within which schooling operates in the United States. Institutional theorists have long noted that a federal system of governance, in which responsibility for policymaking is divided among multiple layers of governance (and among multiple agencies within each layer) facilitates institutional fragmentation, making more difficult the creation of coherent policy and posing a significant barrier to implementing systemic reform in education (Robertson & Judd, 1989; Smith & O'Day, 1990). A striking feature of the U.S. educational system—of policymaking nested within a federalist context and reinforced through the theology of localism—is that it has taken over a century to create a more tightly coupled, yet still too fragmented, system of schooling. This is not altogether surprising given that it requires a reconstruction of institutional power relationships at multiple levels (Skowronek, 1982). Thus, while "the state" has become much more involved in coordinating educational reform policies, the structural impediments of federalism have lead to a "fragmented centralization" of education policies, whereby the educational system is becoming ever more centralized, yet still fundamentally fragmented by its institutional design (Meyer, 1983, p. 181; Rowan & Miskel, 1999). However, Fowler (2000) suggests that the shift toward state control over education reflects a "gradual 'hollowing out' of local control until only its empty shell remains" (p. 144).

Thus, the rising state can best be understood as an ongoing effort by state and national policymakers to more tightly couple a massive educational system that has been loosely coupled both by constitutional design and political tradition, although the evolution of the modern U.S. state suggests that the limitations imposed by constitutional design can be overcome.[6] Significant external, environmental pressures, including increasing international economic competition, limited resources, and an aging and increasingly impoverished, diverse population, place tremendous pressure on an educational system that has not always been outcomes-focused (or whose outcomes are now judged to be insufficient or inadequate for today's needs). As a result, even though the United States has a long history of local control over education and a loosely coupled educational system, it need not always be so. As Rowan and Miskel (1999) point out, it is possible for organizations "to exist in a weakly elaborated technical or institutional environment at one point in time, but, after concerted institution-building, to be in a strongly elaborated technical or institutional environment at a later point in time" (p. 365). With the rising state presence in education, that time may be at hand.

The issue is what impact the rising state will have on the educational system in the United States. Are "top-down, bottom-up" reforms (as suggested by the rhetoric of state and national lawmakers) workable or merely a political slogan designed to placate opponents? Answers may be found in institutional theory and research. The inescapable conclusion from institutional theory and research is that "with greater centralization of power comes greater uniformity" (Spring, 2002, p. 117). This uniformity, or homogeneity, is the product of three distinct isomorphic processes: coercive isomorphism (regulations, mandates, rewards, and punishments); normative isomorphism (professional codes, standards, certification, and accreditation); and mimetic isomorphism (modeling and copying success) (DiMaggio & Powell, 1991). These three processes are common components of educational reforms promulgated by state and national officials and, thus, it is not surprising that these processes would produce greater uniformity and homogeneity throughout the educational system, leading to a more tightly coupled system (Fusarelli, 2002b). As James (1991) observes, the state impact on education extends "far beyond the control that can be exercised directly through regulatory devices" (p. 174).

Significantly, however, at least some of these isomorphic processes are voluntary and could be viewed as locally chosen initiatives. Thus, a more tightly coupled educational system, one in which the rising state plays an ever-greater centralized role, does not eliminate local control or flexibility, even though it encourages and induces greater uniformity and institutional isomorphism. Fowler (2000) suggests that the most effective method might be to distribute power, control, and decision making authority both upward (from the district to the state level) and downward (from the district to the local level)—with the state specifying the outcomes and local schools responsible for achieving those outcomes however they so choose. McDermott (1999) and others call for a "new institutional ordering" in which some functions of schooling such as "the distribution of resources and other equity-related issues" are centralized and other functions, such as control over educational programs (teaching and curriculum), would be decentralized to the individual school level (p. 122). Such an approach might produce greater flexibility at the local level, enabling schools to be more responsive "to communities' distinctive preferences and needs" (McDermott, 1999, p. 122), although a system with mandated or targeted outcomes determined at the state or national level would probably not tolerate or provide much room for local variation.

In conclusion, as the rising state has steadily developed and increased its institutional capacity to engage in systemic reform, educational policy has become more tightly coupled, which, in turn, has produced in general a greater degree of policy coherence, led to improvements in student achievement, and less inequities in student outcomes by subgroup in several states (Fusarelli & Fusarelli, 2003; Fusarelli & Johnson, 2004). Increased state control and federal involvement in education are, on balance, a good thing, which will, over time, lead to a more coherent, tightly coupled, more organized, and more equitable system of schooling for all children than does the current system of educational governance and control.

Notes

1. Hirschland and Steinmo (2003) point out that the federal government had a substantial influence (perhaps its greatest influence) over education from the period of the founding of the Republic until the Civil War, during which time the national government was the premier educational resource provider (in the form of land grants and the distribution of proceeds from sales of federal land) to states to establish public schools. At the time, state and local governments lacked the capacity and fiscal wherewithal to establish a comprehensive system of free public schools. As James (1991) observes, "Beginning with the Northwest Ordinance of 1787, the federal government provided new states with land grants to support [the establishment of] common schools" (p. 178).

2. For similar conceptual clarity, I use the term "national" rather than "federal" throughout this chapter because the latter means a system of power divided among different levels of government as opposed to its popular use referring to the national government.

3. Thus, the rising state is not a recent phenomenon but rather has steadily increased its power, scope, and authority over education over the last forty years.

4. Four percent of Title I funds may be set aside for school improvement activities, with 95 percent of that going directly to schools and districts, leaving the remainder for state education agencies (Archer, 2006).

5. Some would argue that the rising state threatens democratic governance of education. Locally elected school board members have criticized loss of local

control on the grounds that it is undemocratic insofar as it makes it more difficult for parents to influence change as power is concentrated at the state capital (Kossan, 2005). However, this depends largely on how one defines democratic governance (i.e., responsibility, control, and decision-making). In higher levels of government (mayors, state legislators, governors, and national executives), you create a more responsive, democratic system because voters can more easily recognize and identify such officials, and voting records suggest that the public is much more likely to participate in elections beyond the local level.

6. This position is supported by the steady growth of national power, control, and authority over many aspects of modern U.S. society—over commerce, the environment, public health, and social security, to name only a few—at the expense of state and local control to a degree unimaginable to almost all of the Founding Fathers.

References

Archer, J. (2006, September 13). Leading for learning. *Education Week, 26*(3), S1–S20.

Beadie, N. (2000). The limits of standardization and the importance of constituencies: Historical tensions in the relationship between state authority and local control. In N. D. Theobald and B. Malen (Eds.), *Balancing local control and state responsibility for K–12 education* (pp. 47–91). Larchmont, NY: Eye on Education.

Bennett, W. J., & Paige, R. (2006, September 21). Why we need a national school test. *Washington Post*. Retrieved September 22, 2006, http://www.washingtonpost.com/wp-dyn/content/article/2006/09/20/AR2006092001587.html.

Bush, J., & Bloomberg, M. R. (2006, August 13). How to help our students: Building on the 'No Child' law. *Washington Post*. Retrieved August 16, 2006, http://www.washingtonpost.com/wp-dyn/content/article/2006/08/11/AR2006081101565.html.

Campbell, R. F., Cunningham, L. L., Nystrand, R. O., & Usdan, M. D. (1985). *The organization and control of American schools*. 5th ed. Columbus, OH: Charles E. Merrill.

Campbell, R. F., & Mazzoni, T. L., Jr. (1976). *State policy making for the public schools*. Berkeley: McCutchan.

Cibulka, J. G. (1995). The institutionalization of public schools: The decline of legitimating myths and the politics of organizational instability. In R. T. Ogawa (Ed.), *Advances in research and theories of school management and educational policy*, vol. 3 (pp. 123–158). Greenwich, CT: JAI Press.

Cohen, D. K., & Spillane, J. P. (1992). Policy and practice: The relations between governance and instruction. *Review of Research in Education, 18*, 3–49.

Committee on Education and the Workforce. (2003, November 7). Seattle schools first in nation to receive red tape relief under No Child Left Behind "local-flex" initiative. Press Release. Retrieved August 31, 2007, http://republicans.edlabor.house.gov/archive/press/press108/11nov/nclb110703.htm.

DiMaggio, P. J., & Powell, W. W. (Eds.). (1991). *The new institutionalism in organizational analysis*. Chicago: University of Chicago Press.

Evans, P., Rueschmeyer, D., & Skocpol, T. (Eds.). (1985). *Bringing the state back in*. New York: Cambridge University Press.

Feller, B. (2006, May 2). College aid qualifications to get stiffer. *Boston.com News*. Retrieved May 4, 2006, http://www.boston.com/news/education/k_12/articles/2006/05/02/college_aid_qualifications_to_get_stiffer/

Feller, B. (2006b, May 9). Rising number of schools face penalties. *Boston.com News*. Retrieved May 11, 2006, http://www.boston.com/news/education/k_12/articles/2006/05/09/rising_number_of_schools_face_penalties/.

Finn, C. E., Jr., & Hess, F. M. (2004). On leaving no child behind. *The Public Interest, 157,* 35–56.

Firestone, W. A. (1990). Continuity and incrementalism after all: State responses to the excellence movement. In J. Murphy (Ed.), *The educational reform movement of the 1980s: Perspectives and cases* (pp. 143–166). Berkeley: McCutchan.

Fowler, F. C. (2000). Converging forces: Understanding the growth of state authority over education. In N. D. Theobald and B. Malen (Eds.), *Balancing local control and state responsibility for K–12 education* (pp. 123–146). Larchmont, NY: Eye on Education.

Fuller, E. J., & Johnson, J. F. (2001). Can state accountability systems drive improvements in school performance for children of color and children from low-income homes? *Education and Urban Society, 33*(3), 260–283.

Fusarelli, B. C., & Fusarelli, L. D. (2003). Systemic reform and organizational change. *Planning and Changing, 34*(3&4), 169–177.

Fusarelli, L. D. (2002). The political economy of gubernatorial elections: Implications for education policy. *Educational Policy, 16*(1), 139–160.

Fusarelli, L. D. (2002). Tightly coupled policy in loosely coupled systems: Institutional capacity and organizational change. *Journal of Educational Administration, 40*(6), 561–575.

Fusarelli, L. D. (2005). Gubernatorial reactions to No Child Left Behind: Politics, pressure, and education reform. *Peabody Journal of Education, 80*(2), 120–136.

Fusarelli, L. D., & Johnson, B. (2004). Educational governance and the new public management. *Public Administration and Management: An Interactive Journal, 9*(2), 118–127.

Gittell, M., & McKenna, L. (1999). Redefining education regimes and reform: The political role of governors. *Urban Education, 34*(3), 268–291.

Goodsell, C. T. (2004). *The case for bureaucracy,* 4th ed. Washington, DC: CQ Press.

Gordon, R. (2006, March 15). The federalism debate: Why the idea of national education standards is crossing party lines. *Education Week, 25*(27), 35, 48.

Grissmer, D., & Flanagan A. (1998). *Exploring rapid achievement gains in North Carolina and Texas.* Washington, DC: National Education Goals Panel. Retrieved June 9, 2006, from http://www.negp.gov/reports.

Helfand, D. (2006, February 27). The ABCs of mayoral control of schools. *Los Angeles Times.* Retrieved February 28, 2006, from http://www.latimes.com/news/education/la-me-nymayor27feb27,1,7324149.

Hirschland, M. J., & Steinmo, S. (2003). Correcting the record: Understanding the history of federal intervention and failure in securing U.S. educational reform. *Educational Policy, 17*(3), 343–364.

Hoff, D. J. (2006). GOP era wrought unexpected changes. *Education Week, 26*(15), 10, 11.

Hornbeck, M. (2006, March 31). Mich. raises the bar for students. *The Detroit News.* Retrieved April 3, 2006, from http://www.detnews.com/apps/pbcs.dll/article?AID=/20060331.

Hui, T. K., & Epps, K. W. (2007, September 5). Advice for Wake schools: Curtail principals' power. *The News & Observer*, pp. A1, A12.

Institute for Educational Leadership. (2001). *Leadership for student learning: Recognizing the state's role in public education.* Washington, DC: Author.

James, T. (1991). State authority and the politics of educational change. *Review of Research in Education, 17*, 169–224.

Jan, T. (2005, November 30). State official wants tougher plan to aid struggling students. *The Boston Globe.* Retrieved December 1, 2005, from: http://www.boston.com/news/education/k_12/mcas/articles/2005/11/30/state_official_wants_tougher_plan_to_aid_struggling_students/.

Kossan, P. (2005, August 9). Laws cut school control at local level. *The Arizona Republic.* Retrieved August 12, 2005, from http://www.azcentral.com/families/education/articles/0809BTS-boards09.html.

Malen, B. (2003). Tightening the grip? The impact of state activism on local school systems. *Educational Policy, 17*(2), 195–216.

Malen, B., & Muncey, D. (2000). Creating "a new set of givens'? The impact of state activism on school autonomy. In N. D. Theobald and B. Malen (Eds.), *Balancing local control and state responsibility for K–12 education* (pp. 199–244). Larchmont, NY: Eye on Education.

Manna, P. (2006). *School's in: Federalism and the national education agenda.* Washington, DC: Georgetown University Press.

Manzo, K. K. (2006, September 6). Fordham pushes national standards. *Education Week, 26*(2), 14.

Mathews, J. (2006, September 3). National school testing urged. *Washington Post*. Retrieved September 6, 2006, from http://www.washingtonpost.com/wp-dyn/content/article/2006/09/02/AR2006090201041.html.

Mawhinney, H. B. (1994). *An interpretive framework for understanding the politics of policy change.* Paper presented at the Annual Meeting of the Canadian Association for Studies in Educational Administration, Calgary.

Maxwell, L. A. (2006, June 21). N.Y.C. schools to gain freedom under empowerment plan. *Education Week, 25*(41), 8.

Mazzoni, T. L. (1995). State policy-making and school reform: Influences and influences. In J. D. Scribner and D. H. Layton (Eds.), *The study of educational politics* (pp. 53–73). Washington, DC: Falmer Press.

Mazzoni, T. L. (2000). State politics and school reform: The first decade of the "education excellence" movement. In N. D. Theobald and B. Malen (Eds.), *Balancing local control and state responsibility for K–12 education* (pp. 147–196). Larchmont, NY: Eye on Education.

McDermott, K. A. (1999). *Controlling public education: Localism versus equity.* Lawrence: University Press of Kansas.

McGivney, J. H. (1984). State educational governance patterns. *Educational Administration Quarterly, 20*(2), 43–63.

Meyer, J. W. (1983). Centralization of funding and control in educational governance. In J. W. Meyer and W. R. Scott (Eds.), *Organizational environments: Ritual and rationality* (pp. 179–198). Beverly Hills, CA: Sage.

Murphy, J. (1990). The educational reform movement of the 1980s: A comprehensive analysis. In J. Murphy (Ed.), *The educational reform movement of the 1980s: Perspectives and cases* (pp. 3–55). Berkeley: McCutchan.

Murray, C. (2006, July 25). Acid tests. *The Wall Street Journal.* Retrieved July 28, 2006, from http://www.aei.org/include/pub_print.asp?pubID=24711.

Olson, L. (2005, December 7). Nationwide standards eyed anew. *Education Week, 25*(14), 1, 24.

Poggio, J. P. (2000). Statewide performance assessment and school accountability. In R. S. Pankratz and J. M. Petrosko (Eds.), *All children can learn:*

Lessons from the Kentucky reform experience (pp. 75–97). San Francisco: Jossey-Bass.

Reeves, M. M. (1990). The states as polities: Reformed, reinvigorated, resourceful. *Annals of the American Academy of Political and Social Science, 509*, 83–93.

Robertson, D. B. (1993). The return to history and the new institutionalism in American political science. *Social Science History, 17*(1), 1–36.

Robertson, D. B., & Judd, D. R. (1989). *The development of American public policy: The structure of policy restraint.* Glenview, IL: Scott, Foresman.

Rowan, B., & Miskel, C. G. (1999). Institutional theory and the study of educational organizations. In J. Murphy and K. Seashore Louis (Eds.), *Handbook of research on educational administration,* 2nd ed. (pp. 359–383). San Francisco: Jossey-Bass.

Sack, J. A., & Trotter, A. (2005, September 7). Schools to tackle a new mandate: Teaching about U.S. Constitution. *Education Week, 25*(2), 9.

Scheurich, J. J., Skrla, L., & Johnson, J. F. (2001). *State accountability policy systems and educational equity.* Paper presented at the Annual Meeting of the American Educational Research Association, Seattle.

Skowronek, S. (1982). *Building a new American state.* New York: Cambridge University Press.

Smith, M. S., & O'Day, J. (1990). Systemic school reform. In S. H. Fuhrman and B. Malen (Eds.), *The politics of curriculum and testing* (pp. 233–267). London: Falmer Press.

Spring, J. (2002). *Conflict of interests: The politics of American education,* 4th ed. Boston: McGraw-Hill.

Stutz, T. (2006, July 10). School reform in state's hands. *Dallas Morning News.* Retrieved July 18, 2006, from http://www.dallasnews.com/shared content/dws/news/nation/stories/DN-edcommish_10tex.ART.North.Edition1.240ca09.html.

Teicher, S. A. (2005, September 8). Everyone is telling teachers what to teach. *Christian Science Monitor.* Retrieved September 12, 2005, from http://www.csmonitor.com/2005/0908/p12s01-legn.html.

Thomas, G. M., & Meyer, J. W. (1984). The expansion of the state. *Annual Review of Sociology, 10,* 461–482.

Tofig, D. (2003, December 12). New learning blueprint: State hopes changes will boost scores. *The Atlanta Journal-Constitution.* Retrieved December 13, 2003, from http://www.ajc.com/friday/content/epaper/editions/friday/news_f39da649f0c0c10010d1.html.

Usdan, M. (2001). *Leadership for student learning: Recognizing the state's role in public education*. Washington, DC: Institute for Educational Leadership.

Welburn, B. L. (2002, Spring). State education governance for the 21st century. *The State Education Standard*. Retrieved June 13, 2006, http://www.nasbc.org/Standard9_Spring2002/Exec._summary_03-02.html.

Wirt, F. M., & Kirst, M. W. (2005). *The political dynamics of American education*, 3rd ed.. Richmond, CA: McCutchan.

Contributors

Enrique Aleman, Jr. is an assistant professor in the Department of Educational Leadership and Policy Studies at the University of Utah. He also serves as a research associate with the Utah Education Policy Center. His research agenda includes studying the effects of educational policy on Latina/o and Chicana/o students and communities. Dr. Alemán has published articles in Educational Administration Quarterly (EAQ) and Educational Policy, and has a chapter forthcoming in an edited book titled, *To What Ends & By What Means? The Social Justice Implications of Contemporary School Finance Theory & Policy.*

Bruce D. Baker is an associate professor in the Department of Educational Leadership and Policy Studies at the University of Kansas. He has authored a multitude of articles on the topics of state school finance policy and the economics of education in journals including the *Economics of Education Review, Journal of Education Finance, Educational Evaluation and Policy Analysis, Educational Policy,* as well as law review journals. Professor Baker has consulted on the design of state school finance policy for state governments in Texas, Missouri, Wyoming, Hawaii, Rhode Island, and New York, and for special interest groups in Washington, Kansas, and other states. Professor Baker is working with Professor Green on a forthcoming book on school finance policy for Merrill/Prentice-Hall.

Kevin P. Brady is an assistant professor in the Department of Educational Leadership and Policy Studies at North Carolina State University in Raleigh, North Carolina. Dr. Brady's research and scholarly interests are in the areas of school law, school finance, and educational technology for school leaders. Dr. Brady's most recent publication, "The Elementary and Secondary Act at 40: Equity, Accountability, and the Evolving Federal Role in Public Education, appears in the *Review of Research in Education.*

Tricia Browne-Ferrigno, an associate professor in the Department of Educational Leadership Studies at the University of Kentucky, earned her PhD in Educational Leadership and Innovation with emphasis in Educational Policy and Administration at the University of Colorado at Denver. While living in Denver, she conducted analyses of state policies and practices supporting teachers seeking National Board Certification and affecting teacher supply and demand in the Commonwealth of Virginia for projects by the Education Commission of the States. Her work is published in *Educational Administration Quarterly, Journal of Research in Rural Education, Journal of School Leadership, Leadership, and Policy in Schools,* and annual yearbooks of the National Council of Professors of Educational Administration.

Bruce S. Cooper, is a professor in the Division of Educational Leadership, Administration, and Policy, in the Graduate School of Education at Fordham University. Dr. Cooper has done extensive research on school finance, organization, policy, and reform. He has served on the editorial boards of *The Educational Administration Quarterly, Journal of School Leadership*, and *Policy and Leadership in Schools.* He has authored and coauthored twenty-two books, and over 275 articles, chapters, and papers, and served as national president of the Politics of Education Association. His most recent books include *Better Policies, Better Schools,* with Lance Fusarelli; *Promises and Perils Facing Today's School Superintendents,* with Lance Fusarelli; *Truancy Revisited,* with Rita Guare; *Optimizing Educational Resources*; and *Career Crisis in the School Superintendency? The Results of a National Survey,* with Bruce S. Cooper, Lance D. Fusarelli, and Vincent A. Carella.

Elizabeth DeBray-Pelot is an assistant professor in the Department of Lifelong Education, Administration, and Policy in the College of Education at the University of Georgia. She has also served as a program analyst at the U.S. Department of Education, research assistant at the Consortium for Policy Research in Education, and research associate with the Harvard Civil Rights Project. She is the author of *Politics, Ideology, and Education: Federal Policy During the Clinton and Bush Administrations*, as well as numerous articles and book chapters on education reform and school desegregation.

Bonnie C. Fusarelli is an assistant professor in the Department of Educational Leadership and Policy Studies at North Carolina State University, earned her PhD in Educational Administration at The Pennsylvania State University. Dr. Fusarelli's research focuses on educational leadership and policy, the politics of education, specifically school reform, superintendents, social justice/educational equity, and organizational change, specifically with school/agency collaboration. Dr. Fusarelli coedited the *Politics of Education Yearbook: Curriculum Politics in Multicultural America*, and her research appears in journals including *Educational Policy, Journal of School Leadership, Leadership and Policy in Schools, Journal of School Public Relations, International Journal of Educational Research, Journal of Cases in Educational Leadership, Public Administration and Management, and Planning and Changing.*

Lance D. Fusarelli is an associate professor in the Department of Educational Leadership and Policy Studies at North Carolina State University. He is the author or editor of five books and more than forty journal articles and book chapters. He coauthored *Better Policies, Better Schools: Theories and Applications* and recently coedited *The Politics of Leadership: Superintendents and School Boards in Changing Times*. His primary areas of interest focus on superintendents, No Child Left Behind, and the politics of education.

Preston C. Green is an associate professor in Associate Professor in the Department of Education Policy Studies at the Pennsylvania State University. He has written articles pertaining to the legal issues surrounding educational access and charter schools. His research appears in journals including *American Journal of Education*, *Journal of Negro Education*, *Journal of Education Finance*, and *Peabody Journal of Education* as well as law review articles. Additionally, Professor Green is coauthor of the *Charter Schools and the Law: Establishing New Legal Relationships*, the only book devoted to the legal issues surrounding charter schools.

Molly Gordon is a doctoral student at the University of Minnesota.

Brendan D. Maxcy is an assistant professor in the Department of Educational Leadership and Policy Analysis at the University of Missouri-Columbia and an associate editor of the *Journal of School Leadership*. He earned his Ph.D. from The University of Texas at Austin in 2004 and was awarded Outstanding Dissertation in the Politics of Education, 2004–2006, by the Politics of Education Association. His research draws on critical and postcolonial theories to examine the interplay of leadership, management, performance, and accountability policies in public schools. Currently, he is studying leadership in schools contending with national educational reforms and intense regional unrest in the border provinces of southern Thailand. His work is published in *Educational Administration Quarterly* and *Educational Policy*.

Kathryn A. McDermott is an associate professor in the School of Education and the Center for Public Policy and Administration at the University of Massachusetts, Amherst, where she is also Associate Director of the Center for Education Policy. Her research interests include state education policy, accountability, and equity. She is the author of *Controlling Public Education: Localism Versus Equity*, as well as numerous book chapters and articles in education and public policy journals.

Judy Meath is a doctoral student at the University of Minnesota.

Philip H. Nisonoff is the assistant superintendent of Schools and the School Business Administrator for the Emerson Public Schools located in Bergen County, New Jersey. An adjunct instructor of School Finance and Doctoral Candidate at the Graduate School of Education at Fordham University,

Phil Nisonoff is a recognized leader among New Jersey school business administrators.

Lawrence O. Picus is a professor of school finance and educational administration at the University of Southern California's Rossier School of Education. He also serves as the director of the Center for Research in Education Finance (CREF), a school finance research center housed at the Rosser School of Education. CREF research focuses on issues of school finance adequacy, equity, and productivity. His current research interests deal with adequacy and equity in school finance as well as efficiency and productivity in the provision of educational programs for K–12 schoolchildren. Picus is a past president of the American Education Finance Association. His most recent book is *School Finance: A Policy Perspective*.

Andrea K. Rorrer is an assistant professor in the Department of Educational Leadership and Policy Studies at the University of Utah.

Karen Seashore is the Rodney S. Wallace Professor at the University of Minnesota. Her research focuses on school improvement and reform, leadership in school settings, and knowledge use in education. Recent publications include *Organizing for School Change*; *Aligning Student Support with Achievement Goals: The Secondary School Principal's Guide*, with Molly Gordon; and *Professional Learning Communities: Divergence, Depth and Dilemmas*, with Louise Stoll.

Mengli Song is a senior research scientist at the American Institutes for Research. Her research interests include educational policy and politics, social network analysis, research design, and quantitative research methods. Her most recent publication on state reading policy won the William Davis Award for the Most Outstanding Educational Administration Quarterly Article in a Volume Year (2005). Dr. Song holds a Ph.D. in Educational Administration and Policy, and an M.A. in Educational Foundations, Administration, Policy, and Research Methods from the University of Michigan. She also received an M.A. in Teaching English as a Second Language from Beijing Normal University in China.

Emanda Thomas is a doctoral student at the University of Minnesota.

Sandra Vergari is an associate professor in the Department of Educational Administration and Policy Studies at the State University of New York, Albany. She is a political scientist whose research focuses on education reform politics and policies. Vergari's work has appeared in policy reports and academic journals, and she is the editor of *The Charter School Landscape*.

Index